Designing History

Documents and the Design Imperative to Immutability

Chris Lee

Set Margins' Publications #37

"The great enemy of property is oblivion, since the loss of conscious master over time and succession leads inevitably to the breakdown of property. Thus the forces of oblivion are antagonistic to the self and property, while all the techniques of mnemonics are their essential allies."

— George Caffentzis, *Clipped Coins, Abused Words, and Civil Government: John Locke's Philosophy of Money*

Table of Contents

Foreword
The Discreet Charm of a Short-Term Rental Agreement

Dear designer, design researcher, design freak: I ask you to forget, for the time being, magazines, logos, and fancy typefaces. Instead, think of bills, coins, spreadsheets, passports, even cuneiform tablets and cryptographic ledgers. Think of *documents*. I get it, that 1969 Milton Glaser poster changed your life, but what about that misleading short-term rental agreement that kept you up at night for weeks?

Banal artifacts like the latter can hardly be called design, you might object. They're often dull, if not just plain bad. Is there anything to say about them, design-wise? Anthropologist David Graeber, author of a clever study on bureaucracy, understood this clearly:

> Paperwork is boring. One can describe the ritual surrounding it. One can observe how people talk about or react to it. But when it comes to the paperwork itself, there just aren't that many interesting things one can say about it. How is the form laid out? What about the color scheme? Why did they choose to ask for certain bits of information and not others? Why place of birth and not, say, place where you went to grade school? What's so important about the signature? But even so, even the most imaginative commentator pretty quickly runs out of questions.[1]

Not only is paperwork boring, he adds, it is also "*supposed to be boring.*"[2] We could say that it is designed that way. Still, why bother? The thing is, my fellow friend, sometimes the most unappealing things, the ones without symbolic depth, are also the most important. In this case, "important" means that they are worryingly close to force, to legitimized violence. Try not to comply with some shady conditions of the aforementioned agreement to see what I mean.

Designing History brightly confutes Graeber's point: Chris Lee makes the important, even when it's dull, interesting. He manages to write a deep, imaginative, and compelling essay on these seemingly transparent artifacts that are, in appearance, purely operational. This book shows us that documents *do* possess an aura—the palpable Sauron's gaze of authority, dominion, *herrschaft*. Here, the transparency and uniformity of the document reflects the opacity and intricacy of power; the merely operational runs on the symbolic structure of the sovereign institution. And, needless to say, this institution not only wants to be in charge, it wants to remain so. That's why the imperative that drives the design of documents is, as Lee clearly points out, that of immutability.

In recent decades, it has become commonplace to extend the concept of design indiscriminately across time and space, as if Chauvet's cave paintings or the Inca *quipu* could be held up as examples of what is understood today, in the modernized West, as design. According to Giovanni Anceschi, in this way design becomes a Hegelian category of spirit, rather than a historically situated idea.[3] This unwarranted extension can only yield valid results if a specific, solid angle is chosen—one that genuinely transforms our understanding of design here and now, instead of clouding our historical awareness with the fog of the present. Chris Lee's perspective, which traces back to Sumer civilization, does exactly this because it lets us rethink design history *as a whole* as a history of documents. And it works: we see the past as present, and the present as past. From this point of view, it is not absurd to speak of micromanagement in the period from 3600 to 3100 BCE (see page 70 for reference).

The author's personal history led him to rethink historiography. He insists that history is not an arid sequence of facts, but a *story*, a narrative based on the interpretation of evidence. For once, it makes sense to speak of storytelling in design. This is where things get challenging, because this book is about the matter of evidence, that is, documents. And documents are not simply historical—they *want* to be so. Lee's theoretical journey is vertiginous, as he tries to rethink design history through documents while historicizing them, such that we are urged to see the document as both form and content, structure and thing, sign and symbol. When we think we have finally landed on an "historiography of the design of history," Lee warns us that the ride is not over yet: there are other forms of history-making, fully legitimate, that eschew documentary evidence and archives, dealing instead with repertoires and performative rehearsals, where illiteracy can be feigned deliberately. And the conflict between these two different mythologies, that of the evidence and that of the repertoire, is true not only for design history, but for history at large.

Let's stay within the design field, though. While the most cutting-edge design historians are busy today with the task of breaking the design canon through the additive, somewhat liberal approach that priorities inclusivity, Lee explains that "it is ultimately impossible to produce an absolutely inclusive canon." So, he transcends these efforts, shaking the very foundation of the history palace. Instead of breaking canonical history, he proposes to rethink canonical *historiography*: don't focus on the petty bourgeois, now post-Fordist design author with their publicity artifacts, but look at the documental debris that surrounds you. Ironically, documents are a much broader "gap in the record" within design history than any poster designed by whoever.

A Reddit user had an idea: "We should put Comic Sans on legal documents, not to legitimize Comic Sans, but to *delegitimize* law."[4] Reading this book, one risks starting to believe that designers are capable of legitimizing authority through their craft: the carefully designed banknote, the calligraphy of old contracts, and so on. Thanks to design, these documents appear more official, more convincing. But, in fact, it is the other way around: it is the narcissism of power that embellishes its immutable claims. It is power that legitimizes design, and not vice versa. Evidence for this lies in the poor and, at times silly, design of documents that still wield significant impact over people's lives. Institutional authority can make even Comic Sans look serious—just think of the CERN Higgs boson announcement in 2012.

So, what's left for designers? With a touch of melancholy, Lee concedes that no design student dreams of designing tax forms—and yet, there is, in *style*, a fascination, even a fetish, with standards and grids, from Josef Müller-Brockmann to Carsten Nicolai. Not many students go to design school to anonymously contribute to anti-imperial struggle—not many, but surely some, especially since politics have become a token of professionalization. Nobody goes to design school to become a saboteur—and yet, the creative industries have eulogized the cheerful hacker, the troublemaker, even the rogue. I'm not sure if this is good or bad, but this book might be more directly relevant than what our humble author thinks.

There is also another path for designers: some of them can provisionally *impersonate* power by means of forgery. From Lee's perspective, counterfeiting emerges as a design practice in its own right, grounded in a theoretical framework which goes beyond the occasional anecdotal account of heroic endeavors, such as the illegal activities of Willem Sandberg during the Nazi occupation of the Netherlands. With these ideas in mind, the more we look, the more we find graphic design. We find forgery "from above" in Orwell's novel *1984*, where Winston Smith amends historical records, and counterfeiting "from below" in Bong Joon-ho's film *Parasite*, where Ki-jung forges a university diploma to make his brother look qualified (while he comments "with skills like this, why can't you get into art school?"). So, here comes the oxymoron: *Designing History* makes forgery legit.

In Lee's hands, design is neither just a technical nor just an expressive practice, but a political one, or more precisely, it is pre-political. It acts on the surface where politics takes place. Lee makes us see the proscenium, not just the stage. This book is ultimately political because it understands that power floats above the murky waters of politics, with documents serving as power's seemingly neutral interface. Its focus on immutability is also a not-so-subtle critique of the imperative to publicity and its high-falutin career aspirations, where the designer becomes ontologically indistinguishable from their clients. (see pg. 21)

An underlying thread running through *Designing History* is its anarchist leaning, with anarchy understood as freedom from external authority. Without giving too much away, I believe the central scene of this essay is the one that takes place on a soccer field, where the refusal to acknowledge an official document is dismissed as illiteracy. Fundamentally, the scene has to do with organization and the extent to which we want to formalize, with a Leviathan-like system, something that could be easily managed informally and horizontally. This is crucial to keep in mind, since designers are often managers by vocation, if not outright bureaucrats.

So, beware. Reading this book, the bureaucrat in you might lose interest in colorful posters and magazines, only to be captivated by the ominous charm of bills and spread-sheets. By contesting the immutability of these artifacts, you might change your perception of design—and, consequently, the design you produce. ✳

Silvio Lorusso
Lisbon, November 2024

1   David Graeber, *The Utopia of Rules: On Technology, Stupidity,*
    and the Secret Joys of Bureaucracy (Brooklyn: Melville House, 2015), 51.

2   Ibid. Emphasis mine.

3   Giovanni Anceschi, *Monogrammi e figure*
    (Florence: La casa Usher, 1981), 145.

4   r/unpopularopinion, "All legal documents should be written in Comic
    Sans," *Reddit*, 2019, reddit.com/r/unpopularopinion/comments/h7xfjl/
    all_legal_documents_should_be_written_in_comic/.

A Note on the Design and Formatting

- The heads of the coin (opposite), derived from Hammurabi's stele, $\downarrow_{145}$ appeals to an impersonal, divine authority as a guarantee of value and meaning. The rod and cord held by the seated deity symbolize the right to measure according to the stability of a divine standard.
-- The tails similarly refers to an authority, but is charged with a death threat at the hands of the bureaucratic entity (the state) that governs the document. The inscription "To Counterfeit Is Death" and others to the same effect are found on American paper currency from around the time of the American Revolution. $\downarrow_{38}$
... The edge form is a skeumorphic vestige of a time when the face value of coinage was protected by the integrity of the reeded edge. This created a normative expectation, which affirmed for the receiver of a coin that it had not been "clipped" to extract some precious metal while retaining its face value. $\downarrow_{118}$

In its appeal to the divine, its derivation of authority from the state and its material effort to foil forgery, this coin (designed by myself, and pressed in an edition of ~5,000 in 2018) indexes three techniques of immutability for securing inscriptions on documents. Its compact format achronologically imbricates multiple eras of statecraft. Exploring this non-linearity is one of the primary conceits of this book's construction. Its contents largely swim against the implicit linear, progressive flow of a bound book (or an eBook for that matter), whose discrete limits of page size or compact spread layout enable its commodification and circulation through a market system. However, the potential resonances and imbrications of the ideas and artifacts in *Immutable* exceed what can be made apparent within such a spatial unit, and reading this book is thus necessarily a disjointed, non-linear experience. Against the typographic conventions that usually orient the reader along a unidirectional trajectory, *Immutable* weaves time and material into a recursive loop; it follows conventional Latin orthography where the pages advance sequentially (1, 2, 3...), but the figures devolve (163, 162, 161...). Throughout, the reader

will find hyperlinks indicated by directional arrows i.e., $\downarrow_{151}$ which are meant to give some emphasis to the historical "rhymes," echoes, and resonances that reverberate across millenia of documental production. These are, of course, only the ones I am suggesting—I hope that other resonances and potential conversations within and even beyond this book's referential horizon will emerge for the reader.

This book's design is inspired by a few sources—Marshall McLuhan and Quentin Fiore's *The Medium is the Massage*; John Berger and Richard Hollis's *Ways of Seeing*; and Roman Cieślewicz exhibition catalog, *Petites Images*. I hope what I've done here speaks with these examples and the mode of designerly cognition that they exemplify. In other words, the reader will find pages populated by text and image, where the delineation between these categories falls apart, and the typographic distinction between body text, sidenotes, and captions is nominal, perhaps more an effect of the limited scope of the page/spread.

Though the irregular experience of reading this book and the technique of hyperlinking probably have something to do with my limitations as a writer, I want to point directly to them as a way of high-lighting the perverse banality of the book form itself and the expectations it generates. With regards to an adherence to the conventions of academic writing, the creative concerns are privileged over the scholastic ones (though these are not necessarily in opposition). Citations are respected, however, pagination/navigation is irregular; image reproduction rights were taken care of to the best of my ability, but many illustrations are processed and stylized, while some images are of my own making and would have no place in any book that claims to be a "legitimate" work of historical scholarship. One of the production conceits (for which I was unable to find an agreeable printer) was to scramble the page signatures before binding, in order to make it futile to try and cite the book: "page 23" in one copy might not be in the same spot in another.

What follows is decidedly not what a tenure review committee in traditional academic disciplines would regard as valid scholarship. Notwithstanding my nominal qualifications as a professor, my mistreatment of the banal standards and conventions of book design aims to probe the formal, designerly standards that demarcate academic legitimation. This is to say that the way that a book is designed, the way it looks, can mark the distinction between one that circulates legitimately, legibly as such, within an academic bureaucracy, and one that does not—if it can be said to produce knowledge, or if it cannot. Against those performative conventions, I present this project as an expository essay: an attempt† at an alternative, achronological, non-teleological, and intuitive (read: academically indefensible) historiography of graphic design that centers the document and its bureaucracies. Its value as a knowledge producing work is subject to debate, and I truly hope that it generates just that.

† This framing is informed by Paul Bailey's current research, which focuses on the visual essay as a genre graphic designers engage in.

Acknowledgements

Designing History/Immutable emerges from several years of intermittent work. If it wasn't going to be the regular vagaries of life changes and self-doubt, the pandemic (and raising a small child in the midst of it) would have threatened to derail this endeavor at various points. Fortunately, there are several people who helped me to see this thing through in spite of it all, and to them, I would like to humbly express the most profound gratitude I can offer.

This project, which began in earnest with a half-year research fellowship at Het Nieuwe Instituut (Rotterdam, NL) in 2017 led by Director of Research, Marina Otero Verzier, along with Tamar Shafrir, Klaas Kuitenbrouwer, and Katía Truijen. I am grateful to the research team and my fellow fellows, Ramon Amaro, Daphne Bakker, and Sara Frikech, for their rich intellectual and creative companionship and help incubating this nascent project.

At the time, I was based in Buffalo, NY, and upon returning, was invited by curator Bryan Lee of El Museo to mount an exhibition later that year of the research and studio outcomes generated during the fellowship. Working spatially afforded a generative opportunity to think through and explore some strategies for non-linear narration that inform the structure of this book. Carl Spartz's technical and intellectual companionship animated (literally and figuratively) many aspects of this work. Humbaba and Diogenes would not have made an appearance in this story were it not for him. Conversations with the composer Colin Tucker deepened my thinking and broadened this project's frame of reference. Mirabo Press (Bob Fleming, Rachel Shelton, and Mizin Shin), Xuanao Zhang, and Leo Grant, each enriched the exhibition with creative interventions.

Freek Lomme (Onomatopee), stopped over in Buffalo on his way to Toronto just before the exhibition was to open. I had the chance to preview it for him and we struck a deal to develop (the forthcoming print version of) the first edition of this publication—the trust and enthusiasm he had for a project that was just beginning to take shape was catalytic, to say the least. Since then, Freek's steady hand and understanding, as this book's development tumbled in and out of focus for a couple of years, was what I needed to eventually get this book back on track.

I am grateful to Liz Park for introducing me to Ben Tiven in the context of a design commission. Ben is a co-founder of Library Stack (librarystack.org), the publisher of the eBook edition of *Immutable*. Without Ben's belief, dedication, investment, and generosity in shepherding this book, I don't know how much longer it would have been stalled, or if it might have simply faded into oblivion. My gratitude cannot be overstated.

I would also like to acknowledge that the work, conversations, and comrades in many of the other activities I've had the privilege of being involved with have influenced the thinking and motivation for this project. Steven Chodoriwsky and Julie Niemi, and our work on reconstituting Tolstoy College, a defunct experimental anarchist college at UB SUNY; my colleagues at the Pratt Institute, Nida Abdullah and Xinyi Li, and our ongoing explorations of curriculum development and radical pedagogy; the cadre of agitators that is the "Communist AIGA," a growing, critical and convivial group: Danielle Aubert, J. Dakota Brown, Andrea Cardinal, Jack Henrie Fisher, Alex Hayashi, Anther Kiley, Jacob Lindgren, Kikko Paradela, Ali Shamas Qadeer, Melissa Weiss, and Lauren Williams.

Towards the final stages of writing, this book benefited greatly from the insightful and enriching feedback of Jennifer Pranolo, Willis Kingery, and Francisco Laranjo. Rachel Valinsky's copyediting was incisive and elevating. I count myself quite fortunate for having some proximity and access to their generosity and intellect. This reprinted and expanded edition has been blessed with a preface written by the illustrious Silvio Lorusso.

Finally, there are those who have given me so much in other ways: their space and time; their interest, intellect, enthusiasm and conversation; their hospitality, and their solidarity (in some cases, their funding)! With some overlaps, and roughly in that order: Josh MacPhee; Ruben Pater; Anja Groten, and Alex Walker, (Sandberg Instituut); Femke Herregraven; Ramiro Espinoza (who made pizza for me and taught me some of the basics of punchcutting); Jordan Geiger and Miriam Paeslack; Ekrem Serdar (Squeaky Wheel); Geoff Kaplan (No Place Press); Pouya Ahmadi (Amalgam, RISD); Jack Henrie Fisher (Counter Signals, University of Illinois Chicago); Ali Shamas Qadeer; Patricio Davila; Silvio Lorusso; Allison Collins (Western Front); Elise Hunchuck; Siddhartha Lokanandi; Kelly Walters, E Roon Kang, and Caspar Lam (Parsons School of Design); Duncan Hamilton (Pratt Institute); David Catterini (CalArts), Jan Hadlaw (York University); David Bennewith (Rietveld Academie); Stevphen Shukaitis and Jürgen Rudolph (Journal of Applied Learning and Teaching); Paul Bailey (De Koninklijke Academie voor Schone Kunsten, Gent); Charles Stankievech (University of Toronto); Thomas Castro (ArtEZ); Clara Balaguer; Public Address; Michèle Champagne (ABZ-TXT); Ramon Tejada, Arthur Roeloffzen (Design Academy Eindhoven); Ilana Altman (The Bentway); Benjamin Thorel (After 8 Books); Marco Ferrari (Design Academy Eindhoven); Peter North (UAL); Aggie Toppins (Washington University); Ian Lynam (Temple University Japan); Chris Hamamoto (Seoul University); Rachel-Emily Taylor and Bryony Quinn (UAL); The Technē Institute (UB SUNY); Deutsche Bundesbank (Frankfurt); The Plantin-Moretus Huis (Antwerp); The British Museum (London); Western Front (Vancouver); The Science Museum (London); and the Bureau international des poids et mesures (Paris).

Designing History

Introduction
Toward Historiography as Ground
for an Antagonistic Pedagogy and Praxis

I
The Trouble (With Graphic Design)

II
Design Imperatives (Publicity)

III
Graphic Design History:
Centering the Document

IV
Historiography

The colonist makes history and he knows it. And because he refers constantly to the history of his metropolis, he plainly indicates that here he is the extension of this metropolis. The history he writes is therefore not the history of the country he is despoiling, but the history of his own nation's looting, raping, and starving to death. The immobility to which the colonized subject is condemned can be challenged only if he decides to put an end to the history of colonization and the history of despoliation in order to bring to life the history of the nation, the history of decolonization.

—Frantz Fanon, *The Wretched of the Earth*

Preface

This book was originally intended to be a post-hoc catalogue for an exhibition held at El Museo in Buffalo, New York, in 2018. The exhibition was developed as a multi-faceted presentation of early research into a project I have been calling *Immutable: A Mineral History of Currency and Typography*. This research was driven by a hunch that an exploration of the relationship between typography and currency could yield insights into graphic design's political dimension. I gesture, perhaps naively, toward a desire to escape the persistent and immovable conditions that make design the alienating activity that it is today.

Since the early days of my work as a designer, I have found the practice of design to be overshadowed by a micropolitical struggle against the inertia of convention and the constraints of finance. Design seemed almost completely circumscribed by the rationality of the market, a disavowed yet radical conservatism, and an under-scrutinized liberal ethics grounded in a culture of promotion and publicity. Design did not and could not embody, for me, the radical, revolutionary praxis I had hoped it might, even vaguely, as a student coming up in a milieu in which Adbusters and Shepard Fairey appeared to offer the only alternative possibilities to vulgar commercialism. The compromises and constraints that are endemic to practicing design professionally are insurmountable because they are essential to what it means to do design and to be a designer, in spite of the acrobatics of the kinds of hyphenated "-design-" acutely critiqued by contemporary commentators.[1]

Yet, as I seek an escape from the inevitability of what one might refer to as "formal design" (wherein what is legible as such is circumscribed by commercial priorities and their attendant pedagogical orientation), this book peeks "under the rug" once more before moving with the intuition that there is still something from graphic design that is worth studying, teaching, and practicing as a means to contribute to and enact struggle. I would be loath to close the gates on the question of what graphic design could be and do, in spite of the overwhelming reasons substantiating the kind of disillusionment that critics like Silvio Lorusso have provided language for. I share Lorusso's disdain for such foreclosures, which he identifies as a mark of privilege and an attitude one ought to be wary of.[2] There is perhaps yet some space for "design" to mean something other than what even the most disillusioned might make of it. If the reader shares a similar feeling, I offer this work as an invitation to think together.

Part one of this book collects, updates, and synthesizes texts I have written over the past few years to iterate my thinking about various facets of this project. Part two, which was originally published in late 2022 through Onomatopee, concatenates an array of collected visual notes, references,

1   See @ethicaldesign69, Silvio Lorusso, and J. Dakota Brown.
2   A sentiment shared in conversation with the author, 2019.

and projects exploring the relationship between currency and typography. These are gathered around the notion of *immutability*, constituting the first crude scratches toward mapping a terrain of practice—while also marking graphic design's current, implicit boundaries—as a place from which to plot an escape. The book manifests as an inquiry in publication form and embodies an impatience with rigid, institutional systems of knowledge production and gatekeeping. In other words, its form and style are decidedly multivalent and aberrant when held against the typical modes of scholarly publication. I hope that it is regarded as a signal, calling to potential accomplices—those dissatisfied with graphic design as it tragically seeks valorization in commerce, in tech, and in the academy—and produces a space for cultivating conspiratorial alliances with poetry, performance, anti-capitalism, and decolonial critique. This is an ambitious goal, offered with humility, and I am grateful for the reader's consideration of what follows.

For me, the primary aim of this project—what I hope it contributes—is a challenge to the way that the canonical historiography of graphic design is narrated, and subsequently, how its attendant pedagogy and practice are imagined and enacted. Through the book's form, the reader is prompted and challenged to approach its contents less as a linear text, and more as a field of resonances to provoke reflection and debate. I would count it as a success if it were able to generate a schism or contribute to existing schisms, such that design history, and historiography itself, might be considered as possible fields of contestation and terrains of critical, speculative, and collective praxis, characterized by an expanded spectrum of concerns, tools, and techniques that constitutes designing, or perhaps even abandoning design itself as a useful paradigm for such a praxis altogether. In other words, this project attempts to rethink the ontology of the designer and what it might mean to design by rethinking what design history narrates.

Introduction
Toward Historiography as Ground
for an Antagonistic Pedagogy and Praxis

This project, *Immutable*, emerges from a synthesis of two aspects of my relationship to design education. The first concerns what gets taught as design. Mahmoud Keshaverz has argued that there is an apparent, prescribed boundary to what counts or doesn't count as design, and who is properly engaged in its discourse. The axiomatic schism of what he calls the "politics of design" appears along the lines of what design school curricula define as such, and is derived largely from the kind of career return on investment that schools promise to (the parents of) prospective students. Graphic design's boundaries become more discernible when, for instance, one considers passport forgery as a kind of graphic design that doesn't get taught in schools. These boundaries circumscribe a domain of "regulated and reg-

4

ulatable" (Keshavarz 2018, 3) forms of design and foreclose a creative and critical mode of attending to what designing *could* entail. As a corollary, the second concern guiding this book has do with the field's historiography and the way it implicitly narrates the historical borders of the field.

The artifacts and figures that populate the historiography that my project outlines are, for the most part, Western. This is not to affirm or defend the knowledge production of Western institutions but rather to locate them as the Other figured by this historiographical work (Weymans, 177–78; de Certeau 1984).[3] While resources like *Decentering Whiteness in Design History*[4] (to name just one significant example) attack the narrow historiography of design by addressing its lack of diversity and inclusion, they do not seem to engage the problem of narration in design history. To do so, I propose, would mean to *center* whiteness in design and scrutinize its imbrications with colonialism and capitalism. Could this yield an indictment of design's quasi-apocalyptic entanglements with the aforementioned "isms" and confront the problem of a canon that resources like *Decentering Whiteness*, to the extent that it might be regarded as a "move to innocence,"[5] seem to misrecognize?

Around ten years ago (as of the writing of this text) I took up a position in the Department of Art at the University at Buffalo—SUNY and found myself confronted for the first time with having to teach a course on the history of graphic design. Although I had studied the field as an undergraduate using texts like *Philip Meggs's History of Graphic Design* (2012), I was unsure of what I would use to teach the course. I remembered it as drudgery and didn't want to put myself and my students through that. One sees, with hindsight of course, Meggs's survey as a rather chauvinistic, stultifying narration of Western, capitalist progress, despite the efforts made over subsequent editions to include (or, perhaps, accumulate) the "contributions" of non-Western references and practitioners.[6] In spite of these efforts, graphic design history is still largely trapped by its assimilation of the

---

3   See note in proximity to "INVESTITURE OF HAMMURABI." Castoriadis, "Castoriadis infers that the very impulse to know about any ("other") society is particular to Ancient Greece and Western Europe because these societies were particularly effective at domesticating meaning within the web of institutions that concretized their intentions. The look "outward," motivated by a desire for autonomy, was about finding other ways of being that exceeded enclosures of meaning."

4   Decentering Whiteness in Design History, "Decentering Whiteness in Design History Resources," last accessed November 29, 2024, bit.ly/decentering.

5   See Eve Tuck and K. Wayne Yang, "Decolonization is Not a Metaphor," *Decolonization: Indigeneity, Education and Society* 1, no. 1 (2012): 1–40.

6   For the historian Hayden White, the writing and interpretation of history cannot be objective and value-free. What is conventionally referred to as "history" (as objective fact) is rather an indeterminate field wracked by the same anxiety that all varieties of humanistic study suffer as concerns whether or not the construction of its statements and claims can attain the status of scientific objectivity. As the *de facto* standard, Meggs's book putatively tells *the* story of graphic design, constructed largely upon the accession of artifacts that serve to narrate the development of publicity and valorize the figure of the contemporary commercial designer. My contention with this status has less to do with its Euro-American parochialism than it does with its teleological regard for technological progress and the expansive reach of design as beneficial. White enables us to think the problem beyond whether a history is true or false—he contends that all histories are represented as stories—and to turn our attention to what makes a history intelligible as such. What makes Meggs's graphic design history intelligible in the West, then, is the way in which it conforms to the colonial mythology of discovery and expansion as a progressive force. See Hayden White, "Historical Pluralism." *Critical Inquiry* 12, no. 3 (Spring 1986): 480–93.

narrative of modernist progress and its struggle to legitimize a language of rational (read: industrial) and ostensibly universal forms by virtue of their being irreducibly elemental (read: machinable)—a tendency that rejects, or rather disavows, the cultural substance and material particularity of locally inflected form as "outmoded," "irrational," "illegitimate," and perhaps even "unethical."[7]

I sought alternatives. The option that stood out, and the one I ended up using, was Johanna Drucker and Emily McVarish's *Graphic Design History: A Critical Guide* (2012). As the title suggests, the book offered some critical tools for studying the history of a discipline to which my students were being initiated. Readers were prompted to always query and reflect on designed artifacts themselves as a materialized instantiation of a broader agenda. Instead of simply reading graphic design history as a linear, teleological flow of male Euro-American geniuses and their masterpieces, Drucker and McVarish ask us to consider the various conditions that have shaped the production and transmission of the artifacts being studied and how these in turn impact the contexts (into which) they (are) actualized. Their book challenges us to recognize how these examples, now regarded as canonical constituents of graphic design, serve as active agents of history— shaping and being shaped by knowledge, identity, labor, technology, politics, economics, and more. In other words, their book contextualizes and politicizes design. It extends a conception of design's agency and impact to concerns beyond its conventional disciplinary boundaries. It sets the stage for reflecting on what design's creative imperatives entail. It suggests that the designed world is a contingent one, available to being *redesigned*.[8]

This was appealing to me, because one thing I hope to do as an educator is to challenge students to think critically about why they do what they do—to generate some degree of inoculation against the uncritical reproduction of a world overcoded by what Mark Fisher has called "capitalist realism" and sedimented in coloniality and bureaucratic stupidity.[9] My thinking was that if students, educators, and practitioners of design, following Drucker and McVarish's guidance, could discern the ways in which design has produced and been implicated in how the world is known and made—and, more specifically, how it has been implicated in the development

---

7   The arch-modernist Massimo Vignelli, for instance, famously opined in the film *Helvetica* (2007) that with the introduction of the desktop computer, the tools for making graphic design become more accessible, enabling an abandonment of tradition and craft. The result: "vulgar" forms, "disease," and "visual pollution." Ironically, what he perhaps misrecognized is the desktop computer and the graphical user interface's status as apotheosis of the industrial formal language of elemental, geometric, machinable forms, and its irreducible unit: the pixel. The progressive reduction of pixel size, such that any image can be captured, stored, and transported digitally—on screen or in print, immediately and anywhere—is precisely the kind of colonizing rationalization that places an injunction on the expression of form according to its rectilinear terms.
8   I'm thinking here of Keith Hart's obituary of David Graeber, in which he lauds the anthropologist and anarchist for his commitment to a form of anthropology that sought to study (ethnic) people as a way to prove that things could be otherwise, that the Western/Northern capitalist order was far from inevitable. Keith Hart, "Obituary: Keith Hart," davidgraeber.org, accessed August 25, 2021, davidgraeber.org/memorials/obituary-keith-hart.
9   See David Graeber, *The Utopia of Rules: On Technology, Stupidity, and the Secret Joys of Bureaucracy* (Brooklyn, NY: Melville House: 2015).

of the settler state and the capitalist enterprise—then perhaps they could cultivate an understanding of the designer's agency and design's transformative capacity, while also gaining sober understanding of its limitations. And perhaps, without too much delusion or hubris as to design's capacities, the student/practitioner could intervene in what it means to be a designer—who a designer is and what a designer does.

I had been thinking about this since graduate school—my first attempt at escaping the alienation of design. There, I presented a thesis project that reflected on the phenomenon of alternative currencies and how case studies of their creation might be studied as models for a politically engaged practice that expands the spectrum of concerns graphic designers typically engage. The research and work emerged from a naïve question, but one that nonetheless continues to be generative for me to this day. As a graphic design student with very little money, I asked myself: "Why can't I make my own money?" My ambition upon graduation was to spend time in a community, get involved in economic justice activism, and be around proponents of the solidarity economy in order to help set up some kind of alternative currency system to render redundant—or rather, to channel into other circuits labor/life—that which would otherwise contribute to reproducing capitalist society. This never came about for a variety of reasons. Notwithstanding an incapacitating analysis of capitalism as a totalizing system with no "outside," my own nomadic precarity didn't help. I needed to submit my skills to the market and just get a steady job, pay rent, save enough money to support my parents in retirement, etc. But mostly, it was that the stakes were too damn high. Historically, the great majority of these schemes have failed, and I was terrified of the potential responsibility I would bear in the high likelihood that my "social art scheme" would fall flat. I shuddered at the prospect of disappointing anyone who might have invested even a little bit of hope in such a project. It was a clarifying moment—conventional design practice has much lower stakes, and I told myself that participating in such a scheme as a designer was vainglorious. Nonetheless, the prospect of designing money cast such genres of form (with their aura of inevitability, and indeed, their banality) as contestable. I still don't seem to have enough money, so I still think about it. At the very least, there's political utility in being able to make that which appears as "necessary and inevitable to be a mere contingency."[10] That's where this project, *Immutable*, comes in.

I share these brief points of origin only to set up an account of what I hope this book does, and what I think it doesn't do.

I understand this as an intervention. Destabilizing the inherited historiography of graphic design, at a minimum, could challenge graphic design pedagogy's inert tendency to be animated by the vague ethics of "service" and "problem-solving," client-oriented, commercial practice. But whose

---

10   Quoted from the famous mural in memory of Mark Fischer at Goldsmiths, University of London.

fucking problems? Such a query steers us toward examining the ways in which graphic design is regularly used by those with financial and political power to shape and control "defuturing" processes from conception to production, storage, and transmission, presenting these actions as both inevitable and good.[11]

This project's own limits map to the question of what design can do in the hands of powerful entities like colonial states and multinational corporations, and what it can do when wielded by their subaltern Others. In fact, this limit is its point of departure. I want to eschew the vanity of thinking that graphic design as we know it can be wielded as a tool to "dismantle the master's house."[12] At the risk of being overly modest, this project is ultimately and simply an exploration of how much of graphic design's normative values are a reflection of its status as an instrument of capitalism and colonialism. It also seeks to cultivate a recognition that the effects of this instrumentality— what graphic design objects help to make real (e.g., private property)—are contingent and subject to the same vulnerabilities as any design object, from obsolescence and replacement to recoding and even obliteration.

This book thus describes a ground upon which another mandate for design might be articulated in order to sharpen an antagonistic distinction in how design pedagogy and practice are imagined, taught, studied, and practiced. In quite schematic terms, this turn is premised on understanding graphic design primarily through its archival function rather than its public one. The key to enacting this shift and generating a schism is to center the banal genre of *the document*, to the extent that it serves as a genre of design's entanglement with colonialism and capitalism. This calls for an alternative pedagogical mandate, charged by the idea that a field of study is "not an object or a terrain that one masters, but a mode of seeking in the world that one cultivates endlessly."[13] My hope is that the kind of reflection and making that emerges from such an orientation resonates with the more substantive and urgent forms of struggle against capitalism and colonialism. Again, the naïve questions are the generative ones: Why doesn't graphic design history teach documents like money, passports, and property deeds? What would it mean to do so?

A brief excursus into historical narration is warranted here. The theorist of history, Hayden White, problematizes the way canonical history is regarded as merely established fact by arguing that history is more accurately understood as a kind of *narrative* composition of statements, which are themselves stabilized by their grounding in observation and evidence (White 1986). While the elements of the historiography I am experimenting

---

11   For Tony Fry, "defuturing" is the term he uses to refer to processes and practices that diminish
      the possibility of an environmentally and socially viable future fomented by unsustainable consumption.
He argues that modern design, driven by short-term goals and profit, often accelerates defuturing by neglecting
long-term ecological and ethical considerations
12   Audre Lorde, "The Master's Tools Will Never Dismantle the Master's House, in *Sister Outsider:
      Essays and Speeches* (Berkeley, CA: Crossing Press, 1984), 110–14.
13   Gayatri Spivak, cited in Emily Lordi (@ejlordi), July 11, 2020, X (formerly Twitter).
      The link is no longer available.

with are founded on artifacts that were, to be sure, designed precisely to *be historical*, their idiosyncratic concatenation plays with, eschews, and mutates the narrative tropes that are often employed in the writing and interpretation of history.

In a published conversation with FRAUD, I learned about the controversy around ancient ceramics found in the Canary Islands.[14] Spanish archeologists have made the argument that Spain's sovereign claim to the islands is premised on a shared ancient origin. The ceramics allegedly support this claim because of the morphological similarities found in Spanish, North African, and Canarian pottery of the period. It implicitly suggests that these apparent similarities are the result of Iberian migration outward from the peninsula. However, there is a pretty significant assumption built into this narrative: What if it was the case that the people who ended up in the Canary Islands went there precisely because they wanted to escape? What if they were ancient refugees, who might today want to have nothing to do with Spain? Yes, the existence of these ceramics, the timeframe of their production, their location, and even the morphological similarities are positive, scientific facts. But the story they might tell is less stable.

Brendan Cormier, a curator at the V&A Museum in London, once shared with me an experience of curating an exhibition of chairs in one of the museum's corridors. At first, the collection was ordered chronologically, from oldest to newest (or newest to oldest, depending on which way one entered the space). Then this same collection was arranged along the lines of their continental origins—Europe, Africa, Asia, North/South America. This, however, suggested an uncomfortable hierarchy. An alternative curatorial conceit had the chairs arranged instead by material (wood, metal, plastic, etc.), then later by production method (hand-crafted, industrially manufactured, emerging technologies).

This anecdote enables us to think different frameworks for the comparison, analysis, and interpretation of the chairs. While each arrangement was implicitly structured by the narrative trope of progressive, teleological development (the movement from primitive to advanced, manual to industrial/digital, and similarly, inefficient and wasteful to rational and sustainable), it also opens up a discussion about the different, potentially insightful registers that were not necessarily recognizable with the other arrangements of the artifacts. In the collection arranged by production method, for instance, we find a narration of the alienation of the anonymous craftsperson in the emergence of the industrial designer as intellectual worker; when arranged by material, a polemic on the environmental impact of industrial production; by geography, a narration of global "cultural exchange" or, inversely, of colonial plunder. The point I am trying to make is that the historical facticity of the chairs doesn't make the way that they are presented

---

14 Chris Lee and FRAUD (Andrey Samson and Francisco Gallardo), "Immutability, Management, Trees," Transmediale, January 30, 2023, 2023.transmediale.de/en/text/immutability-management-trees.

any contestable with regard to what stories get told and what assumptions are sedimented about design and the world it shapes and is shaped by.

Graphic Design Pedagogy, Blind Spots

Let's come back to graphic design, or rather its pedagogical blind spots. What exists in the way of theoretical literature around graphic design has relatively little to say about what documents *are*, and offers little help in cultivating a critical understanding of either how they come to be or what they do as designed things. This lack seems to suggest that documents are taken for granted, a *fait accompli*, or even a quasi-natural phenomenon, outside what is understood as the subjective activity of designing. Although the document may represent design's most profoundly consequential genre, design pedagogy seldom regards it as a form and format for students to consider, much less explore, as a viable field of study and practice. No one is to blame here—students don't usually apply to design school with fantasies of designing tax forms, and there aren't very many commissioners for this kind of work anyway.

Before lamenting this, James C. Scott reminds us to proceed with caution in engaging vestigial artifacts and documents of the state because these necessarily privilege the viewpoint of centralizing authority and relegate to oblivion worlds that tend not to produce intentional documental traces (Scott 2009, 33–34). This suggests that there is a blind spot in the shape of those obliterated by this power, or perhaps more fortunately, those who managed to evade the imposing gaze of authority by eschewing forms of governance facilitated by documents, instead cultivating lifeways that left few, if any, legible residue. Rather than simply testifying to a lack of identitarian representation in design history that should be grieved, this "gap in the record" corroborates the notion that some ancestors were able to escape into actual and historical shadows, and implicates the document as complicit in facilitating the availability of people and things to the gaze of hierarchical administration. The documental forms considered in this project are almost entirely vestigial traces located within the halls (or perhaps more likely, the dusty stacks) of power, created to make the world legible and manageable from the position of the administrator's desk. Indeed, they are *created* and as such, are also contestable—that is, available to the critical and creative modalities of graphic design practice.

Documents as the very material basis of any historical narration remind us that they are, in their very function, historio*graphical*. And historiography is a genre of design; its terrain is where currency and typography overlap. At first glance, this may seem idiosyncratic, arbitrary, and achronological. Yet, it resonates with Keith Hart's recognition of *money* and *language* as vehicles of memory.[15] Pointing to the imbrication of these phenomena helps to frame

---

15   "[M]oney considerably expands the capacity of individuals to stabilize their own personal identity by holding something durable that embodies the desires and wealth of all the other members of society. An aid

and narrate notions like standardization, visual epistemology, and govern-ance as political dimensions of design, and to cast them as realms of criti-cal/creative study and exploration. Furthermore, if historio*graphy* as a genre of design is inherently about settling claims and making it possible to utter as fact such statements as "this is New York City" vs. "this is Lenapehok-ing" (which are, instead, historical contingencies), a study of how history is designed to serve an agenda and to naturalize dominating claims suggests that this theater of conflict be understood as a matter of the politics of re-membrance. As an initial provocation in reconsidering how we might think about, teach, and practice graphic design, an essential scholarly question for the design student might be, "How is memory/knowledge designed?" and then, "What does this look like?"

Currency and typography happen to be two coterminal categories of graphical form locatable within the conventional boundaries of the field. Currency is perhaps the more peripheral of the two, if one judges by what school curricula—circumscribed by the market demand for design labor—call graphic design.[16] Even granting that their status as genres of design is incidental at best, it may be more salient to recognize them as being imbri-cated on their own terms: a five-thousand-year-old story built on vestigial traces of power to constitute an uncountable number of documental arti-facts, because to document—to hold a memory so as to be able to teach/show it—is precisely what these artifacts were designed to do. What I'm proposing is that spending some time in this entanglement of currency and typography (and their documental functions) brings us to a focus on the document (as a form) and documenting (as an agenda), and challenges many assumptions about what a designer is and does. One of the consequences of doing so is the articulation of some reflections not only about how certain people design documents and why, but also about how documents, in turn, design people and the world they live in. Perhaps it is within this dialectic that graphic design might understand its political stakes.

This reckoning with *what is at stake* has been neglected in graphic de-sign's disciplinary imaginary. Graphic design tends to be taught, through history and studio courses, as an affirmative, client-oriented, commercial practice. The canonical forms that delineate what has been (and now is) design, and the attendant skills and principles to be identified and under-stood from these examples, privilege the commercial, client-oriented prac-tice of the designer, who is characterized as an individual, petit-bourgeois auteur.[17] It is rare, if ever, that things like passports, tax forms, property

to memory, indeed···. Communities exist by virtue of their members' ability to exchange meanings that are substantially shared between them." See more in Keith Hart's, *The Memory Bank: Money in an Unequal World* (London: Profile Books, 2000), 259–61.

16   While typography sits squarely within the boundaries of graphic design, one would be hard-pressed to find even a superficial undergraduate or graduate course on currency design, though these are often acknowledged as having been designed. Books like David Standish's 2020 *The Art of Money* attest to this, as do the many design contests and exhibitions of money that have been held around the world. However, these almost invariably play in the representational register.

17   Silvio Lorusso's *Entreprecariat* brings much more nuance and depth to my pithy characterization.

deeds, driver's licenses, shop receipts, and money are taken up in design pedagogy, in spite of the fact that these forms are rather ubiquitous and enmeshed with profoundly transformative forces. Such unglamorous forms tend not to appear in the career fantasies of young designers.[18]

A critical, design-oriented study would begin by asking broadly: how has graphic design been an instrument of state-making, colonialism, and capitalism? It would also reconsider the constituents of graphic design historiography, not as a teleological apology for how graphic design is imagined, taught, and practiced today, but rather to implicate its centuries, if not millennia, of violent entanglement with the operations of great administrative entities like colonial states and capitalist enterprises (henceforth simply, bureaucracies). This is resonant with what the anthropologist Laura Nader has called "studying up"—that is, studying those in power—to produce an analysis and critique of that which has been kept in the dark from the perspective of those of us below (Nader 1972). Most importantly, this orientation of study also opens up a creative field of possibilities for antagonism.

To that end, *Immutable* is composed of themes and examples filed into an imaginary dossier—its own *j'accuse*, mounting the artifacts of empire as evidence of its own vaunted crimes. In the broadest sense, this is a narrative about graphic design as a technique for creating and reinforcing (colonial, capitalist) memory as progressive and inevitable. Documental memory is deliberately characterized as an act of "creation" and follows Johanna Drucker's insight that "visualizations are arguments made in graphical form" (Drucker 2014, ix–x). Indeed, what is created when we're talking about documents is an argument, a claim, a memory, and an attempt to objectify and sediment these as inscriptions in an immutable form—to place these outside of the entropy of movement through time and space, and more crucially, the contingency of the political.

Graphic design artifacts already often perform, rather incidentally, an indexical function. As its artifacts accede from the social quotidian to the historical, they inform what is knowable as history and put into relief the notion that history is itself a signifier. This can be elaborated on in at least two senses. The first is that a designerly consideration of history is meant in a very material, technical sense: things that are designed to be historical are things that are designed to transmit and store inscriptions, allowing them to move through space and time while stabilizing the integrity of their form. This immutability is key to their status as a document. The second is that—to the extent that claims, memories, and knowledge are actively *given form*—they are contestable and contingent: one way or another, things could have been formed otherwise and other things could have been claimed. One would do well to always query any historical nar-

---

18   Consider what it means for a person to be "undocumented," and therefore illegible and "illegal."
      Consider the violence called down upon this person to reinforce the validity of a distinction with
being "documented" (legible, legal).

rative as to whose memory, claims, and knowledge it centers.[19] What does it explain and naturalize?[20] Who benefits from a story being told a certain way? As a historiography of the design of history, this book also tries to be aware of how it itself is designed while eschewing a performative disavowal of bias that humanistic disciplines sometimes seek in the construction of their statements: processes of selection, editing, sequencing, and layout, to say the least, have rhetorical effects, and this book tries to be self-conscious and playful about how they are deployed.

For instance, the running text throughout this book (a linear convention) lays out a narrative that is only nominally chronological, sequential, and progressive. However, it tries to bypass the implicit pathology therein through a variety of intuitive and idiosyncratic moves. If reading the running text is like traveling down a river, not only is this river meandering, but one's trajectory is sure to be thrown off, tangled, trapped, turned over, and twisted by the intervention of notes, anecdotes, tangents, and the ccasional rock that appears unexpectedly while one strains for a clear navigational clue on the bank. Design and layout gestures trip over banal graphical conventions and act out a resentment for simplification, coordination, and standardization—snubbing the ways in which these values have been deployed as design imperatives in service of colonial management, administration, and governance.

Readers are invited both to engage with the book in a straightforward manner, or to wander diagonally through the pages, landing on and spending time with anything that sparks an interest at any given moment. Part two of this book is designed in a way that the ideas, artifacts, and stories it juxtaposes are arranged into digestible bundles that can be concatenated into a variety of readings and discussions. The spatial and sequential proximity of the page elements only suggest what I think are the most salient readings. Another way of looking at this book is that it tries to enact a circular sense of time rather than the kind of linear sequentiality embodied by conventional documentary forms. As a conceit, it is counterposed to the way that colonial/administrative/legal notions of linear time are coextensive with traditions like patrilineal naming, and the intergenerational inheritance of property and wealth (often, if not always, derived from heinous exploitation).

In broad strokes, part two of this book is arrayed with a set of documentary artifacts that serve as portals to prompt a consideration of design's role in manifesting and circulating the interests of administrative power, and iterates a narrative of immutability as a primary imperative in the design of documents. The imperative to immutability is recurrent in each

19   "My body will be no more than the graph that you write on it, a signifier that no one but you can decipher. But who are you, Law who transforms the body into your sign?' The act of suffering oneself to be written by the group's law is oddly accompanied by a pleasure, that of being recognized (but one does not know by whom), of becoming an identifiable and legible word in a social language, of being changed into a fragment within an anonymous text, of being inscribed in a symbolic order that has neither owner nor author." Michel de Certeau, *The Practice of Everyday Life*, trans. Steven Rendall (Berkeley: University of California Press, 1984), 140.
20   Ruth Frankenberg's study of the way that racial whiteness is ostensibly "unmarked" as the normative ground against which othered racial identities are marked is illuminating in this respect.

13

"sub-section" (they're more like waves), which explores the various ways that documental design artifacts try to satisfy the aim of deflecting the entropic decay of time and space, and to resist dispute.

What is arrayed herein to explore the facets of immutability as a design imperative is not exhaustively comprehensive, much less inarguable—there are certainly many, many gaps. The reader in search of a teaching resource that presents facts to be transmitted and consumed through rote memorization, rather than ideas to be considered and debated, has picked up the wrong book. This book is an essay, in the French sense of the word: an attempt that necessarily trespasses disciplinary spaces that I, as a graphic designer educated in a glorified trade school, have no official business working in (that is to say, for which I lack the correct papers). I hope to offer provocations as much as a much-needed space for treading on well-respected conventions. I hope to be able to dissolve some institutionalized boundaries; open up new paths of exchange and registers of study; and challenge traditional institutional/colonial notions of who makes knowledge and who is the object of study of other peoples' knowledge. That said, I welcome responses and insights coming from discussions about historiographic methodology and oral history, two fields in particular which this project ventures into with humility, and possibly naïveté. My sincerest wish, however, is that this book serves as a resource for unpacking the relationship between form, technique, history, and politics for students, educators, and practitioners of graphic design, as well as anyone engaged in a struggle for how things are known and remembered.

Before embarking on this voyage to alien territories, it will be helpful to orient ourselves by first establishing a point of departure. Where we're coming from and where we're headed are distinguished by two different sets of imperatives that frame graphic design praxis. The former tends to be lively and colorful, amicable and hospitable. This is a place where things are sold, announced, and published—it interpellates an audience. Graphic design, here, is driven by what I will call the *design imperative to publicity*. But leaving this place doesn't put us in the clear. Beyond its threshold lies, by contrast, a banal and arid ground, violent and unforgiving. It is a disputed territory, riven by conflict, and suffused with open antagonism. Here, graphic design is motivated by what I am calling the *design imperative to immutability*. Here, design objects are filled in, stored, and securitized, to interpellate people and things as recombinant ciphers, subordinated by administration. This, however, should not be understood as the destination, but as a terrain that is necessary to wander for a while before abandoning both territories.

I
The Trouble (With Graphic Design)

Our point of departure: the recognition that graphic design is troubled and troubling. It is troubled by a crisis of relevance and its marriage to commerce and capitalism, and the question of whether or not it can do something about it can be tracked in the literature from Ken Garland (1964) to Silvio Lorusso (2023). Its canonical history, however, gives us examples of the ways it has battled illiteracy, inefficiency, and injustice; artifacts ranging from war propaganda to counter-cultural protest art index a moral aspiration, a precedent to emulate, and a cultural ideal. Yet, in the face of the intensifying normalization of systemic racism, war, fascism, and environmental catastrophe—all aspects of capitalist/colonial imposition—graphic design struggles to reckon with a troubling romanticization of its impact (Laranjo 2014).While the extent of its capacity to intervene has largely been limited to designing campaigns and speculative proposals, or to taking on so-called "wicked problems" through competitive challenges within the cultural sphere, the question remains as to what can be done—what capacities, tools, and weapons can designers wield in one hand in order to undo the harm to which it has been accomplice with the other? While asking this question earnestly, designers hesitate to admit that design has been rather unconvincing in meaningfully antagonizing capitalism/colonialism, even if (or more likely because) it has been one of its lackeys. Design, for instance, fetishizes "progress" while misrecognizing, in the luster of its advancing front, a wake of misery and destruction.

The conundrum of graphic design's inertia in the face of catastrophe is partly a matter of its vocabulary of forms being constrained by the grammar established by its historiography. Notwithstanding a few exceptions, there seems to be relatively little consideration, reflection, or critique of graphic design as an instrument of capitalism/colonialism.[21] The prevailing historical narrative tells us that the canonical genres of form that constitute graphic design typically include things like writing systems, typefaces, signage, books, posters, identity systems, campaigns, websites, etc., arrayed as a progressive telos which takes us from cave paintings to moveable typography to the Internet. Taken together, these constituents of graphic design historiography figure a discipline in which progress is defined primarily as a struggle to overcome the friction of time/space, in order to transmit messages as widely and as quickly as possible. The hyper locality and illegible particularity of cave paintings are taken as the departure point in conventional design history, from which the Internet can be teleologically affirmed as the apogee of communication media due to its

---

21   The groups, programs, and/or publications depatriarchise design and Futuress (Basel), Decolonising Design, Interference Archive (New York), *Modes of criticism* (Porto), and *CAPS LOCK: How Capitalism Took Hold of Graphic Design and How to Escape from It* by Ruben Pater (Valiz, 2021), among others, as well as various unaffiliated individuals, form but a handful of examples in an immense field.

putatively universalizing immediacy. What graphic design historiography includes, and how it narrates the relationships between what it includes, thus shapes the imaginary horizons of what students come to implicitly understand as its disciplinary purview—what it is, the kinds of sociability it mediates, and who practices it. In other words, this history suggests to its readers that graphic design's historical mandate is to colonize its dark, illegible peripheries by promoting, demanding, and imposing the kind of universalizing rationality that would connect the world as one big society/market. Put yet another way, design historiography's modernist commitments aim to position graphic design as a liberal utopian instrument that will resolve the cacophonous irrationality of the world and harmonize it along the lines of some kind of inevitable consensus.

As a field of practice and study, graphic design largely lacks the language for recognizing and reflecting on its alignment with the destructive, "defuturing" impact of capitalism/colonialism (Dilnot et al. 2015, 15). *Immutable*'s counterintuitive suggestion is that we ought to look at the occluded counterforms of design history, represented by documents, designed as such, in an attempt to examine this silence, and to reckon with the culpability of design. I should be very clear from the outset that there will be no comprehensive resolution or absolution for design—it may be irredeemable. However, what I am interested in is working through design's indictment—to name its crimes—as the premise upon which to ask the reparative question: how to recover what it has damaged, to undo what it has wrought, and to unlearn (or abandon) it in favor of a praxis engaged in giving form to anti-capitalist and decolonial sociability.[22] To this end, let's go back to *1984*, incidentally the same year Apple releases its first personal desktop computer, the Macintosh.

1984s

Winston Smith, the protagonist of George Orwell's *1984*, is a graphic designer. He works at the Ministry of Truth in the Records Department, editing historical documents ("photoshopping" JPGs, and hacking PDFs, surely). He rewrites history to align with the policies and pronouncements of Big Brother. Winston secretly hates the Party, and he hates being a graphic

---

22   The poet Eunsong Kim decries the "uncreative writing" processes of Kenneth Goldsmith's conceptual poetry. Goldsmith was famously criticized for his tone-deaf reading of the autopsy report of Michael Brown (the Black teenager killed in 2014 by police in Ferguson, MO, sparking the Black Lives Matter movement) as a piece of conceptual poetry. She argues that the conceptualist, algorithmic techniques he employs for generating form are consistent with a capitulation to the managerial logic of capitalism. She sees such processes as resignation to the impossibility of producing new forms or articulating and valorizing other points of view, and to the absence of revolutionary irruptions and radically subversive ways of being outside the prescriptive grid of capitalist hegemony. Under such conditions, the options available to the poet are constrained to the horizon of rearranging its existing components in novel ways. For Kim, quoting Audre Lorde, "··· poetry is a form against standardization, and an attack on her is an attack on the emergent." See Eunsong Kim, "Poetry without Poets," in *Forms of Education: Couldn't Get a Sense of It*, ed. Aeron Bergman, Irena Borić, and Alejandra Salinas (Seattle, WA: Institute for New Connotative Action Press, 2016), 46. She asserts that there is indeed still much that needs to be said—much that has been erased, suppressed, silenced, marginalized, invalidated—many points of view, ways of knowing and being that exist or could exist beyond, underneath, in the margins, and in spite of capitalist/colonial inevitability. Could poetry/poiesis provide insights for articulating a counter position to graphic design?

designer. He struggles to manifest his own desire in spite of it. He writes a personal diary, and he falls in love. To Winston, these are the only things that are true, but he learns that truth is located neither in his desires nor in anything outside of them. He learns, when his poetic resistance is punished, that truth is a matter of power. Big Brother's gaze, the Party's official language—"newspeak"—and the practice of "doublethink" make his humanity unthinkable, unsayable, and unknowable.

This Orwellian allegory gives us a way to see form and form-making as actuators of the ways one sees, knows, makes, and acts upon the world. Clive Dilnot's 1984 essay "The State of Design History" provides an articulation of Winston's angst when he asks: "To what extent can history contribute to what design is and what a designer does[?]" (Dilnot 1984, 5). What other words are there for making thinkable, knowable, and actionable other conceptions of design? What concepts, precedents, tools and forms can equip us for a break from its current horizons?

Similarly, Frantz Fanon challenges us to peer over the edge of what has been given, to see the history of the colony not as one that drives toward its modernization, but as the history of the plunderous extension of the metropole (Fanon 2004). Ananda K. Coomaraswamy is famously quoted: "We are proud of our museums, where we display the damning evidence of a way of living that we have made impossible" (Coomaraswamy 1947, 7). Ariella Aïsha Azoulay impels us to imagine what could have been, had the colonial theft of world-making artifacts not taken place—had the art museum, that palace of colonial memory, not been an agent of dispossession. Her insights on "unlearning imperialism" and imagining "potential histories" provide a compelling exit strategy (Azoulay 2019). But before we embark on exploring these escape routes, let's first try to anticipate some traps we'll find along the way.

"Good Design"

There have been a small handful of coordinated public attempts at reconciling graphic design with its complicity in systems of domination. They have mostly taken the form of self-conscious handwringing, stemming from the ascendance of design as a facet of the NATO bloc's soft power apparatus. Yoko Ono's counsel that weapons of war be replaced with paint has been taken to heart—the world is increasingly covered in a glass and steel shade of neoliberal blue, with a wash of green for good measure.

The "First Things First" (FTF) manifesto, for instance, agonizes over this entanglement and attempts to escape its orbit by vaguely articulating a politics of refusal (Garland 1964). Its recirculation in the year 2000, published by *Adbusters* and other professional and academic periodicals at the time (i.e., *Items* in The Netherlands, AIGA *Eye on Design* in the US, and more), tweaks and updates the modest and vague declarations of the original, which carry with it an immobilizing ambiguity.[23] Between 1964 and the year 2000, the manifesto itself added only eleven more signatures from high-profile contributors, primarily if not entirely from NATO countries. The signatories of the FTF manifestos—dispersed across networks, loosely organized, if at all, in studio clusters, and perhaps exemplary of the so-called "Professional Managerial Class" (Winant 2019)—have proven unable to coalesce into a coherent political entity or a force with any capacity for coordinated systemic antagonism—not in the sixties, not in the aughts, and not now. They represent a subjectivity whose agency is enacted at the scale of the atomized designer. The vagueness of the FTF language reads as a "first-world" designer problem. Urgency, clarity, and a militant analysis are evidently muted by proximity to power, capital, and a comfortable distance from both the systemic and direct physical violence these entail. The manifesto's performative signaling is akin to the self-congratulatory domestic peace movement against the American War (in Vietnam), and the complete erasure of successful Viet Cong resistance forces within Western narratives. Such liberal political horizons beg for a clearer distinction—at the very least, between refusal and action. Metahaven might have sealed the coffin of morbid designer guilt in the opening of their text "White Night Before a Manifesto." In recasting so-called information overload as the infinite multiplication of "surface," they mapped graphic design to a speculative and immaterial domain that, by virtue of its boundlessness, is void of any meaningful antagonism. "Surface is not territory. Territory, which is actual and geographical (for that reason limited in supply), can be contested and may become the site of an actual conflict, a physical confrontation. This cannot happen on, or to, a surface. Surface is to territory what speculative capital is to gold" (Metahaven 2008). One thing that is confounding about FTF is that it casts designers as actors complicit, if not outright implicated, in the crimes of capitalism—an indication of great power—yet essentially unable to do anything about them other than "hope that our society will tire of gimmick merchants, status salesmen and hidden persuaders, and that the prior call on our skills will be for worthwhile purposes" (Garland 1964).

---

23 This equivocation was also noted by Metahaven in *White Night Before a Manifesto* (May 2008) and it still applies to the renovations published in 2014 and 2020 (*firstthingsfirst2014.net* and *firstthingsfirst2020.org*). While the sincerity of these iterations is not in doubt, Metahaven point out that "its signees are not outraged, but 'increasingly uncomfortable.'" One wonders if regular updates, by dint of their repetition, won't start seeming more like a form of self-flagellation for a fractional set of formally trained designers.

The signatories "propose to share our experience and opinions, and to make them available to colleagues, students and others who may be interested."[24]

Global design (for good) festivals like What Design Can Do? (WDCD),[25] attempt to pick up where FTF, then and now, have left us by formalizing and coordinating efforts to see design put to "better" use. But such initiatives can be just as problematic, and perhaps even more damaging, in their patronizing solutionism. The Amsterdam-based design festival, for instance, started in 2011 as "a platform to showcase design as a catalyst of change and as a way of addressing the societal issues of our time."[26] In annual conferences held in Amsterdam, Mexico City and São Paulo, as well as on the festival's blog, designers from around the world are invited to respond to challenges ranging from the quest to scale up clean energy to the so-called European refugee crisis.

These challenges privilege design as a problem-solving, solutionist activity and tend not to reckon, in spite of themselves, with their topic of concern systemically. Indeed, the second paragraph of their description of the Challenge program on the website states that:

> WDCD's Challenge programme is a space where the creative community can pilot, test and scale new innovations led by design and design-thinking. Participants range from young professionals to creatives, designers, students, social entrepreneurs and start-ups.
> Challenges provide the global creative community with the connections, resources and funding to help their ideas thrive.[27]

Such "challenges" treat crisis and catastrophe as opportunities for designers to demonstrate their benevolence and intellect. They paradoxically suggest that design is not already political—that the world hasn't already been affected by design-inflected "progress." It's an omission that suggests that the ways in which the world is wrought through design are marked as a kind of inevitable natural phenomenon. They fantasize about the agency of the individual designer/studio operating autonomously against systemic forces, without regard for the operational dimension of a design object resting on massive organizations (consider that a coin is just a piece of metal without a state recognizing it as a legitimate form of money, or that a passport only "functions" as such under the gaze of an armed border agent). The writing for WDCD's 2015–2027 "Refugee Challenge" belies an empathetic regard for displaced people, figuring them instead as props in design's performative virtue signaling.

---

24   "First Things First" manifesto designishistory.com/1960/first-things-first.
25   The initiative What Design Can Do (WDCD) is exemplary of design solutionism which, in failing to ask the question "What has design done?" largely reproduces the imposing coloniality of design.
26   "Mission," What Design Can Do, last accessed November 28, 2024, *whatdesigncando.com*.
27   This quote seems to be the updated copy, replacing the following, which is no longer on the website:
"The objective of this challenge was to call upon creative thinkers to use the power of design to come up with real life solutions to global problems. Our aim was to demonstrate *the potential impact that design can have* on our lives, and to encourage designers to use their skills and creative thinking to embark upon political activism." See "Challenges," What Design Can Do.

The graphic designer, researcher, and writer Ruben Pater has noted that although the competition invites submissions by refugees themselves, the promotional imagery and language are addressed more to non-refugee participants. He observes that images like the one depicting "refugees standing in line, covered with blankets, aided by UNHCR workers," are followed by the tagline "here's your chance to make a difference" (Pater 2016). One gets the sense from this image/text arrangement that the people in the photograph are not the people who are being offered a "chance" to enter a design competition but rather are aspects of a situation for the *designer* to "make a difference." This is reminiscent of Azoulay's critique of the myopic, self-serving colonial notions of progress, characterized more commonly as modernizing and civilizing projects, and less as a destructive force. Just as egregiously, perhaps, it also mirrors the hubris of the designer, who misrecognizes the power they serve as the power that they wield.

The path outlined for the challenge generally follows the conventional life cycle of product pitches for a commercial endeavor. Winning submissions are engaged in an acceleration program in which concepts are developed "into working prototypes and business plans." This process narrowly applies design as a vehicle of commerce and perhaps, by extension, policy. As such, it is an invitation that forecloses on the possibility of soliciting ideas that may truly be antagonistic to the entities that help to create the very conditions that produce the refugee crisis (there's no "business plan" for the dissolution of the system of nation-states and their borders, for instance). It disqualifies an analysis of the forces that underwrite the funding and resources that participate in producing the problem in the first place. Designers are in effect asked to operate politely within the realm of their increasingly institutionalized and professionalized forms of labor.

While the desire to help may be quite sincere, one wonders if there isn't another horizon of analysis, a different approach to the "refugee crisis" (read: ongoing effects of colonialism and capitalism) besides one that is ensnared by the publicity-oriented hubris of WDCD. Pater's criticism is even more insightful when he frames the competition within the context of an ascendant right-wing populism fomenting xenophobia and fiscal austerity measures that cut funding from the pillars of the welfare state (the arts, healthcare, social services, etc.) in favor of a society more deeply structured by the market. He cautions that the good intentions of "design for good" which inform the WDCD Refugee Challenge could exacerbate the crisis by covering for, or encouraging, the withdrawal of European states from their humanitarian and social welfare programs. One could go even further and call out the historical role of these states in producing such crises in the first place—the responsibility of former colonial powers to unconditionally restore and repair the damage wrought on the people and places from which their wealth, and many of the refugees fleeing to their shores, have come.

II
Design Imperatives (Publicity)

FTF and WDCD are trapped, along with the more vulgar commercial practices they try to create distance with, within a domain of design that I call the *design imperative to publicity* (What I'll refer to henceforth, schematically, as Design$_I$). This imperative emerges from an ontology of design that casts the "capital-D" Designer (henceforth Designer$_I$) as producer of communication artifacts aimed at a public for the benefit of a client/commissioner trying to maximize, or at least optimize, the cost of reaching as many people as it can. Susan Sontag's exegesis on the poster points out that this paradigmatic genre of graphic design "presupposes the modern concept of the public—in which the members of a society are defined primarily as spectators and consumers."[28] Designer$_I$ emerges from a historiography that narrates the history of this figure as an agent who strives to communicate to an increasingly global public. This Designer$_I$ is valorized as such by a market composed of clients/commissioners seeking their services to make artifacts of publicity (henceforth Artifacts$_I$). In fact, it doesn't make much sense to ontologically distinguish Designer$_I$ from their clients. Designer$_I$'s value is tied to their ability to render communications artifacts and deliver these to a mass audience. Designers$_I$ are fundamentally interpellated by a canonical design historiography (henceforth History$_I$) which valorizes a client-oriented commercial pedagogy, wherein what is prioritized is the production of workers who are certified and prepared to furnish the requirements of publicity.

I reiterate here the above in a more concise schematization so that it can be held up to another schematization later on for comparison: **History$_I$** circumscribes **Design$_I$**. These are populated by **Designer$_I$**, who is charged with the making of **Artifacts$_I$** (inculcated in its attendant techniques).

Let's postulate that Designer$_I$ is trained and valorized as such through gate-keeping institutions (and sometimes even through specific networks of social media/peer recognition that are not so far from the institutions).[29] Again, Designers$_I$ are recognizable as such by dint of the kinds of things they make—artifacts that presume the mobilization of technologies for producing, storing, and transmitting messages aimed at large audiences that are sometimes, depending on the available budget for market research, figured through the lens of reductive consumer profiles (i.e., "lattes & strollers" for the young urban family, or "pick-up trucks & fishing poles" for the suburban homesteader).[30] This Designer$_I$, by definition, can't be disentangled from an expansionary logic driven by the relentless

---

28 Susan Sontag, "Posters: Advertisement, Art, Political Artifact, Commodity," in *The Art of Revolution: 96 Posters from Cuba*, ed. Stermer Dugald (New York: McGraw-Hill, 1970), 196–218.

29 There ought to be a study that concretely maps the overlaps between the graduates of certain schools and social media following.

30 Insert Starter pack meme. Silvio lorusso?

search for new audiences/friends/followers/consumers. This Designer$_I$ works for the benefit of the client. Even design artifacts that fall outside of these conditions—because they are made by the self-driven designer for ostensibly non-commercial purposes—are defined in relation to the (lack of a) client. Being formally trained in graphic design means becoming a Designer$_I$.

The canonical category of form factors I will dare to identify as universally privileged in the studio/classroom includes an array of artifacts ranging from typography, logos/corporate identity systems, brands, books, magazines, posters, websites, signage and wayfinding, advertisements and campaigns, and other genres and formats of publicity. Student assignments tend to be framed primarily by the transmission of technical, formal knowledge cultivating literacy in, and adherence to, the conventions of legibility and "good design."[31] Ethical/aesthetic concerns tend to be overcoded by language inherited from pop-psychology-inflected marketing, and generally adhere to a mandate to create legible and accessible communication work for such constituencies as the "target audience." These tendencies can be understood as being axiomatic of Design$_I$.

Career Outlook and Curriculum

A cursory examination of "Career Outlook" webpages from a variety of graphic design programs in North America offers an impression of the discipline's conventional boundaries.[32] Below, a few examples:

> Graphic Design graduates leave RISD [Rhode Island School of Design] prepared to work in almost any field imaginable—from education to film, television, publishing, retail and more. Alumni follow a wide range of individual paths, including running their own design studios, working for large corporations, specializing in web and interactive media, and creating everything from package design to title sequences for film and television.[33]

> You can pursue studio courses in areas of practice such as: Brand strategy, Editorial and publication design, Interactive communication, Motion graphics, Packaging design, Typeface design, Wayfinding and information systems[34]

> ROI: Return on Imagination. Graphic Design alumni are thriving in an array of fields, with jobs that include:

---

31   One may often encounter this phrase in design education contexts and never know what exactly this means. Still, there might be resonance with what Thomas J. Watson Jr., former president of IBM, is often quoted as having said in a 1966 memo: that "good design is good business." Its apocryphal status among designers is less an affirmation of business and more an attempt at valorizing design through its proximity to the world and financial resources of commerce.
32   While digging deeper and wider among North American schools and beyond will show a variation with a debatable degree of departure in orientation from those listed here, it remains true that no schools are attempting to attract graphic design students with the prospect of becoming passport designers.
33   "Digital Commons @ RISD," Rhode Island School of Design, last accessed November 28, 2024, digitalcommons.risd.edu/graphicdesign/.
34   "Discover OCAD U Graphic Design," OCAD U (Ontario College of Art and Design University), last accessed November 28, 2024, ocadu.ca/academics/undergraduate-studies/graphic-design.

— UI designer for Uber
— Graphic designer for motion pictures such as
Nope and First Man
— Fashion technology designer
— Brand designers for Chobani, Everlast, and more
— Designers at agencies including Paperwhite in NYC and FleishmanHillard
in Washington, DC[35]

Typical formats include branding and logo development, posters, books, package design, apps, websites, and interactive design. Students learn to articulate a critical and theoretical perspective and develop graphic design skills, such as type design and traditional letterpress. Strong craft and presentation skills are emphasized throughout. Students achieve the highest level of design excellence through critiques, reviews, and workshops. Recent employers include Apple, Anthropologie, LACMA, Guess, Metro, and Capitol Records.[36]

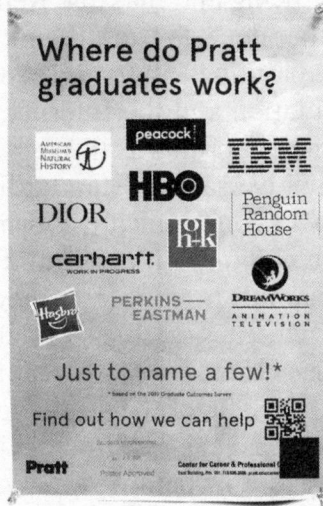

These examples map a domain of agency and intervention animated by the prospect of addressing a public through mass networked media. Or at the very least, they promise an engaging career involving high technology and working for national and international brands, prescribing student (and parent) aspirations before they even enter the classroom studio.

Design$_I$'s orientation is reinforced in curricula via the canonical history of graphic design, whenever it is available as a course, and implicitly naturalized where there is no such course offered. The design theorists Clive Dilnot, Tony Fry, and Susan C. Stewart cast design history as a form of "ontological design" (Dilnot et al. 2015, 29). They argue that the production of history invariably bears an agenda that narrows the discursive breadth and disciplinary imagination of practices like graphic design. This is exemplified in the de facto accession of Phillip Meggs's *History of*

---

35 "Graphic Design at MICA," Maryland Institute College of Art, last accessed November 28, 2024, mica.edu/undergraduate-majors-minors/graphic-design-major.
36 "BFA in Graphic Design," OTIS College of Art and Design, otis.edu/programs/undergraduate/bfa-graphic-design/index.html.

Graphic Design as the primary textbook demarcating the boundaries of what it means to be a contemporary graphic designer and to do graphic design today.[37]

Johanna Drucker critiques Meggs's book for uncritically adopting the methodology and narrative modality of art history. Its concern with provenance, much like art history, is expressed as a concatenation of artifacts that are ordered primarily along the lines of a linear, teleological chronology. Transposed to graphic design as a techno-progressivist model of history, Meggs's narration "works against analysis of ideological forces; it naturalizes sequence as a self-evident fact" (Drucker 2009, 61). Rather than seeing designers as political actors and design as a political and historical force in and of itself, this tendency suggests that these Designers, and the Artifacts, they create are outside of the social, political, economic, and ideological conditions of their being and making. Remember, Meggs's history figures a telos of design that departs from the indecipherable, local particularity of pictorial cave paintings and is directed toward the universalizing rationality of computation and the Internet. In other words, it casts the activity of graphic Designers, primarily through a narrative lens of technological progress, toward a universalizing standardization of the production, transmission, and literacy of communicative form. This of course fails to acknowledge the Western colonial inflection of this universalism, where imperialism and global capitalism appear as inevitable and, to borrow a concept from the field of whiteness studies, rather "unmarked" (Frankenberg 2001). Drucker observes that for Meggs, changes in the appearance of designed objects are symptomatic of the aesthetic tendencies of extraordinary individuals, and appear as incidental, self-evident markers that neatly illuminate the invariable path to where we are today.

Drucker also argues that by neglecting the codependence between graphical object, technology, and "circumstances of production and use" (62), and by simply situating the historical appearance of canonical artifacts within the flow of technological progress, Meggs denies the reader any tools for discerning the political, economic, epistemological, and ontological consequentiality of the episodes and artifacts he describes. She turns to his narration of the advent of moveable typography as applied in Gutenberg's printing press, observing that, while Meggs provides an informative description of techniques like punchcutting, matrix casting, and the development of an alloy specifically designed to withstand repeated pressing, he never suggests that the standardization and modularization that are part of letterpress technology imposes rationality on human production in a way that broke with the holistic guild approach and provided

---

37   I would also note that from my own anecdotal survey of studio/classroom contexts, in which I ask students why they chose to study graphic design, the answers often range from something to the effect of, "I want to do art, but my parents want me to get a job," to "I want a career in advertising." Even before one encounters the canonical history or normative program descriptions, graphic design's disciplinary boundaries seem to be circumscribed by artifacts and desires endemic to commerce and the market.

a model for attitudes towards knowledge production as well as labor. The fragmentation of processes into distinct parts that had to fit—literally in the case of letterpress is part of larger changes.... [T]he printing press exemplifies the organizing principles for discourse formation in the larger social order. The rationalization of sight according to perspectival principles and the introduction of mapping systems to organize space according to a mathematical representation register related and equally striking shifts aligned with these organizing principles" (Drucker 2009, 62)

The other ontological consequence of this techno-progressive parochialism, Drucker argues, is the figure of the ostensibly autonomous Designer$_1$, freely making creative decisions independently from the conditions that constitute their subjectivity.[38] For Meggs, she argues, "designers are conceived as acted on, not complicit" (64). In addition to enacting a kind of "mirage of an unmarked whiteness,"[39] these blindspots also echo a capitulation to what Mark Fisher calls "capitalist realism" (2009), given that most Anglophone graphic design students engage this as the main source for learning a history of their chosen discipline.[40]

Auteur

Today's Designers$_1$, largely inculcated as a kind of atomized, post-Fordist worker in a field constantly struggling to pin down its value proposition, maneuver to position themselves in whatever flow of capital design can latch on to. Authorship, persona, and charisma are values that aid in producing market distinctions, and legibility (measured in likes, followers, and connections, in addition to formal credentials) is to varying degrees equated with legitimacy, longevity, and relevance.

In a famous debate that took place in Amsterdam in 1972, Wim Crouwel admonishes Jan van Toorn for asserting too much subjectivity in his commissioned work. An excess of opinion and affect, rather than a prioritization of the business objectives of the client, jeopardizes the relevance of a practice and undermines its credibility, he argued. This is illustrative of a persistent and pervasive ethical position that emerges with the protagonists of modernist graphic design, as many in the field sought to align themselves with capital flowing through business and commerce. One position seeks the valorization of graphic design on the basis of the singularity of the Designer$_1$ as auteur—and ostensibly, as provocateur (taking as inevitable its interdependence on a client, van Toorn)—while the other is staked on the valorization of graphic

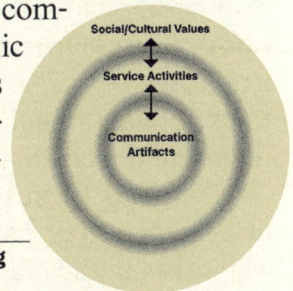

Social/Cultural Values

Service Activities

Communication
Artifacts

---

38   Suguru Ishizaki's service design diagrams offer a possible tool for mapping the forces that enable and constrain a design artifact and its attributes, effects, meanings, etc.

39   Incidentally, the so-called "2016 Design Census Survey" showed that the graphic design field in the United States was ~73% white at that time.

40   Meggs's book has been translated to Chinese, Hebrew, Japanese, Korean, and Spanish (Heller 2018), however, I am unable to speak to the status of this book in graphic design curricula in these countries.

design for its utility in facilitating the agenda of clients—helping to rationalize business and public administration (while disavowing its performative anti-subjectivity) (Poynor, 2015).

Crouwel's brand of "total design," for instance, which favors austere, aesthetic restraint in an embrace of mechanical rationality, and developed for large corporate clients and multinationals, articulated form in consideration of the constraints presented by the telecommunications technology of the time and an administrative requirement for bureaucratic harmonization (read: documents) across the expanding geographies of corporate/capitalist organization. He was distinguished in the market precisely for this kind of work, and the accession of the corporate identity as an elemental genre in graphic design education today testifies to this. The development of corporate identity is narrated in the canonical historiography of design as an indicator of the progressive trajectory of Western democracy and capitalism, and is associated with the putative neutrality of internationalist tendencies like the so-called International Typographic Style.[41] Those familiar with Meggs's textbook may recall that in his narration of graphic design history, the development of corporate identity design is oriented toward globalization as the force behind the development of the Internet—a tautological construction that aligns such phenomena as a progressive inevitability. As the infrastructure of an emergent "global village" (McLuhan 1967), the Internet represents for Meggs an ideal monumental achievement as a corrective Other to the kinds of irrational, conflict-laden tribal particularities that Crouwel accuses Van Toorn of reproducing (irresponsibly and self-indulgently). This attitude is itself an echo of Adolf Loos's racist "Ornament and Crime,"[42] which feared the kind of aesthetic irrationality expressed through a "narcissism of minor (national) differences," to use Freud's famous phrase, and was associated with the World Wars of the twentieth century.[43]

Yet, both figures are inextricably dependent on the client and their publicity imperatives; as such, they are exemplary of the capital-D Designer, who exists in the market as an auteur and continues to win lucrative work

---

41   Also known as "Swiss Style."
42   Adolf Loos, "Ornament and Crime," in *Programs and Manifestoes on 20th-Century Architecture*, ed. Ulrich Conrads, trans. Michael Bullock (Cambridge, MA: MIT Press, 1970), 19–24.
43   Sigmund Freud, w, trans. David McLintock (London: Penguin Classics, 2002).

by virtue of their visibility in it. Though it is quite self-evident, Van Toorn's critical interventions and formal experimentation are ultimately recuperated in the tacit approval of the client who *allows* his critical designs to be actualized publicly. The self-scandalization his interventions produce may even be beneficial to the client, who is thereby able to show themselves as receptive to criticism, transparent, and accountable to the public. The condescending air of Crouwel's admonishment to serve the client faithfully hallucinates about an evacuation of subjectivity as dispassionate transparency, and rests on the performativity of the designer's disciplined technocratic execution. This impasse, and FTF's vagueness, also bely a kind of passivity by suggesting that Designers$_1$ maintain a strategic holding pattern until an opportunity appears to do more "meaningful" work (for an NGO, a cultural organization, a not-for-profit community group, etc.) to rescue them from their current patrons. The Designer$_1$ is deeply entangled with the market, which mobilizes their labor (for profit, or not), sustains the valorization of the Designer$_1$ as a "problem-solving" agent (whose problem?) equipped with the tools to "improve" (what and for who?) and "renew" things (what is discarded?), but trapped by their intermediary position between client and public and thus doing work that is circumscribed by an imperative to publicity.[44]

Incidentally, there is a rather meaningful counter-position to such figures and their artifacts$_1$, which also lies within the domain of the Design$_1$, but actualizes a different order of opposition than what I aim to suggest later. While this position is not our destination, we shall make a slight detour to it, if only to better map the impasse I wish to posit.

OSPAAAL and the *Atelier Populaire*

A reminder that we're still looking at potential traps, and that one may be found even in an area that is almost inarguably righteous (unless, of course, one is more of a reactionary). The Organización de Solidaridad de los Pueblos de África, Asia y América Latina (OSPAAAL), founded in 1966 immediately after the Tricontinental Conference in Havana, Cuba (only two years after the publication of FTF), as well as the proliferation of Ateliers Populaires across France in and around the May '68 uprisings, are two instances that illustrate graphic production animated by political struggles, which overlap in their opposition to capitalism and imperialism.[45]

---

44   A common genre of graphic design school assignment entails redesigning or rebranding something, refreshing it, making it "better," and distinguishing oneself from one's peers through work measured against something old, which is cast as inherently problematic.

45   The neutered narration of OSPAAAL, and the omission of the *Ateliers Populaires* from the de facto textbook on graphic design history by Philip B. Meggs and Alston W. Purvis is illuminating. The Ateliers Populaires were conspicuously, though perhaps not unsurprisingly, absent from Meggs' *History of Graphic Design*, while OSPAAAL is given around two pages in the fifth edition. The treatment of OSPAAAL in these pages is characteristically uninsightful, unreflexive, patronizing, and barely conceals a dismissive, American disdain for these "Third-world" posters and their "ideological" content directed at what the authors render, ironically, in quotations as "'Yankee imperialism." See Meggs and Purvis, *Meggs' History of Graphic Design*, 5th ed. (Hoboken, NJ: John Wiley & Sons, 2012), 457–59. Johanna Drucker and Emily McVarish's *Graphic Design History: A Critical Guide* include both OSPAAAL and the Ateliers Populaires as sidenotes on pages 280–81.

OSPAAAL was a propaganda office and studio that promoted revolutionary left-wing internationalism, led by agents trained in Madison Avenue advertising agencies (Chak 2019). It models a collective designing subjectivity and agency, in contrast to a Western capitalist/colonial world and the atomized designer who inhabits it. OSPAAAL directed their efforts toward the cultivation of an internationalist consciousness antagonistic to the very forces about whom the signatories of "First Things First" could only wring their hands. It is worth mentioning that while the FTF document itself is formally resonant with modernist tendencies of the International Typographical Style and the sober restraint typical of northern/Central European publicly funded social democratic design—rational, dispassionate, and utilitarian—OSPAAAL's stylistic tendencies were boldly idiosyncratic. Sometimes psychedelic and always deeply coded, their designs were charged with affect, often featuring copy set in multiple languages calling to an audience united in their struggle against Euro-American imperialism. This imperialism was increasingly represented by corporate modernism and public administrative modernism, as seen in massive (colonial) urban development projects of the era, such as Brasília in Brazil and Chandigarh in India.[46] This formal, graphical contrast between FTF and OSPAAAL indexes two positions within a field of imperial/anti-imperial antagonism. However, it may also be suggested that these formal tendencies, beyond their indexicality, can function as equipment, embodiment, assertion, and claim. On the one hand, the rationality of the grid, and the fetish of legibility and universalism manifest in high-modernist graphical form, while appearing outwardly progressive, belying a tacit coloniality—a desire for the kind of accountability/transparency that enables containment and managerial control, unencumbered by irrational ornamentation and unpredictable subjective flairs. On the other, the highly particular inflections of OSPAAAL's posters; the culturally specific references and codes; the affect of idiosyncratic, colorful hand-painted forms; and their internationalism eschew imperial languages of form.[47] The posters' copy often appears in Arabic, English, French, Spanish, and Chinese. Their forms affirm particularity and stand in contrast to the accountability and formal transparency of corporate design. What they depict comes from the shadows of mountains and jungles[48]; their forms evade managerial scrutiny and refuse the empiricism of colonial epistemology.[49] As Susan

---

46   J. Dakota Brown's excellent pamphlet, *Typography, Automation, and the Division of Labor: A Brief History*, concisely sketches the divisions of design, typographic, and printing labor. His analysis highlights the complex relations that underwrite what is mistakenly understood as the "product of a singular detached mind." In his description of the impact of Apple's Macintosh computer's arrival on this division of labor, he gestures to the valorization of the grid in modernist, corporate design—as an instrument of technical/professional communication that provides precise measurements and coordinates from the designer's conception of an outcome to pre-press. Its rectilinear rationality is elemental to the graphical user interface of the Macintosh and becomes discernible as an artifact of managerial aesthetics. Brown, *Typography, Automation, and the Division of Labor: A Brief History* (Chicago, Other Forms, 2019), 28.

47   Drucker's insightful treatment of this concept can be consulted in *Graphesis*, 28–40.

48   James C. Scott casts such terrain as illegible to the state, and, as such, consonant with the strategies of the non/anti-statist subaltern in eluding governance.

49   What if design historiography gave more space to the internationalism of the anti-imperial struggle,

Sontag observed, the aim of the posters was to "raise and complicate consciousness—the highest aim of the revolution itself" (Sontag 1999). Well, yes, but...

The Atelier Populaire (AP) was spawned amid the upheavals of May '68 in France. Beginning with the occupation of the print studios at the École des Beaux-Arts in Paris, the "popular workshop" spread to other occupied print studios across the country. The Atelier produced and freely distributed propaganda posters in support of an uprising that seized the country for seven weeks. An account of the studio's production tools illuminates the political significance of graphical techniques and form. The story of the first AP poster goes that a lithographic print, output in an edition of fifty at the printing workshop of the Beaux-Arts, was being delivered to a local commercial print gallery to be sold to raise funds for striking factory workers. The courier's path, however, required traversing a barricade set up by protestors. While trying to pass through, the posters were snatched by the protestors and distributed and pasted on walls throughout the city. This was an epiphany. The revolutionary potential of the poster lay not with the traditional mechanisms of production and distribution (i.e., refined lithographic prints on proper archival paper destined for collectors of the middle and upper classes), but with the radical appropriation of these mechanisms by the people. The students returning to the print workshop sought cheaper and faster modes of production: serigraphy (silk-screen printing), cheap ink, and rolls of newsprint donated by sympathetic newspapers enabled an amplification of production and distribution. Atelier were established as students across the country occupied institutional spaces and their equipment, set up on the street, and organized councils to decide what would get printed (Deaton 2013).

Downplaying entities such as OSPAAAL and phenomena like the Atelier Populaires within canonical texts highlights a bias inherent in design history. It shows that creative endeavors undertaken collectively and driven by a sense of urgency and discontent, a commitment to a cause, opposition, the pursuit of liberation, speculation on a shared identity rooted in the struggles of the marginalized, and the fostering of solidarity against imperialism and capitalism, as well as against various forms of unjust discrimination, often receive little attention in historical narratives intended to uphold the primacy of the Designer$_1$'s existence.[50]

rather than the internationalism of the typographic style championed by the vertically integrated multinational corporation?

50   This is not to lament individual authorship *tout court*, nor is it to suggest that such examples don't exist outside of the territorial domain that is typically centered in design history. OSPAAAL posters are attributable to individual artists, but this is more important perhaps to the internal bureaucracy of the organization, the bourgeois collector, and the art historian than to the posters' primary audience. There are an uncountable number of instances of work for which rightful attribution has been denied or trivialized, especially—one must imagine—given the prevalence of cishet white males in the canonical history, of artifacts not created by them. Similarly indicative of historical blind spots, there is the apocryphal anecdote (which nonetheless illustrates the limitations of archaeological study) according to which an archaeology professor lecturing on an excavated bone fragment marked with thirty or so notches conjectures that the notches are

These works, however, don't have to be framed primarily through the lens of publicity. It could also be said that the more salient driver of this work was the production of an international leftist imaginary. Sontag, in her introductory essay to *The Art of Revolution: 96 Posters from Cuba* (1970) points out that according to some radicals, revolutionary art can only truly be produced and experienced collectively. The Cuban Revolution, in contrast to other revolutionary events in states like China and the Soviet Union, eschewed the didactic, mass theatrical spectacle as exemplary of this attitude. Rather, "the struggle of Blacks in the United States, the guerrilla movement in Mozambique, Vietnam, and so forth" (Sontag 1999) were contemporaneously interpellated by OSPAAAL's prints, which effectively served as movie posters for militant struggle imagined as a kind of collective art proper to revolution.

Nevertheless, one might consider that today most students do not enroll in design school to become anonymous poster designers for anti-imperial struggle and make graphics that attend to explicitly political spaces and discourses (anti-capitalism, anti-fascism, decolonial struggle, etc.). Or at the very least, that school prospectuses are not written to promise such a practice to prospective students. The incidental inclusion of examples like OSPAAAL and the Ateliers Populaires (if they appear at all) read as a kind of tokenism that allows canonical design historiography to project some semblance of social relevance while carrying on with business as usual. However, since this kind of solidarity work is not usually well compensated in a domain of practice circumscribed by commerce, its artifacts are largely irrelevant as a source of "inspiration and emulation."[51]

Furthermore, movement-based graphic artifacts have generated discourse and practice that tend to manifest in formats and forums more familiar to the street and to the realm of popular education and activism/organizing. These spaces and discourses are effectively illegible to institutionally and commercially grounded ways of seeing and knowing design made for publicity. These artifacts don't sell things *per se*; they are not obviously useful as precedents for the kind of practice that students are being initiated into. This kind of design deals with a designer subjectivity/agency distinct from that of the Designer$_1$ in that community partners, anonymous workers, grassroots organizations, and so on inform the role of the designer-as-intermediary, as an ethical and political position.

decorative, or that perhaps they represent a lunar cycle, but that their true purpose can't be known. A female student proposes instead that the notches might have been made by a woman recording a menstrual cycle, something that the male professor had not considered.

Tangent: Karenleigh A. Overmann suggests through the deployment of material engagement theory that even though the notches might not have initially been made to render some kind of quantification (that they may have been ornamental), they nonetheless provide an opportunity, once made, for numerical cognition to emerge, or be applied. See Karenleigh A. Overmann, "The Role of Materiality in Numerical Cognition," Quaternary International 405, Part A (June 2016): 42–51.

51   This phrase comes from the front cover flap of *Meggs' History of Graphic Design* (fifth edition).

Here students are encouraged, or perhaps even expected, to mine history for stylistic references. Sontag points out that the poster designers of OSPAAAL used stylistic ambivalence as a way to blur the "latent dilemma for the artist in a revolutionary society of having an individual signature." (Sontag 1999)

This kind of designing agency sometimes eschews the range of subjective qualifications attendant to the Designer₁: instead of author, director, visionary, star, etc., you have: partner, facilitator, organizer, committee member... but also counterfeiter, forger, saboteur, criminal....[52] The latter of these, to reiterate, are not typically the kinds of attributes one finds on a design school prospectus or a job description of any kind. Neither are these the kinds of subjects that enter design competitions and participate in prestigious residencies or festivals. Their traces are, by definition, more marginal, illegible, and illegitimate to gate-keeping institutions that define the formal boundaries of the field.

To be sure, the designers working in those modes are doing the good work and fighting the good fight, and this kind of discussion and practice has been more substantively engaged by others.[53] The two configurations of the designer/design object counterposed above (vulgar commercialism vs. principled activism) are not meant to suggest that the latter is the progressive departure from the former (that the commercial ego-driven Designer₁ is the antecedent to the improved/more favorable Purpose-driven Designer₁). Rather, it is to say that in spite of their being meaningfully opposed, they figure an impasse in that they are both circumscribed by *the design imperative to publicity.*

As an attempt to move beyond this, I propose a third, more banal and deflated variant of design, which is animated by a design imperative to *immutability*, and premised upon a different ontology and configuration of the designer/design object. Clive Dilnot provides a nudge in this direction· when he misappropriates Arthur Pulos's affirmative appraisal of the settler colony that is the United States as a work of design. He quotes Pulos's 1983 *American Design Ethic:*

> Design is the indispensable leavening of the American way of life. It emerged
> with the need of the colonists to transform the wilderness into a secure
> haven and expanded as a natural component of the industrial revolution in
> the New World. The United States was in all likelihood the first nation to
> be designed to come into being as a deliberate consequence of the actions
> of men who recognized a problem and resolved it with the greatest benefit
> to the whole. America did not just happen: It was designed."
> (Dilnot 1984, 5-6)

---

52 See Mahmoud Keshavarz. *The Design Politics of the Passport: Materiality, Immobility, and Dissent.* (London: Bloomsbury, 2018)

53 Some examples include Tings Chak's work and advocacy through the Tricontinental Institute for Social Research; Patricio Dávila's edited volume, *Diagrams of Power: Visualizing, Mapping, and Performing Resistance* (Eindhoven: Onomatopee, 2019), an excellent compendium of critical visualization practices; Kevin Lo's studio work through LOKI and Sheila Sampath's work through The Public, as well as their movement work, which exemplify the ways design can be driven both by care and by oppositional commitments; Josh MacPhee's organizing, writing, design, publishing, and archival work through Interference Archive, which help to build and reinforce cultures of resistance; Ruben Pater's work and writing, which continue to inspire students and practitioners to question the assumptions of their discipline; and the Design Justice Network (designjustice.org), which challenges us to rethink the assumptions that ground design practice by centering people who are often marginalized by design.

Taken at face value, this characterization enables, I propose, an indictment of design's entanglement with colonial imposition and capitalist progress/violence—challenging the presumed yet woefully limited notion that design is a progressive force, or that it might even be politically agnostic. (Dilnot 1984, 6)

Dilnot's 1984 essay "The State of Design History" asks: "To what extent can history contribute to what design is and what a designer does?" (5). To give this question more facets through which to refract pedagogical questions, one might also ask: could an alternative "discursive formation" (Foucault 1972) aligning alternative concepts, precedents, tools, and forms to those found in History$_1$ supply another conception of graphic design pedagogy, praxis, and subjectivity/agency?

III
Graphic Design History—Centering the Document

My own interest in the document began with an exploration of various forms of alternative currency, of which there is an incredible variety of precedents, ranging from local time banks to labor-union tokens to cryptocurrencies. The result was a series of small projects—writing, workshops, posters, and a publication—that index some precedents and insights from the realm of alternative currency design. In aggregate, these projects postulated currency as a genre that entails a spectrum of concerns beyond those usually addressed in graphic design history, pedagogy, and professional practice (for instance, how governance imperatives and the operational considerations around regulation and enforcement are manifest in the graphics of securitized documents).

The document came to be, for me, a tool for reflecting the assumptions of, and exposing the ideological investments implicit within, the conventional bounds of $Design_1$ studio pedagogy. However, plotting an exit from $Design_1$ and toward what I'll refer to as $design_2$—an ontology of design that centers the document—only offers a mirage of escape. $Design_2$ is not $Design_1$'s Other. Rather, it is its superstructure.

To be sure, my ambition is not to propose a graphic design curriculum that trains students in the way of passports, property deeds, and money—preparing them to become administrative officers and proficient designers of bureaucratic forms. Rather, it is to attune the student to $design_2$'s systemic consequentiality and to investigate the ways in which the subordination, marginalization, and oppression that it can participate in might be identified, addressed, and abolished. Speaking to the latter point, I quote the geographer Ruth Wilson Gilmore who has said that:

Abolition is not *absence*, it is *presence*. What the world will become already exists in fragments and pieces, experiments and possibilities. So those who feel in their gut deep anxiety that abolition means knock it all down, scorch the earth and start something new, let that go. Abolition is building the future from the present, in all of the ways we can. (Gilmore and Lambert 2018)

In other words, as a question of design pedagogy and practice, an *abolitionist* orientation affirms the emancipated forms of exchange and sociability that already exist, and inquires about the radical imagination of other, more liberated and non-oppressive but perhaps antagonistic ways of being that may have been overcoded by the document. This is resonant with what Ariella Aïsha Azoulay calls "rehearsal" (as a practical concern) and "potential history" (as a political project), that offer an affirmative charge and propose a praxis of actualizing that which *could have* been had the quasi-apocalyptic forces of colonialism and capitalism not been brought to bear on so much of the world (Azoulay 2019). Such interlocutors help plot a path toward graphic design history, pedagogy, and practice that could adopt a more oppositional mandate.

To get there, one more section of the terrain of design needs to be charted. This place is populated by documental artifacts that are designed and imposed as instantiations of a managerial, administrative mandate. It is grounded in a story of design that centers the document—with a historiography no longer produced through the accession of the genius/masterpiece, but through the accession of the document (and the bureaucracies in which it circulates). This story reconsiders the agency of designing and shifts the frame of subjectivity from the Designer$_1$ to the designer$_2$—or, that which may be more commonly understood as bureaucracy.

DESIGN: The Imperative to Immutability (Not Auteur, but Authority)

I'll start by iterating the schematization of design$_1$ toward a *Design Imperative to Immutability*, or design$_2$. Design$_2$ is figured by a history$_2$ that interpellates *bureaucracy* as designer$_2$ and as the author(ity) behind artifacts$_2$—that is, in broad strokes, the *document* and its attendant array of techniques are mobilized to achieve immutability. These techniques are fundamentally different from those used to achieve publicity because their aims are different. To put it crudely, the former seeks broad dissemination, while the latter seeks permanence.

By way of elaborating this mandate and function, let's look at Johanna Drucker's review of Richard Hollis's book, *Graphic Design: A Concise History*, in which she highlights the standards for accession he applies to his historical narrative. This will serve as a model for identifying design$_2$'s fundamental imperative. She brings to our attention that:

His introductory remarks identify three roles for graphic design that distance his model from Meggs: (1) identification, (2) information and instruction and (3) presentation and promotion. This meta-language of the function of graphic design establishes his study as the analysis of actions.... He grounds his study in the idea of design as functions a designer enacts within a system of social relations of production and reception. (Drucker 2009, 66)

While I agree that this provides a more critical framework for the analysis of the discursive formation that comes to be known as graphic design, I would shed the neutrality of Hollis's terms and recast these with the following three questions: (1) Who wants to know? (2) What do they want to manage? (3) What are they arguing? This framework implicates the commissioner and begs the further question: what agenda does the design artifact embody? Applying a similar framework to history$_2$ while shedding the passive inflection of Hollis's terms, the functions that designers enact may be: (1) arguing, (2) claiming, (3) remembering (as a function of giving form to knowledge and reifying information). This is to say that when it comes to the design of documents, the *designer$_2$*'s questions are primarily concerned with how to render an inscription—which is inherently unstable and contestable—*immutable* against the entropy of movement through time and space, and against contestation. The problem of movement is largely material and technological. The document's primary concern is largely one of stabilizing contingencies as "known," that is to say, located safely beyond dispute. Again, the essential query, the one that frames design decisions as political is: Who wants to know, and why?

While the second part of this book explores what these functions might entail in practical terms, the task for now is to depart from Hollis's retention of the Designer$_1$ as an individual creative agent.[54] Focusing on Hollis's attention to design's functions can be adapted to querying the design of things like money, contracts, passports, and more. To do this, we shift our gaze from the individual subject of the Designer$_1$ to posit a designer$_2$ whose creative praxis entails a spectrum of practical concerns that exceeds that of the traditional Designer$_1$.

Designer$_2$ generates and circulates the kinds of artifacts and inscriptions that can determine who can and cannot traverse militarized border spaces (i.e., passports); they usually interpellate all people along the lines of a cisnormative gender binary (i.e., identification documents); they make one available to conscription, taxation, and public education (i.e., evidentiary documents like reports and orders); they are the basis upon which legality and illegality are defined (i.e., legislative documents); they reinforce one's exclusive claim to a colonized piece of land (i.e., maps, property claims); and so on. It's important to note that each of these functions is ultimately related to some force that can back the arguments, claims, and memories inscribed therein. A passport, for instance, doesn't "function" as intended without the scrutinizing gaze of an armed border agent. The document thus suggests a broader scope of designerly concerns. The designer$_2$'s agency *vis-à-vis* the document is conducted on the level of the systemic. For this to make sense, the subjectivity and agency of the designer$_2$ are located in entities like state bureaucracies and multinational corporations, and away from the Designer$_1$, who rather serves as a technician in relation to these. Such a designer$_2$ has been illegible within a design history modeled on art historical frameworks. Instead, this shift in historical subject initiates an alternative narrative subtended by the design imperative to immutability.

---

54   In the proceedings of the "Graphic Design: History and Practice" conference at the Free University of Bozen-Bolzano, Hollis gives an insightful presentation advocating for a thematic rendering of graphic design history that would equip students with a contextual understanding of canonical artifacts of publicity so as to prompt consideration of the context and forces that constrain and enable the individual designer/author today. He leaves intact, however, the publicity orientation of design (he highlights "identification" here). Richard Hollis, "History and the Graphic Designer," in *Graphic Design History and Practice*, ed. Antonino Benincasa, Giorgio Camuffo, Maddalena Dalla Mura, Christian Upmeier, and Carlo Vinti (Bolzano: Bozen-Bolzano University Press, 2016), 24–25.

Design History Designs the Designer

History is made when archives accession and "process"—
as it is called—*records of interest.*[55]

—Lisa Gitelman, *Rethinking Attachment*

Perhaps for as long as graphic design history has been taught, it has privileged a narrative of design's progressive orientation toward mass production and mass communication, implicitly normalizing the values of a largely Western colonial/statist/capitalist order.[56] It has, for instance, glossed over the significance of labor, particularly gendered labor, and instead fetishized technological progress and individual (male) genius as the drivers of history. It has centered Euro-American sources and neglected an entire planet's worth of practices, people, and places—an unfathomable multitude of worlds. In doing so, it has cast design as an agent of progressive modernization (defined in ways that occlude the violence that this has entailed) and submerged entire ways of being actuated by artifacts often trivialized, for instance, as craft. Design, in other words, has been designated as an agent of "progress."[57]

Within this discursive space, there are indispensable efforts being made by designers, historians, and educators to challenge design's canonical parochialism with the inclusion of more diverse sources and precedents. While I believe it an important political and pedagogical project to broaden design's spectrum of references, I would humbly point to the traps and limitations of the corrective politics of inclusion, particularly when the valorization of non-Western, non-male, non-white, etc., others' "contributions" is premised on their proximity to reference points and frameworks of accession prescribed by the established canon. The design of W.E.B. Du Bois's sociological information visualizations, while undoubtedly treasures, have been assessed in a way that measures their value against, or at least in relation to, the standard of European modernism's ostensibly universal (but more aptly mechanical/industrial) principles of form and cognition. While their minimalist geometric rationality may echo and indeed precede the modernist tendencies seen in twentieth-century European graphic design, to label these "modernist"—as was done in a 2017 blog post—is dissonant.[58] Doing so signals that the accession of Du Bois's work

55   Lisa Gitelman, "Rethinking Attachment," *The New Everyday: A Media Commons Project*, June 29, 2010, mediacommons.org/tne/pieces/rethinking-attachment. Emphasis mine.
56   Benedict Anderson's exegesis of "print capitalism" does much to account for the technological, economic, and political implications of the European formation of moveable typography in relation to the emergence of nationalism. This ought to highlight the techno-progressive blind spots of more conventional narrations of moveable typography graphic design history.
57   Where "progress" is problematized as the modus operandi of empire. See Azoulay, *Potential History*, 18.
58   This may be the first significant introduction to a broader graphic design audience, preceding the more well-known book by Battle-Baptiste and Russert. Maria Popova, "W. E. B. Du Bois's Little-Known, Arresting Modernist Data Visualizations of Black Life for the World's Fair of 1900," *The Marginalian*, October 9, 2017, themarginalian.org/2017/10/09/w-e-b-du-bois-diagrams/. For a more substantive treatment, see Silas Munro, "Introduction to the Plates," in *W. E. B. Du Bois's Data Portraits: Visualizing Black America*, ed. Whitney Battle-Baptiste and Britt Russert (New York: Princeton Architectural Press, 2018), 49–105.

to the graphic design canon is premised on formal/stylistic similarities, in spite of the fact that these graphics sought to challenge Euro-American modernity's participation in the subordination of Black people. It ignores design history as a matter of ideological construction and reproduces the habits of History₁.

Similarly, while the acknowledgment of the Asian advent of moveable typography corrects the hubris of the Eurocentric Gutenberg story, it also tends to give a pass to a more confrontational reckoning with the legacy and role of the European printing press in the emergence of colonialism, nationalism, and capitalism.[59] In a text challenging the relative popularization of "decolonization" in design, Ahmed Ansari invokes Frantz Fanon's observation that "[B]lack people modify their speech, body language, and actions to 'prove the existence of a [B]lack civilization to the white world at all costs,' [pointing] to [an] awareness of the colonized that they exist in relation to a colonizer."[60] Ansari (via Fanon) laments the fetishization of inclusion in the form of a liberal politics of representation/recognition, rather than articulating something more substantively decolonial.[61] Many artifacts, and the cosmologies they reify through use and circulation, are simply incommensurable with a normative and conventional notion of design, and do not therefore accede to the canon for consideration by students in shaping alternative disciplinary horizons. These artifacts often lack the kinds of attributes and functions that Hollis, Meggs, and even Drucker/McVarish, would seek to qualify accession to the story of graphic design.[62]

While one can appreciate the affirmation of cultural ego that examples like the two mentioned above give to the people and places who find relation with these forms, there are two issues that should give us pause. The first is that such inclusion can entail a form of "body language modification" that seeks recognition according to the apparent values and priorities of Euro-American institutions and audiences. Here, accession ultimately affirms the Eurocentric standpoint and gaze as a regulatory, referential mark from which other forms are measured and valued. The second is that "contributions" (to the hegemonic center) that are valued on the basis of their chronological precedence accept as valid the narrative trope of a linear progressive historiography as value-free and uncontroversial,

---

59   See S. H. Steinberg, *Five Hundred Years of Printing* (London: Penguin, 1955); and Benedict Anderson, *Imagined Communities: Reflections on the Origin and Spread of Nationalism* (London: Verso, 2006).

60   Ahmed Ansari, "The Work of Design in the Age of Cultural Simulation, or, Decoloniality as Empty Signifier in Design," *Medium*, January 4, 2017, medium.com/@aansari86/the-symbolic-is-just-a-symptom-of-the-real-or-decoloniality-as-empty-signifier-in-design-60ba646d89e9.

61   "Of course, dressing up in the language of decolonization is not as offensive as 'Navajo print' underwear sold at a clothing chain store and other appropriations of Indigenous cultures and materials that occur so frequently. Yet, this kind of inclusion is a form of enclosure, dangerous in how it domesticates decolonization." Eve Tuck and K .Wayne Yang, "Decolonization Is Not a Metaphor," *Decolonization: Indigeneity, Education & Society* 1, no. 1 (2012): 3.

62   See also Joi T. Arcand, Chris Lee, and Winona Wheeler, "I'm a Little Too Rebellious for That: A Conversation with Joi T. Arcand and Winona Wheeler," *C Magazine*, no. 141 (Spring 2019), cmagazine.com/issues/141/im-a-little-too-rebellious-for-that-a-conversation-with-joi-t-ar.

and turn the process of redressing history into an untenable, unwinnable race, in which the value of coming first obliterates other forms of valorization and meaning making.

There is another schism that might help dissolve the inevitability of the canonical Eurocentric forms and formats that tend to be taught in graphic design history and studio pedagogy. Azoulay inverts the Western museum's tendency to narrate affirmatively its collection, not as a cache of stolen artifacts (extracted violently from the worlds they would have otherwise helped to constitute), but as props in the teleological justification of the advances of Western civilization. Centering *the document*—the material basis of historiography—and inverting its status as evidence in the narration of civilizational progress by regarding it instead as evidence of crime proposes a more violent rupture of the canon—a rupture through which evidence can be mounted to indict graphic design as an agent of colonialism, coloniality, and capitalism. This immediately prompts a few questions: How then might centering the document shape the design student's disciplinary imaginary, their sense of agency, and the array of theoretical and practical concerns that designing entails? Can a designerly intellect and creativity be mobilized to confront the kinds of violent operations of colonial property deeds, border regimes, the carceral state, etc., as enabled by documents? Can the design student abandon the vague ethical paradigm of "problem-solving" to question whose problems are being solved, and instead enact forms of antagonism toward the powers that be?

I won't pretend that graphic design will magically bring about the dissolution of the modern world system or the so-called "capitalocene."[63] But I do propose that we consider document-centered design as a framework through which to "study up"[64] (on those in power). That is, can graphic design education be adapted to study and indict the way that design$_2$ artifacts$_2$ have served as instruments of epistemological violence, while facilitating and enabling other more brutal forms of violence?

To reiterate: Yes, indeed, we ought to recognize and affirm that the Asian advent of moveable typography independently precedes its European counterpart. But it is just as crucial to maintain a confrontational stance and "upward" pressure that tries to account for the critical role played by moveable typography in the European development of capitalism and colonialism. The publication of the massive compilation of design history references under the banner of De-centering Whiteness in Design History Resources (DWDHR), for instance, while undoubtedly rich and convenient, might fall into the trap that Dilnot described—it is ultimately impossible to produce an absolutely inclusive canon. Such efforts implicitly subscribe to the liberal fantasy of universal inclusivity and consensus by failing to

63   See Jason W. Moore, "The Capitalocene, Part I: On the Nature and Origins of our Ecological Crisis," *The Journal of Peasant Studies* 44, no. 3 (2017): 594–630.
64   See Laura Nader, "Up the Anthropologist: Perspectives Gained from Studying Up," in *Reinventing Anthropology*, ed. Dell Hymes (New York: Random House, 1972), 284–311.

recognize antagonism as a constitutive feature of politics and history. A linear, techno-progressive, and fundamentally Eurocentric narrative thus persists as an inevitability upon which reforms are proposed.

Databases such as DWDHR do not narrate history, though they might, at best, provide some resources for alternative narratives. De-centering Whiteness inadvertently maintains whiteness' ontology, echoing Frankenberg's critical assessment of whiteness as a subject position devoid of its own content, but defined by the claim that "I am not the other."[65] The "not-white" entries into the database accede partly on the basis of their non-whiteness. But they also are eligible/legible as candidates for accession because they are recognizable within the rubric of categories that have already been established as proper to this formerly only white domain of study. A more substantively alternative historiography lies, however, in recognizing historiography itself as a field of conflict.[66] History$_2$ takes a different approach to the problem of Eurocentrism. Instead of taking on the quixotic task of writing a universal canon, history$_2$ chooses to *center* whiteness by concatenating the "progressive" achievements of the colonial state and capitalist enterprise, and the documents they produce. The model for this is Azoulay's indictment of the Western museum, not as a place where the progress of human civilization is narrated, but as a repository containing evidence of the crimes of colonial/capitalist theft and shattered worlds.[67]

History$_1$ has led to mistaking an account of apocalypse for a mythology of civilizational progress. This misinterpretation overlooks the revolutionary impact of Gutenberg's press, which can be seen as being more about the emerging violence of capitalism in Europe than a triumphant techno-progressive march toward industrialization, driven by enlightened ingenuity and entrepreneurial innovation. The conventional account of the European press also perpetuates the flawed assumption that there is a direct correlation between literacy and democratization, or the apocryphal and passive notion that Latin script's modularity was key to the successful

---

65   See Frankenberg Ruth, "Mirage of an Unmarked Whiteness," in *The Making and Unmaking of Whiteness* (Durham, NC: Duke University Press, 2001), 72–96.

66   Gerda Bauer, for instance, demonstrates that women (in Germany) are largely omitted from graphic design historiography because their field of practice was largely commercial, craft-oriented, and/or educational. This placed such practitioners and their work outside of significance in a design history that narrates the progressive force of modernism tacitly constructed around networks composed primarily of intellectual, avant-garde men. While this is lamentable, in its indication of the persistence of patriarchy, one also hesitates at the prospective value of "being integrated into a burning house" (as famously expressed by Martin Luther King Jr.), when there are many underexplored ways that women and other underrepresented constituencies can be valorized in design history. Gerba Bauer, "Women and Graphic Design in the History of Design and Design History," in *Graphic Design: History and Practice*, 39–59.

67   "The imperial movement of progress is pursued on the one hand as if along a single, straight line of advance, while on the other, it operates in a suicidal cycle where the new can hardly survive the constant and renewable threat of being declared unfit by the newest. The new is an imperial incentive, a requirement, and a command, but it is framed as an inspiration and a promise in ways that separate it from the violence it involves. Pursued for the sake of itself, it is above all a force, destructive and unstoppable. The new unfolds in a particular temporality—that of historical progress—without which nothing can be announced as new. The principle of the new has become the source of its own authority; the newness of the new has become its sole *raison d'être*, and—like colonial expansion and capitalist growth—it has become voracious and insatiable." Azoulay, *Potential History*, 18.

proliferation of moveable typography in Europe (but not Asia).[68] Instead, history$_2$ suggests that without European printing, the VOC (De Vereenigde Oostindische Compagnie, or, The United Dutch East India Company) could neither issue a mass public offering of stocks in its highly risky colonial ventures—thereby distributing that risk on a national scale and creating the first publicly traded multinational (read: colonial) corporation—nor could it generate the conditions for the world's first stock exchange in Amsterdam (giving birth to the immense force of globalized financial capitalism). The historian of print S. H. Steinberg reminds us that Gutenberg's primary business was in job printing—quotidian artifacts like calendars and, perhaps more salient to our discussion, things like papal indulgences. Thus, history$_2$ suggests that the advent of writing in ancient Mesopotamia should be understood as having more to do with accounting than with literary achievement; so too can printing and the Internet—which marked revolutionary turning points in a story about documents—be understood as having more to do with finance and property than with romance and mystery.

---

68   Elizabeth Eisenstein, Fréderic Barbier, and other historians of European print have suggested this reasoning without accounting for—as Benedict Anderson, James Burke, Janet Abu-Lugodh, and others have done—the increasing surplus wealth derived from colonial extraction, the emergence of a merchant class, and the modern bourgeois state they fought for and won, in generating an increased demand for printing services.

IV
Historiography

Graphics make and construct knowledge in a direct and primary way.
*Most information visualizations are acts of interpretation masquerading
as presentation.* In other words, they are images that act as if they
are just showing us what is, but in actuality, they are *arguments
made in graphical form.*[69]

—Johanna Drucker, *Graphesis: Visual Forms of Knowledge Production*

History$_2$ is derived from Drucker's observation, transposing "information
visualization" to historiography as a creative, contestable, and ultimately
political formation. Frantz Fanon's critical recognition in the epigraph
above—that history is not simply a dispassionate concatenation of chronological facts, but rather a field of contestation, a selective picture constructed
self-consciously and systematically—resonates in turn with what Michel
Foucault might call a "discursive formation."[70] The historiography of
Western nation-states, for instance, at least since the nineteenth century,
has been critiqued as an ideological apparatus used to justify claims over
contestable territories (e.g., "we have always been here; or, our domination is justified because we have brought [our] order" (Fielder 2000, 19). In
other words, *history is designed* to sediment as fact that which is otherwise
contingent. What a historiography of history$_2$ addresses are things that are
designed to be historical—that is, things that are intended to carry memory
and produce information (Hobart and Schiffman 1998; Beller 2017), to
function as (Gitelman 2014), to attempt to place outside of dispute subjective claims (Latour 1986), and to sediment these as immutable (Drucker
2014; Taylor 2003). This history$_2$ is constituted by the various "records of

69   Johanna Drucker, *Graphesis: Visual Forms of Knowledge Production* (Cambridge, MA: Harvard
     University Press, 2014), ix–x. Emphasis in the original.
70   The first of the discursive unities/formations Foucault comments on are discourses constituted upon a
     known object, i.e., madness. But since such a thing as "madness" is not knowable in any stable way—
it doesn't have a fixed definition—the discursive unity around the object is then figured by the changes in how
the object is constituted by the statements in which it is made. The second of the unities/formations has to do
with *how* statements are made. For instance, medical scientific discourse is constituted as such through "the
group of rules, which, simultaneously or in turn, have made possible purely perceptual descriptions, together
with observations mediated through instruments, the procedures used in laboratory experiments, statistical
calculations, epidemiological or demographic observations, institutional regulations, and therapeutic prac-
tice···." A third framework of discursive unity/formation may have to do with the grouping of statements based
on their foundation on a set of established concepts (i.e., the classical analysis of language and grammar includes in its conceptual architecture such things as the noun, the predicate, the verb, etc.). However, Foucault
notes the regular emergence of new and/or derivative concepts, or concepts that are incompatible with the
established set. He doubles back and instead offers that perhaps the unity of language analysis can then be
justified around the simultaneous appearance of a set of concepts and their succession by other concepts. He
describes the fourth unity/formation as being premised on themes (i.e., evolution), or rather the possibility of
divergent statements on a theme.
       However, Foucault is ambivalent about these principles, or rules of formation. He doubts that any of
these principles will be definitive and without gaps and doubt, and he offers what I see as an emancipatory
possibility: "...[O]ne may be compelled to dissociate certain *oeuvres*, ignore influences and traditions, abandon definitively the question of origin, allow the commanding presence of authors to fade into the background"
and so "one is forced to advance beyond familiar territory, far from the certainties to which one is accustomed,
towards an as yet uncharted land and unforeseeable conclusion." See Michel Foucault, *The Archaeology of
Knowledge; and The Discourse on Language*, trans. A.M. Sheridan Smith (New York: Pantheon Books, 1972),
31–39.

interest" (Gitelman 2010) generated in the course of administrating the development and perpetuation of colonial institutions like the state and the corporation, entities for which maintaining radically contingent claims to power and authority were at stake.[71] The artifacts foregrounded in this history$_2$ instantiate imbrications of language and money, or what anthropologist Keith Hart calls "the memory bank." Hart's metaphor of the bank, which implies the storage of memorial inscriptions, intersects with media historian Lisa Gitelman's formulation of the document's functions as a producer of knowledge (read: evidence)—what she calls the document's "know/ show" function, which represents a dual status as dormant file and proof, activated precisely in moments of controversy and conflict. The document is thus cast as an *argument* over the legitimacy of one claim or another. The document's knowledge-producing capacity is attributed an ontological stake and a violent charge in Jonathan Beller's assertion that *information*—reified in documentary formats—cannot be extracted from the capitalist logic of the commodity form. Such forms violently transpose complex and thick "lives to another domain" (Beller 2017, 30) in which living beings are reduced to the onto-epistemic *claim* that they are simply numerical units available to the murderous rationality of managerial calculation.

This book offers a preliminary foray into constructing a document-centric design history$_2$ with a congerie of reference images and captions. It is a narration that spans roughly five-to-six thousand years, where "minerality" serves as a thematic/material subtext underpinning various aspects of the design for immutability—mineral as substrate, mineral as standard, mineral as conduit, mineral as weapon.[72] These aspects of "minerality" variously immunize the integrity of inscriptions and claims "against both any alterity that might transform [them] and whatever dares to resist [them]" (de Certeau 1992, 216). These are the broad strokes of a history$_2$ that centers documents precisely because they were designed to function as the material constituent of history. Ultimately, this is an exploration of the role that designing documents plays in legitimizing power, and an experi-

---

71   In "The Principles of the New Associationist Movement," Karatani Kojin also observes that the state and capital are two sides of the same coin: "Capital and state are two separate things in their modus operandi. Capital belongs to a principle of exchange, while state belongs to the principle of plunder and redistribution. Historically speaking, it was in the stage of the absolutist monarchical state that they were combined. The state necessitated the development of the capitalist economy in order to survive and strengthen itself; while the capitalist economy has had to rely on the state, because it has not been able to affect all productions to make them part of it, and what is more, it continues to be dependent even upon un-capitalized productions such as the reproduction of humans and nature. Thus, after the rise of industrial capitalism and bourgeois revolution of state, the two joined together and came to form an inseparable amalgamation, yet at the same time sustaining their own autonomies." See Kojin Karatani, "The Principles of the New Associationist Movement (NAM)," May 18, 2001, NetTime, last accessed November 28, 2024, nettime.org/Lists-Archives/nettime-l-0105/msg00099.html.

72   A deep-time media history that spans the inert to the intermediary to the malicious application of the mineral is laid out in Jussi Parika's *The Anthrobscene* in which he quotes Thomas Pynchon's novel, *Against the Day*: "'But if you look at the history, modern chemistry only starts coming in to replace alchemy around the same time capitalism really gets going. Strange, eh? What do you make of that?' Webb nodded agreeably. 'Maybe capitalism decided it didn't need the old magic anymore.' An emphasis whose contempt was not meant to escape Merle's attention. 'Why bother? Had their own magic, doin just fine, thanks, instead of turning lead into gold, they could take poor people's sweat and turn it into greenbacks, and save the lead for enforcement purposes.'" Thomas Pynchon, *Against the Day* (London: Vintage Books, 2007), 88, cited in Parika, *The Anthrobscene* (Minneapolis: University of Minnesota Press, 2014), 55.

ment in theorizing legitimacy through a designerly lens, elaborated via the categorical/mineral frames mentioned above. In short, it is a historiography that narrates the development of a praxis circumscribed by a design imperative to immutability.

This mapping of the techniques of immutability offers starting points for measuring the extent to which design operations might be seen as political operations, and vice versa. Formally, my intention is to sketch a kind of tangential narration and an experimental, nonlinear, non-teleological way of writing and reading history. In the second part of this book, I ask the reader to attune a part of their readership to the nonverbal paratextual and hypertextual signals (recalling the term in the way it was discussed by Samuel Delany and Octavia Butler)[73] emitted by the images, as well as other kinds of verbal and nonverbal referencing, to orient one's senses toward texture, form, and picture and discern resonances across pages.

Following Dilnot's and Fry's postulation that history does indeed shape the theoretical, practical, and pedagogical horizons of a discipline, I propose the following consideration while reading this book: can foregrounding the document as a constituent of graphic design history, as its (anti)hero, create the proper basis for identifying the field more completely with the capitalist/colonial enemy? Before proceeding with this, or any other consideration, some outlines for apprehending an ontology of the document will be helpful.

Designing Documents

"Redemption" is . . . really more a matter of destroying the entire system of accounting. In many [Ancient] Middle Eastern cities, this was literally true: one of the common acts during debt cancelation was the ceremonial destruction of the tablets on which financial records had been kept, an act to be repeated, much less officially, in just about every major peasant revolt in history.[74]

—David Graeber, *Debt: The First 5,000 Years*

As mentioned before, graphic design history affords little space to the broad spectrum of things that could be included in the genre of the document, in spite of the fact that this genre is implicitly historiographical. The theoretical literature around capital "G" Graphic Design, has had relatively little to say about what documents are, and offers little help in cultivating a critical understanding of how they come to be designed.

Teaching the document doesn't serve a pedagogical orientation that would supply graduates to a field overcoded by the market and commercial

---

73   Octavia Butler and Samuel Delany, edited transcription of discussion at MIT, Cambridge, MA, February 19, 1998, web.mit.edu/m-i-t/science_fiction/transcripts/butler_delany_index.html.
74   David Graeber, *Debt: The First 5,000 Years* (Brooklyn, NY: Melville House, 2011), 82.

practice. By keeping documents and their function outside of the questions of design, they have been positioned outside of the realm of creative, interventionist practices, and as a corollary, denied the potential for political contestation and escalation.[75] This is lamentable if one recognizes that the violence described in the above quotation suggests that documents have played a definitive and profound role in producing and maintaining unjust relations of power for thousands of years.

David Graeber's observation in the epigraph to this section shatters the fallacy that design$_2$, particularly when it entails the making of documents, can be reduced to a neutral and technical, let alone expressive, activity. Instead, it posits that designing documents is inherently political, and that what is at stake is the validity of claims about *what is*. In other words, designing documents is a matter of producing and reinforcing *claims*, *memory*, and *knowledge* through various *defensive* techniques of documentary inscription. Documents exert an onto-epistemological force—they reify categorical schematizations of the world that enable management, administration, and command; they lay claims; they work as evidence in situations of dispute and aid in the imposition of policy; they stabilize the boundaries of what is known and remembered; adjudicate who you are and where you can go, how much you're worth, what you own, your rights, your obligations, and so on. This array of actions is animated by the imperatives and impositions of bureaucratic power, and its attendant techniques developed through statecraft and capitalist administration.

The landscape architect and theorist James Corner reminds us that things such as private property (the *raison d'être* of capitalism and colonialism) exist primarily by virtue of their rendering across a range of documents like maps, property deeds, bank documents, and so on (Corner 1999). The passport, for instance, only functions as such within a context structured by the political arrangements made among a global system of nation-states. Such things are reified and defended by the "legitimate" violence of states precisely because their claims are as thin as the substrates of the documents upon which they are inscribed. But let's be sure—the graphical artifact only forms part of the picture. In addition to this marriage of the weapon and the word ("armas y letras") (Illich 1980, 70), documents are made functional, legible, and legitimate (legal) within what Michel de Certeau calls a "scriptural economy" (de Certeau 1984) For the media historian Lisa Gitelman, the document and the bureaucracy within which it circulates are co-constitutive. David Graeber's succinct characterization of the police as bureaucrats with badges (another kind of document), and guns, is acute and clarifying.

---

75   This is not to say that the only plausible form of resistance to violent instantiations of the document can come through design, but it is to suggest that other forms of "non-designerly" resistance, for instance document destruction, counterfeiting/forgery, and armed struggle, could be transposed into a design education that genuinely seeks to cultivate engaged practitioners. (Perhaps as a minor in counterfeiting, because they still gotta get jobs in the meantime, you know).

At face value, to say that a document is a designed thing is not such an interesting statement. However, if we were to ask *how*, by *whom*, and *why* documents are designed, then we're on our way to expanding the spectrum of designerly concerns from those usually addressed within the agential horizon of Designer$_1$ toward that of designer$_2$—the bureaucracy. The *how* is not exclusively a technical or practical question. *How*, is more interested in stretching the creative modalities of graphic design practice, and pedagogical imperatives by situating the document among its range of objects. At the same time, this is less about inclusion and more about giving consideration to the occluded innards of graphic design's canonical history. Furthermore, this effort is not meant to inflate the capacities and agency of design. Rather it is to probe the false inevitability of capitalism and colonialism/ity by casting these as coextensive with their documental forms—that is, to say that documents are designed is to suggest that what they claim and sediment is actually vulnerable to contingency.

What Is a Document?

In what follows, I shall array some functions and aspects that suggest a general idea of what a document is and does. This is by no means comprehensive, but I hope it is substantive enough to hold together the various constituents of a history$_2$ of design in part two of this book.

KNOWLEDGE PRODUCTION / EVIDENCE (KNOW/SHOW)

In her book *Paper Knowledge: Toward a Media History of Documents*, media historian Lisa Gitelman describes the document as having a dual purpose, which she calls its "know/show function" (Gitelman 2014). The document, she explains, is a knowledge-producing artifact, but it also plays an evidentiary role in helping to settle moments of controversy. For instance, a passport produces knowledge of a subject interpellated by the global system of nation-states and their attendant border regimes and agents. Its inscriptions produce and stabilize as information: a name (rendered according to a standardized orthography); a date of birth (rendered in an informatic format, aligned with an established convention for marking time); a gender (usually according to one of two cisnormative categories); a nationality (a status which is itself tautologically produced by the very object of the passport); and perhaps other biometric information (which renders the individual body legible as a kind of unique signature of itself, knowable and identifiable). All of this, of course, is rendered in the authorized typeface, on the authorized and securitized paper, using the authorized binding, and so on—signaling to the border agent the authenticity and the legitimacy of the document under inspection. As for the evidentiary function—documents are designed to *show* information in order to make and support claims.[76] The passport, like most documents, is primarily

---

76   Etymologically, the word document is rooted in the Latin *docere*—to show, to teach, to cause to know.

dormant and filed away. It is usually activated only in a moment of potential controversy, where its presenter uses it to try and settle some kind of claim—in this case, the right to traverse a border (another contestable graphical mark on the ground). The document thus produces and sediments attributes that might otherwise be unknowable in any precise, stable way, but are made legible as such for the sake of the disciplinary gaze of the border agent.

What's more, Gitelman dissolves the ontological bounds of the passport as a discrete, physical object. The border, the border agent, and the database against which the passport's information is checked, thus appear in one view as co-constitutive elements that enable the passport to function as such. In other words, as a designed object, the passport (along with the system that constitutes it) works to validate one's claim that one is one the state says one is, and that one has the right to pass, or is prohibited from traversing this or that border space (Keshavarz 2018). The armed border agent brings to this configuration a violent capacity to impose policy—which one might say is primarily the general policy of compelling people to be *legible* to the state's bureaucracy and *available* to the imposition of policy. Gitelman describes such a scenario as a "triangulation" between the document, the modern individual, and authority—that is, the authority of the printed object, and the authority of the bureaucracy which valorizes and recognizes it.

This document/bureaucracy configuration is salient because it makes discernible the operational and political dimensions as well as their functional scope. To reiterate, documents don't exist and function as discrete objects divorced from any context. Rather, they are co-constitutive of the bureaucratic systems within which they circulate, and whose reductive, schematic gaze—the onto-epistemological imposition embodied in the information they carry—often requires a violent capacity to contain the excess of its claims. This concatenation of inscription, database, and force is also reminiscent of what Bruno Latour might refer to as an *alignment* of *allies* (Latour 1986) mobilized to reinforce the validity of statements and claims.[77] Identifying the tools and methods of the designer$_2$ as being inclusive in this way, especially in the case of violence/force, helps to clarify the stakes and identify potential areas of intervention, up to and including forceful resistance.

INFORMATION

Johanna Drucker's study of graphical interfaces elaborates on this further.

---

77   I am partial to the use of these terms because *alignment* suggests a graphical dimension—consider the reductive, instrumental rationalization of the world according to the graphical logic of the spreadsheet, which enables its management and exploitation; and *allies* for the way it suggests the political (where there are allies, there are enemies, or alliances with the other's enemies). The provocation herein comes from a desire to study ways in which one might enact antagonism toward hegemonic ways of knowing and remembering. See James C. Scott, *Seeing Like a State: How Certain Schemes to Improve the Human Condition Have Failed* (New Haven, CT: Yale University Press, 1998).

She directs us to the basic, critical understanding that "most visualizations are acts of interpretation masquerading as presentation... they are *arguments* made in graphical form" (Drucker 2014, ix, emphasis mine). Particularly significant to the question of the design of documents is her brief exposition on the graphical logic of Mesopotamian clay tablets.[78] It should be noted that the inscriptions these carried were primarily records of transactions, financial, and contracts/obligations mediating relationships in which some kind of economic value and contingency was at stake. The range of things given graphical form in early writing—what people were concerned with remembering—primarily includes symbols for commodities and marks for representing their quantities. In other words, the earliest known form of writing doesn't come into being for the sake of literary expression or even religious devotion, but rather for the purposes of accounting (Hobart and Schiffman 1998). The authors of obligations and agreements recorded through inscription required that they travel through space and time, but also against ambiguity and dispute, by virtue of their ability to hold the integrity of their form and meaning, that is, by their immutability.

Drucker calls our attention not only to the semantic value of these inscriptions, but also to their more precise valorization through a syntactic grid that structures the graphical space, providing a scaffolding of rows and columns—a coordinate system for ordering signs into categories, sequence/time, hierarchy, and enabling comparison, combination, and calculation. She recalls Denise Schmandt-Besserat's observation that the grids commonly found on ancient documents (whether visually implicit or explicit) served an orthographic function as "a point of reference against which the basic graphic properties of sequence, direction, orientation, size, and scale can register their significance" (Drucker 2014, 85). When a document is implicated in a contentious relationship, its object/ivity/hood and the mediation that it endeavors to supply[79] become contingent on its correct interpretation, aided by the establishment and adherence to orthographic *standards* and *conventions* of writing and reading.[80]

---

78   I also wish to note that the technical aspect of these ancient inscriptions suggests that "typography" precedes any sort of manuscript as a form of writing. The tablets practically make a self-evident case for this—they are marked by pressing, the symbols are arranged according to an implicit grid, and the morphology of the signs is thus standardized by virtue of a consistently reproducible action. This is of course a back projection made deliberately to align more modern, familiar instantiations of typography with political consequence. If the first "graphic designers" were working to mediate commercial and political relationships through documuments—that is, if in essence, they were bureaucrats—then it casts, at the very least, the idea of the designer as auteur as reductive, ideologically loaded, and contestable.

79   See David Graeber's *Debt: The First 5,000 Years*. To paraphrase severely, Graeber upturns the conventional progressive narrative about the evolutionary transition from primitive barter to the advent of money as the basis of a society in contemporary credit-based economies. He argues instead that primitive economies operated on the principle of credit exchange: If we are neighbors in an ancient village, and you need something from me, then I can lend it to you with a reasonable expectation that I can ask something of you later. This kind of credit-based exchange is evidently unmediated by a documentary object like a contract or money.

80   Further to the political dimension of typography and printing, see Benedict Anderson's *Imagined Communities: Reflections on the Origin and Spread of Nationalism*, 2nd ed. (London: Verso, 2006). Anderson casts the historian and the grammarian—through the technologies of moveable typography and printing, driven by bourgeois capitalist enterprise (what he calls "print capitalism")—as protagonists in the birth of nationalist struggles. Printing subordinated local habits and cultures of writing to a standard centralized around administrative print languages. The standardization of written vernacular languages, and their popularization through education, expanded the audience and market for printed products.

In drilling down and attending to the role of the inscriptions that documents transmit *as information*, the work of Michael E. Hobart and Zachary Sayre Schiffman (1998) proves instructive. They make a helpful material distinction between *information* and *commemoration* to clarify an understanding of the relationship of the former to memory. They argue that information operates as abstraction and rhetorical universalization: information is not the thing that it represents, yet its categories also stand for all the things that it *could* represent. In other words (and in pictures) a symbol of a duck does not stand for any actual duck in particular, but typifies that which could be understood *categorically* as "ducks." By contrast, this is distinct from commemoration (co-memory), which is a matter of immediate and shared presence, embodied experience, and knowledge outside of inscribed objects.[81] Commemoration recalls knowledge iteratively, and its instantiations vary in the details of their performance; it relies on subjective storage and immediate transmission; it lacks transparency, accountability, and objectivity, and is thereby disqualified from holding the status of information. Information, on the other hand, by virtue of the (relative) immutability of its inscribed form, is that which is abstracted from experience and made combinable with other pieces of information in order to facilitate analysis and rationalize action. For instance, the knowledge/memory and performance of tying a knot are produced/recalled in the actual tying of a knot. *Information* about knots is sedimented in reproducible, mobile (Latour 1986), and immutable inscription. For Hobart and Schiffman,

> [w]riting did not spring forth fully formed as a technology of communication, much less one communicating speech. Its genius resides in the fact that it originated as something apart from both picture drawing *and* the spoken word, something absolutely new. At its inception, writing was neither more nor less than the very quintessence of information—the classificatory aspect of language abstracted from the flow of experience and rendered visible. The origin of writing therefore constitutes, at one and the same time, the first information technology and the birth of information itself (Hobart and Schiffman 1998, 34).

Where Hobart and Schiffman tend to address information in somewhat neutral terms (e.g., that it comprises mental objects, abstracted from the "flow of experience"), Jonathan Beller puts a finer point on the political significance of the term. He argues, as previously mentioned, that information

---

81 For Hobart and Schiffman, commemoration ought to be understood more as the enactment of a polity's coherence and as a primitive form of memory storage, passive until recalled at some point as information and evidence. The distinction they make between memory and commemoration also maps to the notions of immutability and mutability, as well as to those of the archive and the repertoire (see Diana Taylor). In other words, an inscription that is unstable cannot really serve as information—the "stuff we abstract from the flow of experience" per se. See Michael E. Hobart and Zachary S. Schiffman, *Information Ages: Literacy, Numeracy, and the Computer Revolution* (Baltimore: Johns Hopkins University Press, 1998), 15. In this sense, the mutability of a claim defies the logic of coloniality and its privileging of the archival inscription. Furthermore, they argue that the tokens and emblems of the earliest forms of writing (count and commodity)—the innovation of their combination (of noun and adjective, name, and number)—figures the distinct caesura between writing proper and absolute orality.

cannot be divorced from the capitalist logic of the commodity form and the potential violence of administrative abstraction (Beller 2014, 30). In other words, information imposes schematic claims that reduce life and worlds in ways that render their complex and plural ontologies into units that are combinable and comparable (with the help of, say, a ruled chart) and made available to the rationality of bureaucratic calculation. Information is thus not an ontologically neutral thing to be simply extracted from the world and presented as such. Instead, it is constituted and circumscribed by the cold and detached managerial gaze that seeks it and acts, sometimes murderously, upon it. Beller's illustration may be a limit case that brings to our understanding the potentially catastrophic reductive rationalization of life and worlds *as information*—inscribed upon the document as an actuation of onto-epistemological claims. From this point of view, the document and its inscriptions, understood as information, constitute a substrate of knowledge production and transmission that facilitates the practices of administration and command, and obscures their violence through banalization.

THE ARCHIVE

As the performance studies scholar Diana Taylor suggests, the document can be implicated as a substrate of coloniality and as an instrument of colonization. Taylor's counterposition of what she calls the "archive" and the "repertoire" is illuminating. To paraphrase, the *archive* represents practices of knowledge production, storage, and transmission carried out through media that would align with the domain of the document—artifacts like passports, property deeds, treaties, etc. Conversely, the *repertoire* entails modes of knowledge production and storage that tend to be stored and rendered somatically, and transmitted through the direct experience of witnessing their performance.

Taylor uses the term "performatic" to describe things like dance, song, recipes, rituals, etc.—forms and formats that can evade and do not necessarily require inscription, and which tend to be embodied and transmitted in the moment of their expression, seldom acceding to the archive.[82] She is careful, however, not to position these modalities of knowledge production and transmission as absolutely exclusive to each other. Colonizers have their performatic forms of knowledge production and transmission, and Indigenous societies have utilized various forms of inscription. However, this does not nullify an implication of the archival inscription—the document—in the quasi-apocalyptic colonization and negation of more "performatic" and Indigenous ways of knowing and being.[83] Indeed, the performative

---

82   For instance, Hobart and Schiffman's example of knot-tying as knowledge is embedded in the living
       practice of sailing, and thus the need for documentation is not necessarily essential to its storage and
transmission. This would be in contrast to the abstraction and objectification enabled by inscription, or by
the maintenance of this knowledge by an autonomous class, as well as institutions of professional knot-tiers.
83   One has simply to think of the colonial erasure, and relative novelty (to the settler) of the name
       Lenapehoking, and its marginalization with the name *New York City*, on documents ranging from tourist
guides and property deeds to drivers' licenses and popular films, graphic design history books, and so on.

presentation of documents is validated in juridical discourse, for instance, by the ritualistic proscenium of the courtroom (e.g., swearing to tell the truth). Antagonizing bureaucratic epistemology can thus be a question of the territorial extent of the proscenium—of what is admitted *into* the record—that is, what is inside the performance, and what outside of it (Coulthard 2014).

I have often referred to a dispute over the use of a soccer field in Yelamu (San Francisco) that took place in 2014 to illustrate this distinction. A widely shared YouTube video records a confrontation in the Mission District between tech bros (mostly white, some Asian) and local youth (mostly Brown and Black) over the use of a public soccer field.[84] One of the tech bros presents an 8.5-by-11-inch permit, ostensibly backing their claim to use the field exclusively for one hour, as authorized by the San Francisco Recreation and Parks Department for a fee of twenty-seven dollars. They expect the youth to leave. One particular tech bro is incredulous that the permit he presented is not recognized by the youth and he admonishes one of the older youth to read it as if it were a problem of literacy rather than of legitimacy. The youth, who can of course read, rejects the permit, countering that the park has never, and can never be "booked," that is to say, claimed by some mere graphical artifact. Instead, he insists, claims about who can and can't be on the field are governed by the principles of pick-up ball—you have seven players, we have seven players—winner stays on. One form of governance is reified in embodied and lived practice among a community of players, commemorated through the iterative "ritual" of playing soccer. The other form of governance is formalized with a document, ostensibly representing a "legitimate claim" designed to be recognized as such by an intermediary public authority should a conflict arise. The document is an instrument for those outside of a common, local understanding of the community to assert a claim. Recognition of the document thus marks the schism between rational political subjects (the white, civic Man) and their irrational, illegitimate others (the ethnic barbarian).[85]

Such documents represent what Bruno Latour might consider "deflated" forms, or what Lisa Gitelman might regard as "genres" of graphic design. They represent the primary constituents of an entanglement between graphic design, coloniality, and power.

Design's Coloniality: Property

What is at stake in the recognition of the contingency and political dimension of the document is the affirmation of testimony, knowledge, and claims that fall outside the statist/colonial forms of legitimacy these underwrite. Dene scholar Glenn Coulthard's critical work on Indigenous land claims struggles is illuminating in this regard. In his book *Red Skin, White Masks*,

---

84 "Mission Playground is Not For Sale," posted September 26, 2014 by MissionCreekVideo, YouTube, 4 min., 35 sec., youtube.com/watch?v=awPVY1DcupE.

85 See Sylvia Wynter, "Unsettling the Coloniality of Being/Power/Truth/Freedom: Towards the Human, After Man, Its Overrepresentation—An Argument," *CR: The New Centennial Review* 3, no. 3 (2003): 257–337.

Coulthard informs us that certain tendencies in Indigenous land claims politics assert an ontology of land as cultural and reciprocal (what he terms "grounded normativity"),[86] as opposed to the colonial, onto-epistemological register of land as commercial and commodifiable. Land claims politics in the Canadian part of Turtle Island have been characterized by an irreconcilable epistemological antagonism, wherein the Canadian state's legal gaze understands land solely as property/commodity, while the more radical elements of the Indigenous struggle reject this, seeing it instead as cultural medium. The Indigenous argument for cultural rights (which the Canadian state insists is distinct from political rights) then figures an ontological understanding of the land as "a field of 'relationships of things to each other'" (Coulthard 2014, 61), as opposed to land as objective commodity with ostensibly stable boundaries, in the form of abstracted private property, valorized as such through colonial dispossession and reified through documents/bureaucracies.[87] Separating land and culture despite their homology allows for a liberal, colonial recognition of Indigenous "culture" on the condition that land is regulated as a commodity. Quoting Paul Nadasdy, Coulthard points out that "to engage in the process of negotiating a land-claim agreement, First Nations people must translate their complex reciprocal relationship with the land into the equally complex but very different language of 'property'" (78). Note that the work of translation seems to flow only in one direction.

To be sure, settler states and the regime of private property they create and govern are reified precisely through documents like maps, treaties, property deeds, and the legal capacity (read: the self-declared right to use force) to adjudicate and back up land claims. Property is something that landscape architect and theorist James Corner would characterize as "phenomena that can only achieve visibility through representation rather than through direct experience" (Corner 1999, 229). Such documents position Indigenous land claims as unrecognized, illegible, unavailable to statist governance, and thus illegitimate. The Canadian state insists on the translation of an Indigenous ontology of land in terms that are legible and reified through the kinds of documents *it* administrates. This way of making claims leaves little ontological possibility for land (and the attendant alternative uses and benefits of land understood differently) outside of legal concepts like usufruct, right to alienate, right to exclude, etc., granted and protected by a state whose Hobbesian mandate is to regulate (through legal, police, and military force) the exchange of land in such a way that it doesn't escalate into internal conflict.

---

86   Glenn Coulthard, *Red Skin, White Masks: Rejecting the Colonial Politics of Recognition*, (Minneapolis: University of Minnesota Press, 2014), 13.
87   The Canadian state uses inclusivity and appeals to disingenuous Western conceptions of universal humanity to maneuver the disavowal of its hegemonic claims to land. Official Canadian multicultural policy is premised on a mendacious history of Canada as always having been characterized by the coexistence of different cultures, starting with the French, English, and the various Indigenous nations. Richard J.F. Day, in his book *Muliticulturalism and the History of Canadian Diversity* (Toronto: University of Toronto Press, 2018) critiques Canadian settler-state multicultural policy as a liberal strategy of pacification.

The Design₂ Coloniality: Typography

The incommensurability of Indigenous claims and colonial claims, a schism drawn along the lines of the document, can also be illustrated in the contention that the Cree syllabary was the first typeface to ever be designed within the settler-state now known as Canada.[88] I am less interested here in the merit that it was the *first*, and rather seek to address the *story* that it was designed at all.

It is useful to note that Benedict Anderson's account of print capitalism casts typography as an actant that compels the standardization of language and the imagination of national communities (Anderson 2006, chap. 3). Following Anderson's accounting of the role that myths play in the production of a shared origin story underwriting nationalistic sentiment, the typographic *history* of Canada, particularly in the context of national/colonial myth-making, designates the settler state and colonization as a benevolent, progressive, and modernizing/civilizing force.

Winona Wheeler (Stevenson), a Native Studies scholar at the University of Saskatchewan, recounts the story of Calling Badger—a Wood Cree elder who received the Cree writing system (which has now been adapted for use in numerous Indigenous languages):

> On his way to a sacred society meeting one evening, Calling Badger and two singers came upon a bright light and all three fell to the ground. Out of the light came a voice speaking Calling Badger's name. Soon after, Calling Badger fell ill and the people heard he had passed away. During his wake three days later, while preparing to roll him in buffalo robes for the funeral, the people discovered that his body was not stiff like a dead person's body should be. Against all customs and tradition the people agreed to the widow's request to let the body sit one more night. The next day, Calling Badger's body was still not stiff so the old people began rubbing his back and chest. Soon his eyes opened and he told the people he had gone to the Fourth World, the spirit world, and there the spirits taught him many things. Calling Badger told the people of the things he was shown that prophesized events in the future, then he pulled out some pieces of birch bark with symbols on them. These symbols, he told the people were to be used to write down the spirit languages, and for the Cree people to use to communicate among themselves.[89]

88 There is also the claim that Canada's first typeface was Cartier, named after the French explorer Jacques Cartier, and designed and released by Carl Dair in 1967. Cartier was commissioned on the occasion of Canada's centenary celebrations and would be used to typeset the Canadian Charter of Rights.
89 Winona Stevenson (Wheeler), "Calling Badger and the Symbols of the Spirit Language: The Cree Origins of the Syllabic System," *Oral History Forum* 19–20 (1999–2000): 19–24.

This story contradicts the conventional (colonial) history of Cree script, which attributes its invention in 1840 to English linguist and missionary James Evans, who allegedly melted the clasps of his tea chest to create type slugs and printed translations of religious texts and hymns. One story, wrought largely from documentary evidence and attesting to the ingenuity and beneficence of the European settler, is plausible and credible—it is considered fact. Evans's printing specimens are preserved and available in archives for researchers; there are other sources that corroborate his story; it is possible to draw morphological and conceptual continuity between the Cree syllabary and Evans's knowledge of Devanagari and Pitman shorthand.

On the other hand, the oral history recalled by Stevenson attributes the creation of the writing system to the spirit world and its transmission through Calling Badger. It leaves no hard evidence (save a literate, living community), no "mobile immutable" (Latour 1986) that can be traced back and verified, nothing to scan and reprint or upload—no original document. Outside of an epistemological framework underwritten by empirical observation, such claims are invalid and reminiscent of fraud, deceit, belief, blind faith, abuse, and dangerous irrationality. It seems hardly necessary to go beyond my own problematic reading of the story as evidence to support a presumption that the Indigenous story would, at best, be trivialized with patronizing curiosity and at worst dismissed as "primitive" mythology.[90]

I propose that the gap between these two stories can be understood as a schematic model of the gap between a European colonial epistemology and an Indigenous one. I point to the conceptual consistency between the contentious typographic histories described above and the Indigenous land claims struggle in Canada. Where a settler-normative epistemology is imbricated with a statist ontology of land as commodity/property, the phenomenon of the typographic object is attributable to a legal individual's authorship as a potential basis for the claim to intellectual property.[91] This would be counterposed to an Indigenous "grounded normativity" imbricated with an ontology of land as reciprocal relationship—a mediating system, like a language, that is immune to private ownership. What I'm suggesting is that the ontological status of the script differs radically according to the possibility of producing empirical evidence. The document—a graphic artifact—thus performs an evidentiary function and affords the narrative for which it does so the distinction of being an immutable historical fact.

---

90   I keep and set in quotes "primitive" to problematize the notion that mythology has been overcome by modernity. Modernity constructs its own myths of progress and benevolence.

91   "The author is a modern figure, a product of our society insofar as, emerging from the Middle Ages with English empiricism, French rationalism and the personal faith of the Reformation, it discovered the prestige of the individual, of, as it is more nobly put, the 'human/ person.' It is thus logical that in literature it should be this positivism, the epitome and culmination of capitalist ideology, which has attached the greatest importance to the 'person' of the author." Roland Barthes, "The Death of the Author," *Image Music Text*, trans. Stephen Heath (London: Fontana, 1977), 142–43.

Perhaps one way to challenge the diminishment of what leaks through the constraints of colonial epistemology could be deliberately enacting illiteracy—a deflection of its insistence on the visible and empirical, and the privileging of objectivity as one of modern, liberal society's tool for guaranteeing validity and legitimacy. This need not be a *wholesale* rejection of such forms of validation, but rather a tactical deflection of the document as an instrument of colonial dispossession, both spatial and cultural. To claim, then, that the script was "designed" (with a documented author as its source) and not "received"[92] (from the Spirit World) would be partisan to a settler-normative form of historical validation.

The invalidating accusation of mythologizing can be inverted to scrutinize the Evans story as itself an element of settler-national mythmaking. This story is agreeable to the official rhetoric of Canadian state multiculturalism. It legitimizes this political program because the diversity manifested by the presence of European settlers on Turtle Island was ostensibly beneficial. What we're dealing with either way are different mythologies. All things being equally mythological, then, the role of the documentary evidence supporting the colonial claim, and the matrix of institutions and bureaucracies that this evidence circulates, as a factor in establishing what is and isn't legitimate, becomes discernible. What could then be ventured is that a deliberate neglect of documentary evidence and empiricism—or what Walter Mignolo might call a form of "epistemic disobedience"—is a politically valid deflection of the persistent settler-normative onto-epistemology of the document.[93] We could also adopt Azoulay's inversion and see typography as evidence of the crime of invasive and apocalyptic colonization. Design$_2$ functions as an instrument of dispossession, alienation, and colonization.[94] The document and its attendant technologies and institutions are mobilized by the settler state and capitalist enterprise to validate its claims and render things like land legible as property and assert empiricism as the ultimate foundation of what can be known, while privileging the visible and the object(ive)—that which is outside of private, subjective cognition and available to public regulation—making illegible and therefore 'illegal' alternative forms of knowledge and sociability.

If indeed a critical studio pedagogy in graphic design is desired, I propose identifying entanglements of design$_2$ with colonial/ism/ity and capitalism through the document, as the ground against which this might be figured. In other words, design$_2$ serves not as a model of progressive achieve-

---

92　This is the term used by Winona Stevenson (Wheeler).
93　The way that "facts" have been eschewed by conservatives and proto-fascists to protect a paranoid conception of the world, an anti-science refusal of COVID-19 vaccination, denial of the rightist insurrectionary violence and emboldened fascism globally, a disavowal of systemic racism, etc., is not what I'm talking about. Epistemic disobedience should be distinguished from ignorance and indoctrination as a mode of resistance that is rather particular to colonized subjects, and premised on resistance to centuries of displacement, attempted genocide, and their legacies of marginalization, systemic oppression, cultural assimilation/erasure, and so on.
94　Glenn Coulthard focuses on the dispossession of land through colonization over proletarianization as the foundation for a decolonial and anti-capitalist political subjectivity.

ment but as an Other against which different kinds of pedagogical and practical questions may be posed and studied. Perhaps a *design₃* could be a space to seek ways of *remembering otherwise*—to counterclaim and destabilize the inevitability of colonial ways of knowing. A different kind of task, orientation, mandate, purview, and range of concerns for graphic design as a critical, antagonistic, and creative discipline.

CONCLUSION

James C. Scott offers that, "The larger the pile of rubble you leave behind, the larger your place in the historical record!" (Scott 2009, 33–34). Although he is, in the context of this quote, commenting on the relative population density of state centers, I appropriate and rephrase this slightly to amplify a partisan bias for the colonized and the oppressed, reading it more as an indictment: "The larger the pile of rubble you leave (in the wake of your conquests) the larger your place the historical record."

If politicizing the design of history were to be reduced to a single agenda, it would be to displace the privileged position of documentary forms legible to the empirical gaze of imperial institutions (universities, museums, and the various "filing cabinets in the sky," to borrow Frank Lloyd Wright's famous quip) as the exclusive basis of legitimate knowledge.[95] Privileging such knowledge effectively violates the worlds of those who leave no legible inscription, and whose ways of knowing *contradict* and *refuse* the literacy of hegemonic institutions. To be sure, the planet has rather been suffused for millennia with unmarked graves strewn in the wake of the colonizer's rampage. These terrestrial scars are themselves the scores that record the colonizer's criminality.

Such marks are the starting point for heeding American anthropologist Laura Nader's call to "study up" (Nader 1972)—to direct a scholarly and critical gaze *up* toward those in power—to cultivate a meaningful understanding of power as the problem against which creative and critical experimentation and exploration is mobilized. Paulo Freire's concept of "naming the world" helps to frame studying up as the search for productive limits from which graphic design might be imagined as a praxis engaged in the production of emergent, emancipatory form. For Freire, the capacity to *name* the world is a transformative and poietic participation in the *making* of the world. To be sure, this capacity to name is not the sole domain of a commanding elite to be imposed on those subordinated to them. Naming, Freire reminds us, can also be undertaken by the oppressed as a matter of being in dialogue (even *with* the oppressor). Freire's description of naming as a recursive, discursive, creative act—where each new name becomes a problem that calls for another new name—is understood as a motivator of the creative impulse, constitutive of what he calls "human-

---

95   See Mike Wallace, "Interview with Frank Lloyd Wright," September 1, 1957, The Mike Wallace Interview Collection, Harry Ransom Center, University of Texas at Austin.

ization," that is, elimination between the oppressed and the oppressor of the oppression that dehumanizes both (Freire 2005).

Naming, as part of the vocation of humanization, thus gives us the diagram: *design* → *designing* → *designation*. To this end, I propose an alternative series of questions orienting graphic design pedagogy toward studying, exploring, creating, and reinforcing, through different techniques of immutability (or against imperialist instantiations of immutability), other ways of remembering, knowing, and claiming. Could these questions explore and generate artifacts that facilitate forms of sociality and preclude the kinds of documental artifacts that are endemic to the managerial/administrative/institutional tendencies of colonial governance? Could historiography be about design$_3$ as a creative, narrative praxis, and would that involve new kinds of writing, transmission, storage, retrieval, and performance? At what point does it stop being useful to retain design$_{1,2}$ as a disciplinary framework? At what point must its institutional and professional horizons be abandoned to meaningfully explore these questions?

Centering the document in graphic design history helps us approach design pedagogy and practice as abolitionist fields. The flipside of casting as Other a history of the document is a divergent, exploratory drive to study and make in relation to existing, non-oppressive, anti-hegemonic ways of knowing and being. The praxis of teaching and learning graphic design ought thus to be fundamentally rethought in ways that center these motivations. We might start, at least in design schools, with the abolition of the reductive informatics of grading—documents that overcode, bureaucratize, and discipline the pedagogical space of the studio. A pedagogy resonant with decoloniality ought to eschew such forms of punitive and retributive discipline, and affirm other illegible, and necessarily unaccountable (at least to a hierarchical, managerial, disciplinary gaze), ways of teaching and learning.[96] This demands a different kind of sensitivity to plurality and new kinds of literacy that exceed the grammar of profession, commerce, and publicity.

Though outside the scope of this book, moving beyond the coloniality of the document can be guided by thinkers like Mignolo, who offers the concept of "re-existing" (Mignolo 2017). This is resonant with Azoulay's criticism of the fetishization of newness, as a means of reconstituting worlds lost to imperialism. Her notion of "rehearsal" equips one with the recognition that potential histories can be enacted now, performatically (Azoulay 2019, 43). Her query about who is authorized to give names, echoing Freire, challenges the epistemological foundations—the meanings we have in common—of our being together (51). One can take this as a prompt to rehearse a field of study and praxis concerned with making knowledge and claims and remembering otherwise against a hegemonic, univocal coloniality. While

---

96 One can say that, ironically, a definitive lack of evidence of grading as a feature of education demonstrates that people have been learning and teaching for millennia without it.

Hobart and Schiffman periodize commemoration as obsolete (or at least in-utile as information), Moten and Harney affirm such social forms through what they also variously call rehearsal, study, speculation, jamming, sitting on a porch together, and so on—forms of sociality enacted within and against some form of imposed, utilitarian, and obligatory situation like the university (Moten et al. 2013, 110). The initial task for a graphic design pedagogy thus figured may be to rap with students on how to "re-exist," "rehearse," and/or generate anew that which has been suppressed by the coloniality of the document. ⊕

On pg. 17, Ken Garland's "First Things First" Manifesto pamphlet (1964).

The photographed poster on pg. 23 was taken at the Pratt Institute in 2022 by the author.

The Diagram on pg. 25 comes from: Suguru Ishizaki, "Service Design and Technical/Professional Communication," in *Proceedings of the 2010 IEEE International Conference on Professional Communication (IPCC)*, Enschede, the Netherlands, 2010.

The dyptich of posters on pg. 26 shows one of Jan Van Toorn's exhibition poster for theVan Abbemuseum (left, 1971), and a Wim Crouwel poster "Vormgevers" for the Stedelijk Museum, Amsterdam (right, 1968). Max Bruinsma writes of Van Toorn's poster:

> "The museum's acquisitions of the previous year are written as a shopping list, with the sum total below the red line. The poster effectively says: "we have spent 273,969 guilders of your taxpayers' money on these works. Come and see whether we did well." Considering the names and the amount, 36 years later one might say it was a healthy investment, but at the time, the point couldn't be missed: this is as much a political statement as it is a cultural announcement." (**Max Bruinsma, "Jan van Toorn: Tactics of Controversy," accessed December 6, 2024, maxbruinsma.nl/index1.html?vantoorn_EN.htm**). It is reproduced here with the permission of the Collection Van Abbemuseum, Eindhoven, and photographed by Peter Cox, Eindhoven.

Crouwel's poster was designed for an exhibition of designers across various sub-disciplines. Although, not for screen-based reproduction, the poster exemplifies his experimentation with the adaptation of conventional forms to the constraints of early digital graphic reproduction. See also his typeface "New Alphabet."

The image on pg. 29 is a a poster produced during the May '68 uprising in France. The text:

| "usines universites [sic] union" | translates to | "factory universities union" |

A claim!

A claim!

Immutable

Preamble

You think you can go from one side of a line in the ground to another, but you don't have the right papers to show the armed man at the gate. You want to keep a dwelling on a piece of land, grow food there, raise a family, host friends, but it is not yours—or so says a piece of paper and the office that holds a copy of it. You memorialize a favor for an acquaintance with a note to call on them when you need something, but this note holds no purchase with anyone else. Your friends and family know you by a loving name and they are your community, yet another piece of paper gives you an official name and declares that you belong to a national community administered by a state. This same document prescribes you a heteronormative gender and status as a citizen, along with the privileges (public services) and obligations (taxation, conscription) that this entails.

Such scenarios are created and mediated by "governmental technologies which assemble scientific knowledge, technical apparatuses, anthropological assumptions, and architectural forms in strategic ways to configure relations of conduct."† The design theorist Mahmoud Keshavarz illustrates this by highlighting the correspondences between "passports [and] other materially made artifacts such as checkpoints and identification databases" in order to instantiate and reinforce contingent claims (like identity, or the right to travel). Documents—the passport, the property deed, the state identity card—are perhaps the most fathomable element of this assemblage, but they are designed to mask the wider forces that back them. *Immutable* explores the design of such documents, which can include governmental impositions designed to facilitate command, taxonomize subjects, facilitate commerce, regulate ownership, and manage public space; or private corporate paperwork that articulates the claims of its stakeholders and their value; as well as numerous other proclamations, projections, designations, and interpellations. These objects are a quotidian and banal genre of graphic design, but they bear the various ways of knowing and remembering that shape our political, economic and cultural space. They have evolved, over millennia, a range of aesthetic, political, and graphical tools to help manifest the authority of their authors, deflect political contestation, and render their claims normative. I call this collection of techniques the design imperative to immutability. *Immutable* examines this cluster of material histories and design strategies, moving achronologically across forms, techniques and political backgrounds.

This book deploys an idiosyncratic constellation of precedents and starting points for theorizing how the transhistorical "design imperative to immutability" might restructure our understanding of design's function. Each section comprises visual notes, references, research, and source materials with extended annotations, captions, and aphorisms. This material cuts across developments in writing, metallurgy, coinage, printing, encryption, cartography, economics, music, law, computation, and communication. These diverse fields are interwoven across five thousand years of artifacts and techniques, each attesting to political efforts to hold a claim or memory intact across time, instantiate value, or project authority. Throughout, we find that no document ever achieves the absolute immutability (or depoliticization) it seeks; every document is met with attempts to subvert, challenge, or invalidate it. It is this interaction with the social sphere that dialectically drives formal innovations, security features, new administrative frameworks, and even outright threats of violence, which in turn propel new forms of subversion and resistance. Forgery, destruction, forking, or refusal can thus all be seen as designerly actions. Sketching an alternative historiography, *Immutable* schematizes numerous recursive or concurrent conceptual developments and technological histories that continually foreshadow (or rewrite) each other across five sections structured loosely around a conceptual, technical, formal, or political toolset:

<u>Proto-Typography, Writing & Grids</u> asks the reader to consider graphic design's origins in the earliest forms of "administration" that emerged from the coterminous application of visual grid systems to organize both writing and landed property. Ancient trade contracts, receipts, promissory notes, and other forms of memorialization were pressed into wet earthen

clay and solidified for preservation. To our knowledge, such artifacts are the most materially durable information storage media to date. The archaeological record shows that what they memorialized were primarily economic transactions and exhaustive lists of objects. Writing first appears to mediate exchange and govern commerce and property—all things around which conflict and violence might erupt. These artifacts also articulate the earliest evidence of graphical thought premised upon attempts at the standardization of writing, the production of conventions, and the sedimentation of authorship, authorization, and authority.

Metals & Mechanization examines automation as a technique of immutability and the evacuation of fleshy, unstable human links in the production and transmission of (official) claims. The reliable repeatability and morphological consistency enabled by metalwork strives for a stable, mechanical objectivity, helping to guarantee the value of a document by establishing a normative standard uninflected by the vagaries of human error or subjective desire. The goldsmith's coin echoes the tools of the Mesopotamian scribe, and anticipates the typographer's punch: metal coinage is but one chapter in the long imbrication of writing and money. Innovations in this area are animated by forgery and counterfeiting, making apparent the need for a political register of design techniques.

Measurement & Standardization traces how developments in the natural and social sciences become instruments of colonial projection. Revolution, metrication, and digitization provide entry points for considering the political dimensions of design artifacts like rulers and maps, which instantiated a bureaucratic gaze that privileges a graphical reduction of the world into calculable and manageable units of space, matter, and time. In other words, the colonial entities that deploy these tools and ways of knowing impose an administrative rationality, which compresses the world into numerical and typographic representations, manipulable through an increasingly global communications and command infrastructure. Colonial power intensifies bureaucracy: vast amounts of paper and massive trade fleets are two sides of the same bill.

Graphic design's entanglement with administration becomes more acute in early European instantiations of <u>Printing & Typography</u>. That Gutenberg's moveable typography is often regarded as the genesis of graphic design betrays a teleological rear-projection of mass communication (that is, mass markets) as the field's primary domain. *Immutable* recasts Gutenberg's invention as the inception of modern capitalism, colonialism, and nationalism, to the extent that it produces the conditions and documental precedents that enable the development of the joint-stock company, the stock exchange, and the first true multinational corporation. Rather than centering literary publishing or advertising, this chapter looks at accounting, certification, governance, and even musical notation to consider how design has enabled managerial coordination and actuated hierarchical command structures.

Finally, <u>Cables & Crypto (or Speed & Displacement)</u> approaches the projection of power and colonial violence as enabled by the long development of global mass communications infrastructures. The oldest enemies of immutability—the entropy of movement in time and space—are vanquished by telecommunications networks hewed into being by the force of imperial might, facilitating the projection of power in radically compressed temporalities while enabling the imposition of violence in expanded theaters to become increasingly precise.

Against this backdrop networked forms of documental memorialization emerge through and against this infrastructure and its progenitors. Blockchain and "artifacts" like cryptocurrencies or NFTs speculate on the viability of decentralized, "trustless" guarantees of meaning and value that subvert the more traditional reliance on direct force and established institutions as guarantors and mediators of documental claims. This phenomenon was accelerated at the turn of the twenty-first century through an imperial war in Iraq, the very region—Mesopotamia— that first gave us inscriptions rendered on clay tablets.

Despite these documental forms being graphic design's most profoundly consequential genre, they have escaped critical or creative scrutiny in the field's largely professionally oriented pedagogy. Their pedestrian visual language often falls at the periphery of what the market and professional designers tend to think of as "graphic design." The field's pedagogy has largely remained mired in the presumptive inevitability of commercial practice. Today, many designers, particularly those who might read this book, are free-floating agents, aspiring to be auteurs lauded for their aptitude for individual problem-solving on behalf of sponsoring clients. Design pedagogy and practice privileges type design and public signage, publications and websites, identity systems and branding, magazines, posters, apps, and ad campaigns, and other subgenres of publicity because, under globalized capitalism, graphic design's charge is to keep capital in motion: to circulate the signs and codes that lubricate commerce and empire. However, when it comes to the document, graphic design is also charged with halting time: fixing the form and meaning of signs, and stabilizing governmentality by locating claims in commonly apprehensible forms, squarely in the realm of the banal and thus more safely outside of contestation. The significance of immutability is occluded by its banality.

Working against reified colonial forms of historiography and graphic design's complicity in them, I aim to contribute a destabilizing element to figure graphic design as a field of contestation for remembering, knowing, and claiming otherwise. I have regarded the precedents and materials hereunder not as accomplishments in a narrative of progress, but as fragmentary forensic evidence of a vast, multiform crime. Can such a history be narrated without the canonical inertia of publicity-oriented projects, or hagiographies of singular practitioners? If so, to what end? To be sure, this is not a parade of "best practices," but rather a sketch that aims to indict graphic design's long entanglement with the villainy of colonialism and capitalism. By examining the graphic forms of documents designed to make and enforce claims—to stabilize the history their author wishes to tell—we can better understand the nature and motivations of the entities that produced them as a basis for articulating clearer counterpositions. Documents cannot function without a reservoir of violence behind them: property deeds require their legal system; the passport requires its border agent; money requires a state— or more recently, an autonomous planetary-scale ledger— to recognize and control its value. Historiography, thus, might be cast as a creative endeavor, where study and making are driven by imagining and "re-existing"—to borrow Walter Mignolo's term—forms of memorialization to subvert, counter, or obviate the capitalist/colonial forms and functions of the document. Historio*graphy* itself could be construed as part of an expanded conception of design.

† Sven Opitz, quoted in Mahmoud Keshavarz in *The Design Politics of the Passport: Materiality, Immobility, and Dissent* (London: Bloomsbury, 2018), 33.

I   Proto-typography, Writing & Grids

163

A massive hoard of clay tablets are recovered from the ancient city of Ur. They record transactions for things ranging from half a million sheep to a single jar of beer. These records, contracts and receipts—pressed then baked into clay substrates—needed to reliably enumerate quantities of things: commodities like livestock, bread, slaves, and durations of time. These tablets promise, claim, and memorialize. ↑163 They have held their form intact across millennia, even as the worlds in which these objects had social, political, and economic meaning have long since vanished.

Consider the advent of *design* in the techniques for administering such disputable claims (i.e., who is entitled to what). These are sedimented into visual codes, semantic signs, and such things as the insignia of state authorities, whose mandate to govern provides an impetus to the development of various techniques of immutability. The standardization of writing, orthography, weights, and measures—in short, the design objects of the incipient state—is directed toward the task of establishing stable administrative norms.

This section inaugurates a story of techniques embodied in documental artifacts—from ancient clay tablets to contemporary cryptocurrencies—that are designed to displace the contingency of human inscriptions and to place a claim beyond the destabilizing reach of contestation.

PROTO-TYPOGRAPHY

Writing begins with pressed forms; we might do well to heed mathematician and historian Peter Damerow's caution (1999) that it developed more as a technique of administration than as a visualization of oral language and literary expression. That is, proto-writing was initially premised on graphical techniques for structuring accountability through the pursuit of durable, archivable inscriptions and the kind of standardization (in units, signs, and the formal way they're encoded) that schematizes the world into manageable, governable bits. Although archaeologist Denise Schmandt-Besserat (2014) has discussed the coterminous relationship between accounting and writing, we might also see these activities as imbricated in what I will call proto-typography—a phenomenon whereby the tool/substrate combination of reed stylus/soft clay conditioned the stability of semantic forms, as well as their consistent repeatability through pressing to actuate morphological and semantic standardization. Early instantiations of proto-typography were designed to address questions of how to represent *who*, *what*, *how much*, *when*, and *where*, writing into being and sedimenting such categories as *identity*, *commodity*, *quantity*, *time*, and *place*. Above all, this pressing "sets in stone" political arrangements (obligations, contracts, debts, property claims, and so on) as *documents*, designed to memorialize and depoliticize these contingencies by attempting to render them immutable—placing them as far outside of contestation as possible.

Imagine that one wishes to establish a claim over a piece of farmland, and to extend that claim to one's progeny (now heirs). Inscribing this claim upon a clay tablet, describing its boundaries, identifying

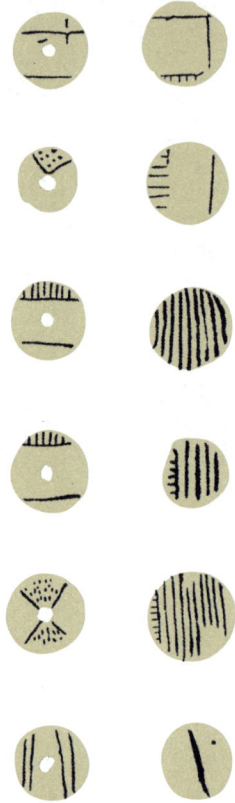

162 These *calculi*, or complex counting tokens, are thought to distinguish categories—possibly of commodities—through a visual system of linear marks. Denise Schmandt-Besserat posits that the increased complexity in the design of calculi coincided with the establishment of "a coercive redistribution economy" (1991) and functioned as an element of ancient state formation because it facilitated record-keeping, standardization, and taxation. Considering the etymology of the word "taxonomy," which comes from the Greek *taxis* (arrangement) and *nómos* (custom, law), it is important to bear in mind that categorization is political because through encipherment it enables governance.

161 Cuneiform inscriptions are pressed into a soft clay substrate with a wedged reed stylus. The combination of these with the action of pressing engenders morphological standardization.

159

Plough	Ox	Reed
Bread	Slave girl	Earth/ Land
Food /Ration	King	Palace /Temple
Day	Star/God (the stable reference)	
Orchard	livestock, sheep (domesticated)	

160 Forms ploughed into clay with a stylus; quantities pressed as dots and tics. Logonumeric tablets include symbols for commodities (Uruk III, ca. 3500-3100 BCE).

159 Proto-cuneiform signs add basic notation for time, political status, and institutions to the scribal lexicon. Two categories of writing exist in the archaeological record: administrative records and lexical lists of thousands of words ordered under categories like animals, cities, professions, plants, etc.

158 Wedge-shaped symbols for clay containers specified by commodity. An early instantiation of the transition to cuneiform. (Uruk III, ca. 3200–3000 BCE).

its owner, and then baking it to set the inscription, perhaps sealing it in a clay envelope, would enable it to travel through space and time, and to resist the more immediate entropy and evanescent instability of the claim rendered orally/aurally. Once hardened through firing, the clay document is securitized, the claim is set, made objectified and verifiable. It is given value by virtue of the fact that it is outside of the subjective enunciation of any interested party. Any attempt to contest the claim by unilaterally revising the inscription will be deemed invalid because of an apparent graphical irregularity between the smooth surface and the settled, that is, "designed," forms of the original inscription. ↓158

Such tablets exemplify the essential aim of documental design: to maintain immutability. They are agonistic artifacts to the extent that they are designed to *deflect direct conflict* about their contents from people who, all things being equal, would be mutually capable of dominating each other (Graeber 2011). As media historian Lisa Gitelman explains, documents triangulate potentially adversarial parties in relation to a third party authority (an adjudicator, for instance) by objectifying an otherwise fallible memory of some political/economic arrangement, and holding its form against entropy and dispute (Gitelman 2014; Latour 1986).

Given that such tablets functioned as administrative documents, and that they held inscriptions about potentially volatile social arrangements (Who owes what to whom? How much? When?), it is clear that these documents functioned as a technique for management, administration, command, and governance; by extension, they were used to memorialize ongoing hierarchical arrangements like debt and coercive tax obligations. ↓133

vs

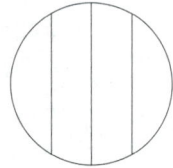

ACCOUNTABILITY
(Cylinder Seals)

"'[R]edemption" is ... really more a matter of destroying the entire system of accounting. In many [ancient] Middle Eastern cities, this was literally true: one of the common acts during debt cancellation was the ceremonial destruction of the tablets on which financial records had been kept, an act to be repeated, much less officially, in just about every major peasant revolt in history."
—David Graeber, *Debt: The First 5,000 Years*

"[O]blivion [is] antagonistic to the self and property, while all the techniques of mnemonics are their essential allies."
—George Caffentzis, *Clipped Coins, Abused Words, and Civil Government*

The earliest use of cylinder seals appeared some 6,000 years ago in present day southwestern Iran. They were used as a form of administrative signature, or to notarize clay documents, and were pressed onto the "latches" of clay envelopes, jars, doors, or directly onto a clay tablet. Clay-baked envelopes, for instance, functioned to securitize the documentation of a transaction,↓111 and contained *calculi*—small clay counting tokens used to record quantities of exchanged goods. Since the calculi were encrypted inside the envelope, their quantities would often be inscribed on the exterior as a reference or label, which itself functioned as a documental claim. This "double document" (Maiocchi 2019) was notarized (authenticated) by an administrative author, identifiable and thus accountable, by the seal.↓56

157 Strictly from the standpoint of visual cognition, dividing a good (formed, for instance, into a pie) equally between the prime numbers of the sexagesimal system (2, 3, less so 5), seems to yield equal portions fathomable as such to interested observers.

156 The glyptic carving from a cylinder seal from ca. 3600–3100 BCE, has been interpreted as depicting pottery, or possibly textile production (Iranica 2011), while two seated figures do some form of accounting with sticks, under the imposing gaze of a managerial figure. This image concisely hints at some kind of political economy, a hierarchical relationship actualized through the production and circulation of administrative documents.

155, 154 Above, a system of cipher discs, one for each sign (0–9, a–f) used in cryptographic hash strings such as those generated by SHA-256. Below, 3D printed as a cylinder seal.

153 The sexagesimal (base-60) number system used in proto-cuneiform notation is thought to emerge from metrological practices for measuring weight. This became the Akkadian imperial standard by decree around the twenty-third and twenty-fourth centuries BCE to rationalize the welter of competing standards for calculation used by different cities and institutions within the empire. James C. Scott gives us a way to understand this tendency as

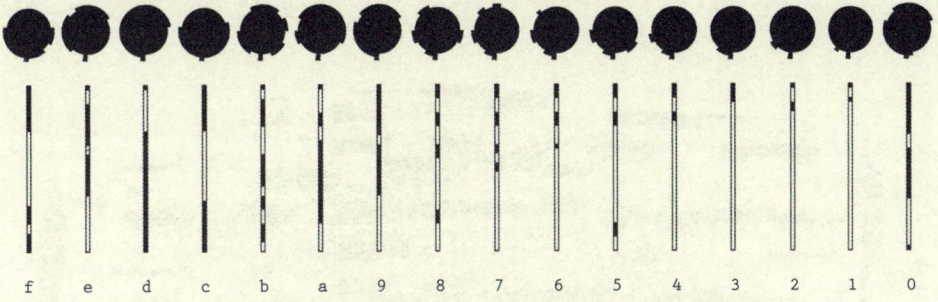

f   e   d   c   b   a   9   8   7   6   5   4   3   2   1   0

154

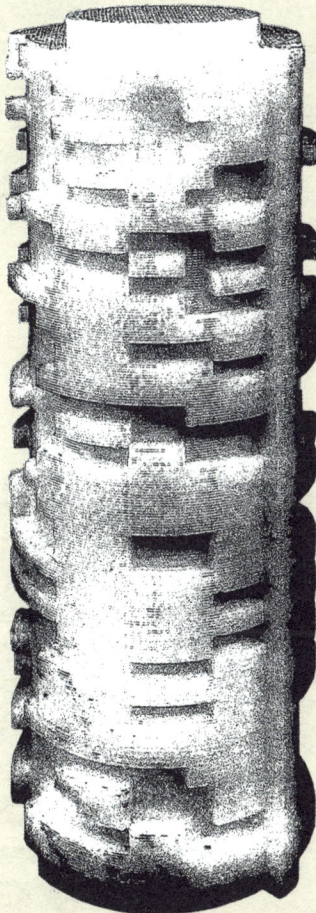

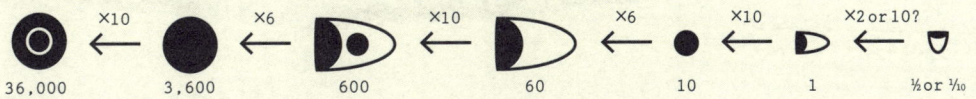

153

something of a source code for the assertion and imposition of colonial claims: "Such projects of administrative, economic, and cultural standardization are hard-wired into the architecture of the modern state itself.... One way of appreciating the effect of this colonization is to view it as a massive reduction of vernaculars of all kinds" (Scott 2009, 12). This apparently also applies to ancient statecraft.

152   As far as we know, clay is the most durable information storage medium. These tablets represent two documental technologies invented thousands of years apart. The 3D printed cylinders ↑154 were pressed into these clay tablets to store SHA-256 strings. However, human cognition is unable to make sense of this potentially machine readable orthography.

151, The proto-cuneiform sign for
150   "day" could represent the sun
ᅌ   rising or setting without a mark to orient the reader one way or the other. In any case, either interpretation could have the same value as a unit of time. Other ambiguities may be more problematic. Two points: First, since proto-cuneiform tablets "represent predominantly quantities..., objects, or persons, institutions, and locations involved... [and] the type of administrative activity that is documented" (Damerow 1999, 8), their formal integrity and the stability of syntactic conventions are crucial to their correct interpretation and the legitimacy of hierarchical bureaucracies's authorship. Literacy and discipline enable command.
Second, cuneiform represents a significant advance in immutability. Using a sharpened tool for *pressing* marks bolsters their resistance to entropy. The inscription's status as document is improved in contrast to proto-cuneiform, where the stylus plows clay to form edges that can crumble when dry.↓47/46

ORTHO·GRAPHY [right•writing]
This tablet↑151 documents grain distribution from a large temple. The glyphs are sectioned by dividing lines, instantiating an early form of graphical thought and visual epistemology. In her book *Graphesis*, Johanna Drucker calls our attention to the grid of lines appearing on such tablets, noting that although these lines do not hold semantic value, they produce a syntactic order and establish orthographic convention. They aid in correctly interpreting (recognizing) the author(ity)'s intent. Drucker quotes Schamdt-Besserat's assertion that such lines function:

whether visibly present ... or implied... as a functional point of reference against which the basic graphic properties of sequence, direction, orientation, size, and scale can register their significance. If the original trace complies with the logician George Spencer Brown's fundamental distinction (as the basis of his Laws of Form) and Derridian *différance* (as the originary process of the possibility of signification), then the ground line is the first cognitive frame, a referential boundary, for putting elements of a graphical system into relation with each other through a common element. (Drucker 2014, 85).

In other words, a grid functions as a technique of orthographic standardization, reinforcing material techniques for mitigating doubt and dispute.↓87/86

Eat/Ration:	abstracted	rotated	simplified
~3000BCE →			~700BCE

◇	B	C	I	J	K	L	M
2				Real GDP growth			
3				Debt/GDP			
4	Country	Coverage	30 or less	30 to 60	60 to 90	90 or above	30 or less
26			3.7	3.0	3.5	1.7	5.5
27	Minimum		1.6	0.3	1.3	-1.8	0.8
28	Maximum		5.8	4.9	10.2	3.6	13.3
29							
30	US	1946-2009	n.a.	3.4	3.3	-2.0	n.a.
31	UK	1946-2009	n.a.	2.4	2.5	2.4	n.a.
32	Sweden	1946-2009	3.6	2.9	2.7	n.a.	6.3
33	Spain	1946-2009	1.5	3.4	4.2	n.a.	8.9
34	Portugal	1952-2009	4.8	2.5	0.3	n.a.	7.9
35	New Zealand	1948-2009	2.5	2.9	3.9	-7.9	2.6
36	Netherlands	1956-2009	4.1	2.7	1.1	n.a.	6.4
37	Norway	1947-2009	3.4	5.1	n.a.	n.a.	5.4
38	Japan	1946-2009	7.0	4.0	1.0	0.7	7.0
39	Italy	1951-2009	5.4	2.1	1.8	1.0	5.6
40	Ireland	1948-2009	4.4	4.5	4.0	2.4	2.5
41	Greece	1970-2009	4.0	0.3	2.7	2.9	13.3
42	Germany	1946-2009	3.9	0.9	n.a.	n.a.	3.2
43	France	1949-2009	4.9	2.7	3.9	n.a.	5.2
44	Finland	1946-2009	3.8	2.4	5.5	n.a.	7.0
45	Denmark	1950-2009	3.5	1.7	2.4	n.a.	5.6
46	Canada	1951-2009	1.9	3.6	4.1	n.a.	2.2
47	Belgium	1947-2009	n.a.	4.2	3.1	2.6	n.a.
48	Austria	1948-2009	5.2	3.3	3.3	n.a.	5.7
49	Australia	1951-2009	3.2	4.9	4.0	n.a.	5.9
50							
51			4.1	2.8	2.8	=AVERAGE(L30:L44)	

149 A record of barley (possibly rations) for which claims are supported by a spreadsheet-like grid. The association of grids with mid-twentieth-century modernism privileging a mechanical rationalization of form, could be reconsidered. Far from being an irreducible element of graphical form, grids are an ancient political/rhetorical technique meant to reinforce the managerial mandate of bureaucracies.

148 A spreadsheet from the 2010 Carmen Reinhart and Kenneth Rogoff study that gave governments scientist cover for fiscal austerity measures and the reduction of broad areas of public spending (social programs, healthcare, the arts, and so on). It claimed that countries with public debt over 90% of their GDP had lower growth rates than countries with lower debt to GDP ratios. In 2013, reviewers examining their work found that the conclusions of the original study were based on a failure to factor in five rows of data into its calculations. ↓72

146 The Great Trigonometrical Survey of India (1802–1871) was conducted by agents of the British East India Company. Its synoptic, colonial gaze is projected and imposed, obliterating the incommensurable plurality on the ground. Just as the surface of a clay tablet must be *pre*-scribed as null (without value), smoothed for inscription (with value), so it is with colonized space—prescribed as null to receive its primary onto-epistemological claim—land-as-property. ↓19

BABYLONIAN SURVEY

This ancient Babylonian clay disc ↑147 is currently the earliest extant example of the application of trigonometry (dating from the eighteenth to the nineteenth century BCE, preceding Pythagoras by more than a millenium). It shows a cadastral survey, mapped to resolve a dispute between two landowners. Such land surveys make apparent an increasing prevalence of private land ownership. Legal documents were produced to govern the distribution of land and settle boundary disputes, heading off the potential for violent confrontation. An old Babylonian poem in which an older surveying student admonishes a younger one illustrates what was at stake in a disciplined adherence to their professional mandate.

Go to divide a plot, and you are not able to divide the plot; go to apportion a field, and you cannot even hold the tape and rod properly. The field pegs you are unable to place; you cannot figure out its shape, so that when wronged men have a quarrel you are not able to bring peace, but you allow brother to attack brother. Among the scribes, you (alone) are unfit for the clay. (Mansfield 2021).

GENERAL PLAN OF THE TRIANGLES.

144

143

145

INVESTITURE OF HAMMURABI

An ancient king receives from the sun god Shamash—
god of justice and truth (seated)—a rod and a coil. ↓140
These are both symbols of divine power. Some inter-
pretations regard these objects as tools for measurement (adjudication, judgement)—surveyors' tools—
representing, by virtue of their divine provenance,
an indisputable standard of measurement. James
C. Scott reminds us that the generalization of one
standard over another is the result of struggle—
in other words, standards are either dominant
or subordinate. ↓104

This image set at the top of the stele makes
the performative claim that the laws inscribed below
it are not the arbitrary decrees of a fallible human king,
but of divine provenance and thus beyond contestation:
"Hammurabi, the king of righteousness, on whom
Shamash has conferred right (or law) am I" (King
2009). The definitions of criminality and the enumer-
ation of their penalties are inscribed thereunder.
The smoothed basalt substrate upon which the laws
are written reinforces these claims by rendering them
effectively immutable. ↓7/6, ↓121/119

145 Hammurabi's stele is a basalt
monument that stands over 2
meters tall. It contains about
4,000 lines of text that covers
criminal, family, property, and
commercial law, expressed as
if/then clauses.

144 A barrel (sphendonoid)-shaped
weight with an inscription
reading:
*One-third legitimate mina
[Belonging to the] palace
of Nabu-shumu-lishir, son
of the Dakkuru tribe
Declared as a known quantity;
Authorized by...*

143 An official weight of 2 mina
(~1kg), used by officials in the
wool industry. Certified in the
storehouse of the temple of
the Moon god at Ur. Reign of
Shulgi, ca. 2094–2047 BCE.

142 Seal of the Bureau International des Poids et Mesures (BIPM), based in the Parisian suburb of Sèvres.

141 The *Tablet of Shamash* functions, among other things, as a land grant sanctified and legitimized by the Sun God. There may have been a boundary marker set on the granted property associated with this tablet to corroborate its validity. This image is superimposed with an image of enslaved people assisting a surveyor in Barbados (Ichirouganaim). Detail from William Mayo's *A New and Exact Map of the Island of Barbadoes in America, According to an Actual and Accurate Survey Made in the Years 1717 to 1721, Approved by the Royal Society & Authorized by His Majesty's Royal Licence* (London: John Senex, 1722).

Castoriadis argues that the very impulse to know about other societies is a peculiarity of Ancient Greece and Western Europe, because these societies were especially effective at domesticating the contingency of meaning(s) within the web of institutions that structured them. Notwithstanding a history of colonial/capitalist expansion, the look "outward" is motivated by a desire to find other ways of being that exceed the ideological enclosures imposed by hierarchical, administrative, statist societies at home. Graeber and Wengrow (2021) show, for instance, that ideas about freedom, equality, and democracy that became popular in the West—ideas often associated with neoimperial claims about the beneficence of Westernization—are largely misappropriations of the critiques of Western civilization by Indigenous intellectuals. ↓8

ROD AND COIL

There is some contention about the symbolism of the rod and ring (or coil) when held by the deity Shamash. One interpretation reads these as symbols of eternal life. The other, as mentioned above, regards these as surveyors' tools. The tapering of the rod suggests that it could also be a peg meant to be driven into the ground, and a point from which to tie off a coil of rope for measuring a distance. When it comes down to a radical dispute over a definition, who can claim the right to arbitrarily define space? Investing this power in a nonhuman deity, outside of human subjectivity (understood as inherently subordinate to the sun god) may serve an ideological function. Enrico Ascalone and Luca Peyronel's (2001) work suggests that the metrology of Ancient Mesopotamia was intrinsically related to cultic activities and the administration of temple economies with embodying concepts like justice and equality. Kathryn Slanski (2013) offers that these are symbols of justice—of what is correct (ὀρθός, *orthós* in Greek). ↑151

Casting a measurement standard as being of divine provenance appears to be an effort to depoliticize the matter and place it within what Cornelius Castoriadis (1991) might call society's "closure of meaning." For him, recognizing such closures as contingent—belonging to the ancient Greek notion of νόμος (*nómos*, or law, custom, read: contingent), and not φύση (*phísi*, or nature, read: inevitable)—casts the struggle for other standards—a different "rod and coil," so to speak—as definitive in the struggle for autonomy and democracy. ↓Coda, 105

BEATING THE BOUNDS

Traditional English methods of defining landed property and legal jurisdiction exposed owners to uncertainty. Property deeds typically included a form of legal description called "metes and bounds," which is usually formulated using natural landmarks and other physical features of a landscape. The trouble was that sometimes these natural, physical features moved over time, or became damaged or destroyed, making it difficult to use them as evidence in an estate claim. "Beating the bounds" is a traditional, ritualistic practice from parts of England, Wales, and later New England. Its aim was to instill knowledge of the established boundaries of a church parish (or some other kind of civil unit, like a town) so that the benefits, obligations, and liabilities could be properly attributed to those who lived within the bounds, while those who lived without could be justly excluded. The participants of this ritual tended to be young boys, ensuring that its witnesses would have a longer lifespan. The ritual involved perambulating the boundaries while beating them with green boughs; sometimes it would also involve violently beating or shoving the boys themselves onto boundary stones, in order to *imprint* them with a memory of the site. The practice solidified local spatial knowledge in the community's oral tradition, while reinforcing the conceptual demand that any real property claim rests on violence. Modern surveying techniques would, at the very least, eventually spare these boys the responsibility.↑146

140 Gunter's chain, designed by English clergyman and mathematician Edmund Gunter (1581–1626), was used for land surveying until the early twentieth century. It served as a legal standard for measuring out property for legal and commercial purposes throughout the British Empire, and enabled the drawing of enclosures. A total chain contained one hundred links, three joints separating each for flexibility. Distinctive tags were placed every ten links from each end.

139 The Ascension Day Incident. Local commoners breach the walls of London's Richmond Park in May 1751 to assert their right to access what were once common lands. This "trespass" took place under the guise of performing the traditional "beating of the parish bounds."

138 Karl Marx's *Capital*, vol. I (ch. 27), narrates the gradual process of enclosing common lands in England and turning them into private property. This had the effect of depriving a great portion of the population access to land and resources to sustain themselves, and forced them into proletarianization—that is, they were left with little choice but to seek employment in industrializing urban centers, and earn a wage to purchase what they might have cultivated through their own labor. ↓119

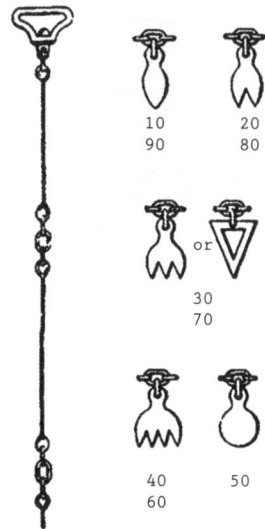

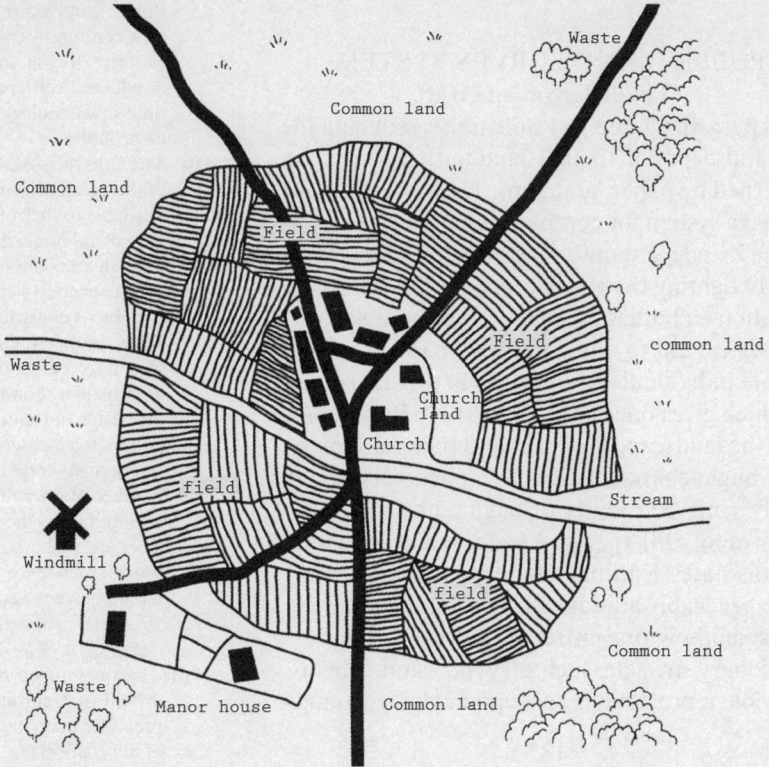

Common land

Waste

Common land

Common land

Field

Field

common land

Waste

Church land

Church

Stream

field

field

Windmill

Common land

Waste

Manor house

Common land

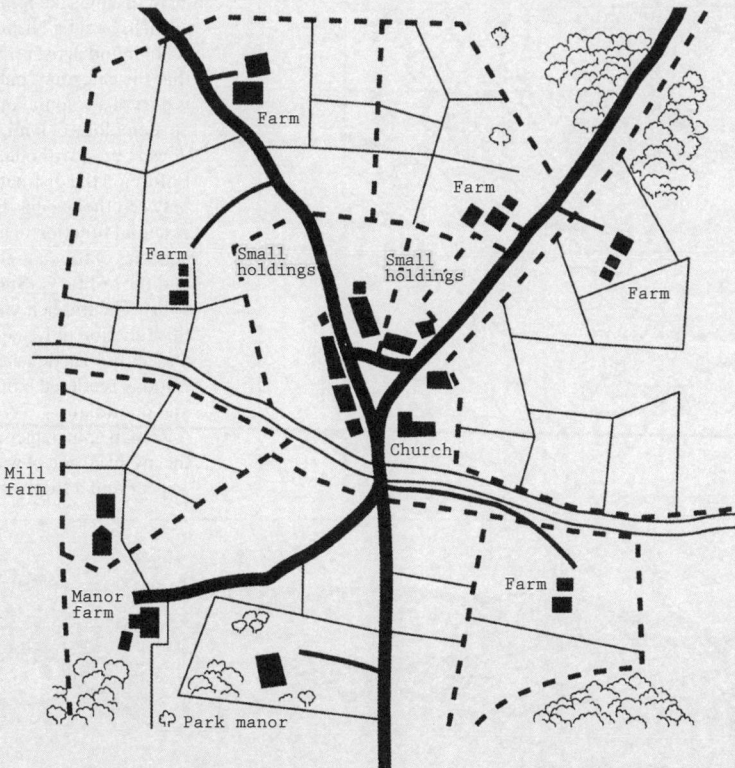

Farm

Farm

Farm

Farm

Small holdings

Small holdings

Church

Mill farm

Farm

Manor farm

Park manor

PUBLIC LAND SURVEY SYSTEM
(The Jeffersonian Grid)

Land is parcelled into 1 × 1 mile units, reducing the plural landscapes of Turtle Island to that which can be governed by paper (and gun). Thomas Jefferson proposed a system for commodifying the land to facilitate its sale and raise funds to repay debts incurred in fighting the Revolutionary War. This standardization embodies the ideals of the bourgeois liberal state, built to rationally govern the property of private individuals. Ownership of private property, which gives one the right to kill in its defense, is what the landscape architect and theorist James Corner might characterize as a "…phenomen[on] that can only achieve visibility through representation" (Corner 1999, 228). ↓100/99 As a feature of the modern bourgeois state's legitimate function and exclusive right to peaceably adjudicate potential disputes amongst land-owning citizens, ↓136 won through revolutionary struggle, such surveys become themselves violent projections cast upon colonized lands.

137

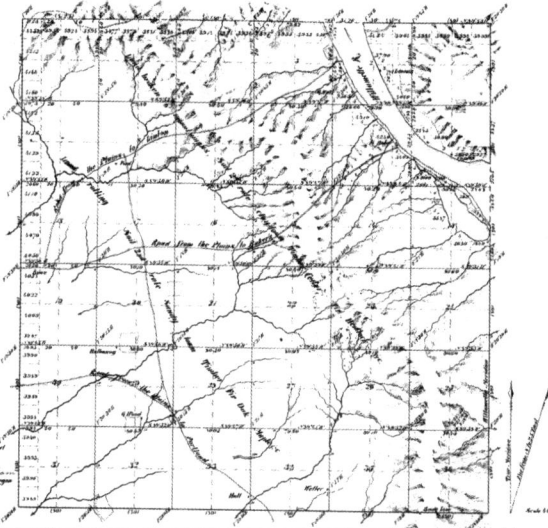

137 Map showing a section of the Public Land Survey in what is now commonly called Northwestern Oregon, imposing a reductive settler-colonial onto-epistemology of land-as-property.

136 The Commissioners' Plan of 1811 renders Manaháhtaan available to the commercial gaze of colonial administration—land commodified as private property and figured as such by its constitutive other, public property. City planners sought to correct the monotony of the grid by commissioning the design of Central Park.

Shannon Mattern observes that (modernist) corporate/ bureaucratic architecture, exemplified by the skyscraper (2017, 42) and urban planning share a preference for smooth circulation enabled by the structural rationality of the grid (126). ↓58/57 ↓87/86

Hailed as an exemplar of progressive urbanism, Central Park was premised upon the destruction of Seneca Village—the first settlement of free Black Americans in New York City.

Leanne Betasamosake Simpson, a Michi Saagiig Nishnaabeg scholar and artist reminds us that the category "public space" is part of a colonial onto-epistemology of land. "Public" doesn't exist without "private." Enforcing the distinction between the two has been the essential function of armed agencies of the state (i.e., police and the military) (Simpson 2016). The implicit violence of this function in Lenapehoking and across Turtle Island is today rendered banal and quotidian.

135 A Roman coin depicting Mars, the mythical god of war, holding a spear and a trophy. ↓25

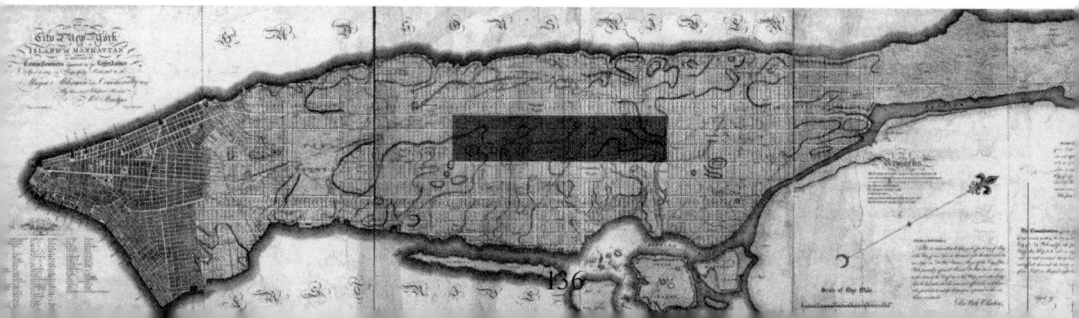

II Metals & Mechanization

135

Metal's material capacity to receive and retain form consistently across innumerable instantiations is salient to charting a history of immutability. The historian Ernst Kantorowicz might have characterized metal coinage as that which helped solidify the proverbial king's claim to territorial sovereignty by enabling the coin of his realm to travel intact across greater ranges of space and time. Vulnerabilities to the integrity of this sign (i.e., forgery, doubt) have driven technological and political innovation.

The techniques and skill sets required to strike metal coinage echo those required to produce inscriptions on clay tablets in the preceding millenia and foreshadow the development of moveable metal typography thousands of years later.

The capacity to (re)produce fungible, stable instantiations of power and value—let's call this *command*—are encrypted through inhuman mechanization. The progressive industrialization of coinage, for instance, seeks to displace the human (the fallible, the political) from the process of creating tokens that circulate to effectuate radically contingent claims about sovereignty and value.

PRECIOUS METALS

Lydian coinage ↕131 minted from electrum, a rare naturally occurring gold-silver alloy, is widely considered to be the first coinage issued by a state anywhere in the world, dating back to the early sixth century BCE. What makes it significant to future developments of coinage is that it is stamped with a seal of the issuing authority as an accountability measure serving two functions: it signals the authorship of the coin, making it an official, constitutive feature of state administration, and it obliges its holder to use it to extinguish their tax obligations to that same issuing authority.

Evolutionary theories of money commonly taught in economics textbooks would claim that the electrum's verifiable mineral composition and natural scarcity (i.e., pure gold and silver), as well as its "portability, indestructibility, homogeneity, divisibility, and cognizability" (North, 7), made it apt for usage as money—emerging putatively as the dominant general commodity from a long evolutionary process wherein the inefficiencies of barter exchange's double coincidence of wants are rationalized (Graeber 2011). While this may be valid from a material point of view, it may be more interesting to approach such tautological theories with skepticism because they tend to back-project today's understanding of money as inevitable and uncontestable.

Some heterodox theories of money argue that anything can and has been designated as money, and states are typically the kinds of entities with the authority to do so. In this view, money's status as such rests in the state administration that issues and recognizes it as valuable. What money means to the state that issues it, at least, is that its holder has contributed something *to* the state. ↗133 As anti-counterfeiting measures, the attributes listed above help regulate and reduce the (financial and political) cost of policing money's integrity. Those who would defraud the state with forgeries expose themselves to being punished by the state. Penalties like imprisonment or death also happen to be, fundamentally, what backs money's value. ↓113 ↓34/33

134 Roman terracotta coin mold (ca. 308–320 CE). This mold was cast from a legitimate gold coin to make counterfeits in bronze.

131 While this coin includes a depiction of a bull and a lion, similar coins from the Aolean city of Cyme, when first circulated around 600–550 BCE, utilized a horse motif, marking an association with the house of Agamemnon and referring to the Greek victory over Troy. ↓18 They were invented by Hermodike II, the daughter of a dynastic Agamemnon of Cyme. She was named after Hermodike I who has been credited with inventing the Greek written script. Cyme's coinage, inspired by the Lydian "nobleman's tax-token," is considered likely the second oldest coinage, and the first used for more quotidian commercial transactions.

134

133   The frontispiece for Thomas Hobbes's 1651 book, *Leviathan* (detail), featuring an image of a sovereign's body composed of his subjects. One of the more famous concepts from this seminal work of political theory is that of the "social contract," whereby (to paraphrase in brief) a state's subjects agree to a set of rights and obligations imposed by their ruler for that ruler's protection from outside enemies. ↓52

132   One side of this Roman Denarius shows tools for minting coinage (tongs, hammer, anvil) and the cap of Vulcan, god of metalworking. The other side depicts Juno Moneta, goddess of memory and mother of the muses. The English words for "money" and "mint" may be derived from her name, suggesting an intrinsic relation between money and the production of memory (Hart 2000, 15, 256–257). Roman coins were minted in the temple dedicated to Juno Moneta. Usages of the word "moneta" in classical and medieval Latin, and its influence on Germanic languages, may have evoked both the "coin" and the "die" used to reproduce morphologically consistent forms through punching (Stewart 1903, 30–31, 39). This suggests that consistent reproducibility is idealized as a basis of valorization. The Roman poet Ovid used the Latin word for "form," *fōrma* (etymologically related to the English word "information") to mean a mold or stamp for making coins (Hobart and Schiffman 1998, 5).

STATE MONEY
(or, Predatory Inclusion [Taylor 2019])

The coin is less a byproduct of the modern state than the very thing that enables it. The coin is paid by the state to the soldier to represent its debt for the soldier's service. It is used to pay the citizen that feeds, arms, entertains, and houses the soldier. From the citizen's perspective, supplying what the soldier wants is the best way to get this coin. The citizen *needs* the coin to pay for the protection the state provides. The soldier is the state's agent of this protection and the state wants its payments, through taxation, denominated in the coin it issues to the soldier—this the only way the subject can legitimately settle their obligation to the state. To fulfill one's obligation to the state is to be within the protection of the state, and not outside of it as its enemy (Hobbes, 1651). This is the value that the coin represents. ↓119 The coin's relative permanence is the inverse of the soldier's immanent death—it vouches for the citizen's contriubution to the soldier (and by extention, to the state) come tax time, even if the soldier is dead (Graeber 2011).

AUTHENTICATION

The term "hallmark" derives from the first Assay Office in London, Goldsmiths' Hall—a kind of early consumer protection agency—and is applied to items made of metal to certify the content and fineness of its consituent noble metals like platinum, gold, silver, and palladium. It is usually only applied after an Assay Office determines that the product in question conforms to the claim made by the manufacturer and to a legally defined standard. The image below ↓ **129** shows punches used by Goldsmiths' Hall to mark goods and certify their precious metal content. Other punches would typically include the initials of the maker of the metalware, a letter signifying the date of certification, or a mark indicating the payment of taxes on precious metals. In total, these serve to legitimize the purity claims made upon the metal and are mandated by a governing authority.

Metalsmithing tools such as these echo the morphological standardization actuated by pressing a stylus into clay. They are also reminiscent of the

131 The reverse side of this ancient Lydian coin shows the mark left by a punch as the electrum is hammered into an anvil die.

130 Typographic punches (left) are typically cut out of a steel bar as a reversed image. It is then used to punch an impression into a softer metal bar (right), usually copper, to create a matrix from which multiple characters can be cast.

129

Sterling silver (traditional mark)

2011

Silver (Sterling)

London

127 The eyes from the cover of *Graphic Design: Visual Comparisons* (1963) by Alan Fletcher, Colin Forbes, and Bob Gill.

126 Allegedly Gutenberg's printer's mark (Paput 1998, 10). Such marks served to identify the printer, certify its provenance, foil counterfeiters, and as a corollary, to enable a political or religious authority to censor books or sanction the privilege to publish (Roberts 2008, 2).
↓66↓80

125 This is an Albus silver coin minted between 1434 and 1459 in Mainz, Germany, the town in which Gutenberg lived and worked. His father was a member of the Mainz fellowship of coiners (Burke 1985, 135).

ability to cut negative reliefs for punches (or molds) like the ones used to strike Lydian coinage. In this sense, coinage foreshadows the development of moveable typography in Asia and Europe through the application of its production techniques to money, actuating its function as document. ↓43 One might thus be able to say that coinage is a prototypical form of typography, to the extent that it is made from dies and is punched/pressed in regular, standardized forms that represent value, both semantic and monetary.

ASSAY STONES (Touchstones) AND HALLMARKS

Touchstones, sometimes called Lydian stones, ↙128 are an ancient assaying tool used for determining the purity of precious metals. The illustration to the left (above) shows touchneedles, an array of precious metal alloy standards of known purity. These would be rubbed against a touchstone made of flint slate (below), leaving a standard against which marks made by the object being assayed can be compared to determine its authenticity and purity (or lack thereof).

Let's return to the topic of state money. To the extent that it is meant for extinguishing one's tax obligations—thereby securing one's entitlement to the protection of/from the state—money systems built upon token designs (coins, bills, etc.) that don't factor in authentication/securitization techniques to protect their value are effectively compromised as an instrument of the state's capacity to command. In light of what's at stake for the state, the recognizability and legibility of a coin as authentic and secure (its legality) ought to be understood as designerly political concerns. From this view, the state begins to appear as a designing agency, and the professional designer simply its instrument.

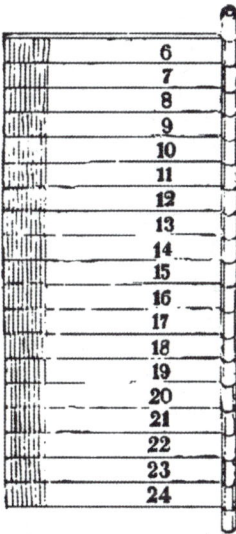

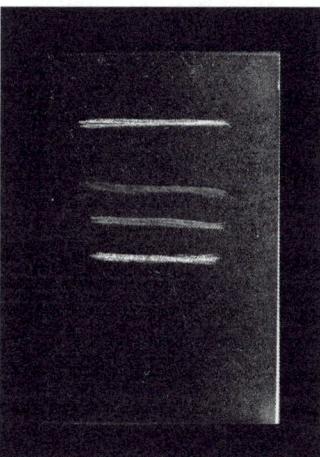

127

128

125

126

METAL TYPE

As suggested above, the tools and techniques of the metalsmith, especially those for making dies and punches, are the antecedent to those of the typographer and printer. Appreciating the political significance of this imbrication entails considering that typography's advent in the West may have more to do with the administrative than with the literary. According to S.H. Steinberg, the earliest dated documents to be composed from moveable typography (1454–55, associated with Gutenberg) are two emissions of papal indulgences. ↓66

> To nine out of every ten readers the sentence that "Gutenberg invented printing" is a shortened form of "Gutenberg invented the printing of books." The inevitable association of Gutenberg's name with the 42-line Bible tends to strengthen this fallacy. For it is not—certainly not primarily—the mechanical production of books which has made Gutenberg's invention a turning point in the history of civilization... When he and Fust preceded and accompanied their great adventure of book-printing with the issue of indulgences, calendars and pamphlets on ephemeral topics, the proto-typographers created what came to be known as job-printing. (Steinberg, 6)

Printing with interchangeable metal typography preceded Gutenberg by two hundred years in what is today Korea, but it was not motivated by a capitalist growth imperative as it would be in Europe. Confucian ethics prohibited the commercialization of books, so the incentive to undertake such a capital-intensive enterprise (and to spawn capitalism itself) was effectively nullified (Burke 1985). ↓43 **cf. Janet Abu-Lughod** While recognition of the Asian precedent is laudable, aiming at the capitalist phenomenon of job printing—the industrialization of traditional scribal labor—gives us a clearer line to such things as papal indulgences, stock certificates, ↓61 and paper money. ↓40 A genealogy of graphic design's implication in the development of capitalism and colonialism eschews a teleological identification with the book and the book designer, in favor of the bureaucracy and document as design history's subject and object.

124
a	Glass gauge
b	Sliding caliper
c	T-square
d	Large flat file, medium rough, for steel and copper
e	Flate file, finer, for steel
f	Heavy hammer
g	Metal saw with exchangeable blades for steel and copper
h	Pliers used in tempering punches
i	Setting-iron
j	Fine file (1–6 cross-sections)
k	Engraving tool (1–4 cross-sections)
l	Drill
m	Light hammer
n	Line-gauge
o	Mirror for reflected light, for engraving
p	Punch-cutting block
q	Holder for magnifying glass
r	Alcohol burner under iron stand with flat plate
s	Fine hair brush
t	Slate slab for facing punches
u	Small kerosene lamp for blackening with soot
v	Sheet of gelatine for taking impressions

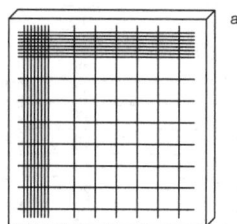

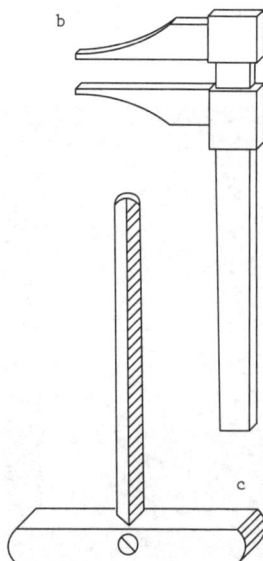

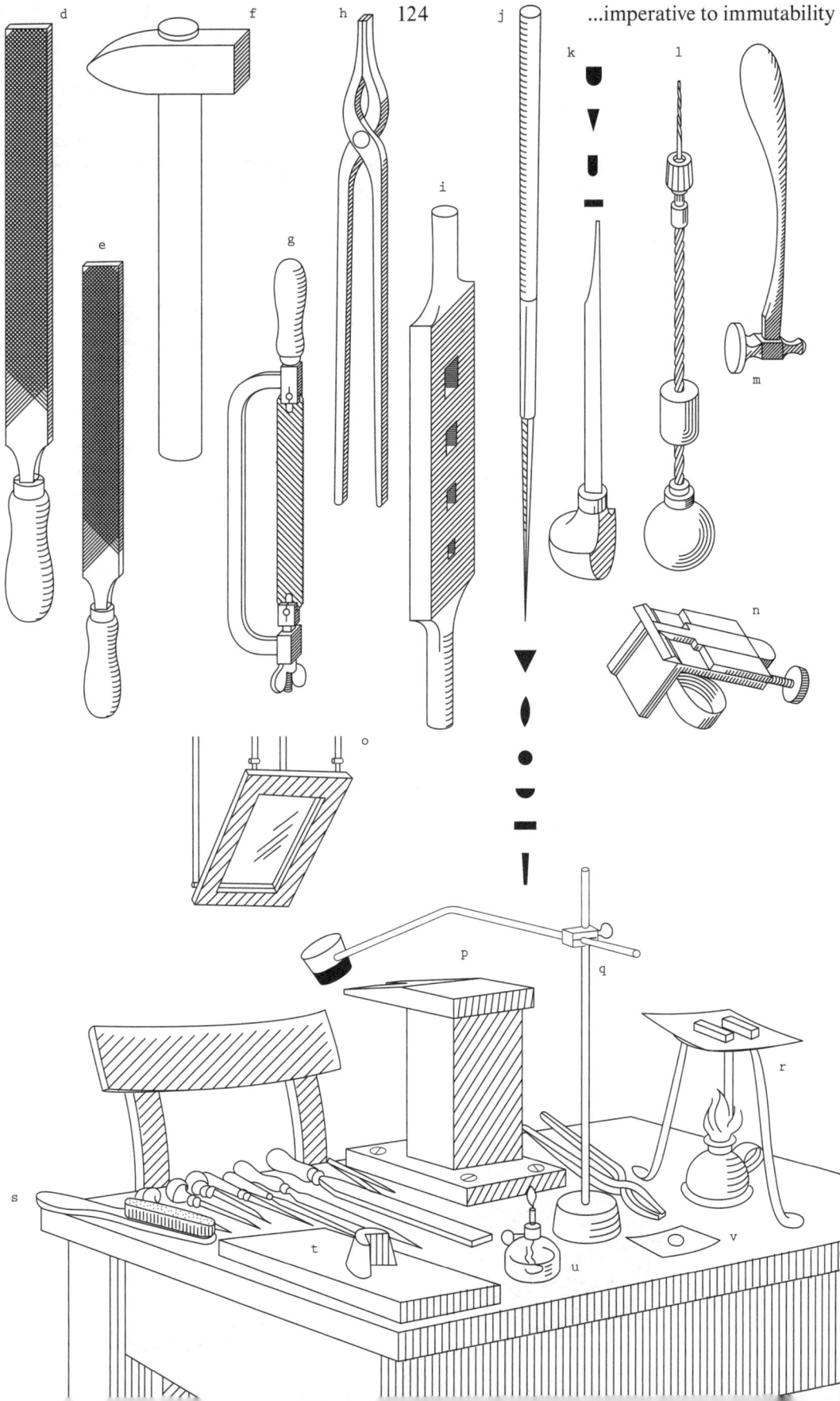

123 An Adobe® Photoshop® error
message appears when opening
a banknote image protected by
the EURion constellation.↓108

MONEY FACTORY
(or, Mechanical Objectivity)

When narrating the significance of industrialization in design history, the factory tends to be privileged over the mint, where the metalsmith and typographer's punch and die would be combined in one of the first ever applications of the Watt steam engine. Matthew Boulton, James Watt's business partner, applied the invention to minting coinage when he established the Soho Mint in 1788. The mint took commissions to stamp coinage for national domestic circulation, as well as for some British colonies. Boulton's facility was equipped with eight steam-powered presses that could strike coins at a rate of approximately 70–80 per minute with a precise morphological regularity such that counterfeits, even with minor flaws, would be easily detectable. The mechanical nature of this production would displace the fallibility of subjective, human intervention. Boulton's machines improved Isaac Newton's innovation of reeded (or milled) ↘120 edges with their precise mechanical consistency. The presses also included a built-in mechanism for counting output. Accountability was ensured as a matter of mechanical objectivity.↓7

Jean-Pierre Droz (a Swiss coin and medal engraver who would be employed by Boulton) developed a segmental collar ↓121 that enabled striking coinage of uniform shape and size, as well as rendering inscriptions on the edge of coins. This technique was witnessed by Boulton and Thomas Jefferson ↓36 at a demonstration given by Droz at the Hôtel de la Monnaie in Paris in 1786. Both men tried to hire him. Boulton was succesful. However, Droz's technique proved unsuitable for the quantity of coinage that a national mint would need to strike. He was succeeded at Soho by Conrad Heinrich Küchler. ↓116/115 The only extant instance of Droz's collar was set to make the Biblical inscription:

"RENDER UNTO CESAR THE THINGS
WHICH ARE CESARS." (Matthew 22:21) ↑133

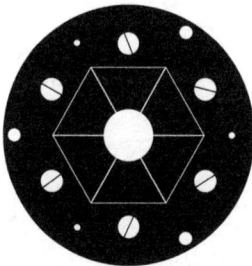

122 The irregular edges of this Ancient Roman coin (141 CE) are typical of preindustrial minting processes: 1) Blank planchets were made from pouring molten metal into standardized molds; 2) These were sandwiched between a metal die set into an anvil and another atop it; 3) The dies were hammered together to impress either side of the blank. Their irregularity frustrates the achievement of morphological consistency, exposing a vulnerability to the money system's validity.

120 A feature appearing on contemporary coinage, the reeded edge is a vestigial skeumorph.↓118

119 British £50 note featuring the portraits of Matthew Boulton and James Watt. The industrialization of coinage troubles the labor theory of value: while mechanization seeks to resolve the fallibility of manual work, the coinage it produces has value only because it serves as a means for extinguishing (tax) obligations to the sovereign (an expanded sense of socially necessary labor?). The labor value embodied in coinage may simply be the provision of a public means for articulating prices—the names of commodities rendered in calculable terms—furnishing a legitimate (legible) visual language (money talks!) such that value can be seen and governed.↓57

EURion field

See-through register of "£" symbol

Watermark

Serial number

Metallic thread

Fifty Pounds

£50

Bank of England

JAMES WATT 1736-1819

© THE GOVERNOR AND COMPANY OF THE BANK OF ENGLAND 2010

I can think of nothing else but this machine

MATTHEW BOULTON 1728-1809

I sell here, Sir, what all the world desires to have - POWER

AA01 001888

AA01 001888

Microprinting

Cotton-based paper

Motion threads and randomly dispersed UV threads (visible under UV light) throughout

118   Edges clipped from coins.
117   Coin with all signs—face value,
      political symbols, etc.—stripped
      away, leaving only features that
      signal securitization.
114   Plate XV from Denis Diderot
      and Jean le Rond d'Alembert's
      *L'Encyclopédie: Monnayage, travail
      de l'or* (1772), showing a massive
      screw press for stamping coins
      that enabled a more mechani-
      cally consistent pressing. Fig. 8
      and Fig. 9 therein represent
      the obverse die for an effigy
      (head), and reverse die for a
      seal (tail) of the coin.↑131

CLIPPING

Considered as dangerous as counterfeiting, the practice of "clipping" coins—that is, cutting off or filing
the edges of precious metal coinage so as to preserve
its face value while reducing precious metal content—was severely punished, occasionally by death.
The reeded edge we see on some contemporary coins
is a holdover of a security feature designed to protect
the face value of such coinage. The presence of such
an edge indicated that the coin had not been tam-
pered with. It was meant to establish a normative
morphological expectation against which one could
discern, at least in principle, whether or not the actual
value of the coin agreed with its face value. There are,
of course, instances in which the issuing authority
debases coinage by diluting precious metal content
with cheaper metals.

CLAIMS. FORM & AUTHENTICATION

This medal, →116 designed and engraved by Conrad
Heinrich Küchler, commemorates the execution of
Marie Antoinette. The young queen is depicted in the
foreground being carted off by soldiers to the guillo-
tine, surrounded by the Revolutionary mob. Under
the employment of Matthew Boulton at the Soho
Mint, Küchler also designed the twopence "cartwheel" →115 which included a number of features that
made the coin difficult for counterfeiters to reproduce. One of these was that sixteen authentic coins
lined up would measure exactly two feet. The precise
specifications of size and weight were intended to
establish a normative standard—a grid, so to speak—
against which counterfeits could be discerned.↑151

116

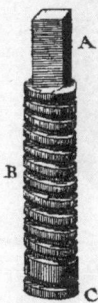

Fig. 1.

Fig. 3.

Fig. 7.

Fig. 10.

Fig. 4.

Fig. 8.

Fig. 5.

Fig. 11.

Fig. 2.

Fig. 6.

Fig. 9.

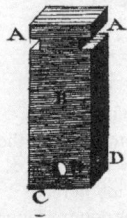

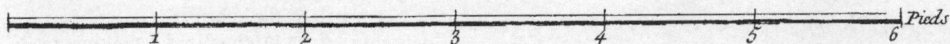

Pieds

1   2   3   4   5   6

Lucotte Del.

Benard Fecit.

Monnoyage, Balancier.

US MINT

Thomas Jefferson thought it crucial to establish a mint that could produce coinage in the United States itself. A national coin would be an indispensable component of a legitimate sovereign state. He failed to convince Droz, who had up to that point developed the most perfect technique for producing morphologically consistent coins, to emigrate to the new country to help make this a reality. Just as with metrication, ↓106 the negotiation of whether or not a standard like a coin was legitimate would be obviated by the establishment of a normative measure against which deviations could be identified as invalid. In other words, rather than relying, as with the colonial paper currency, on the impracticalities of enforcement through severe punishments like the death penalty,↓34/33 the possibility of a the documents' subversion would be effectively foreclosed by the impersonal, dispassionate mechanical rationality of the machine. Precise morphological standardization functions as a defense. ↑119

    Plans drawn up by Jefferson in 1784 called for establishing uniform standards for money, weights, measures, and possibly even time. In a draft of a report from 1790 Jefferson proposed that: "Rain Water, as the most homogeneous substance, be referred to as the standard for weights, and a cubic inch of that be called an ounce. Let the cubic inch, or Ounce of Rain Water be the standard of weight for the Unit or Dollar" (National Archives). Jefferson's statecraft was comprehensive and his commitment to decimalization exemplifies this: he was acquainted with the notion through the work of the Flemish mathematician Simon Stevin's book *De Thiende*, published by Christophe Plantin in 1585 (Struik 1959, 477).↓77

113 25 sol "Assignat" issued by the French Revolutionary government, printed under the direction of Jean-Pierre Droz. The text on the ribbon reads "the law punishes counterfeiters with death / the nation rewards the informer."↓131

112 Decimalized denominations of US currency, from top to bottom, 1¢, 10¢, 25¢.

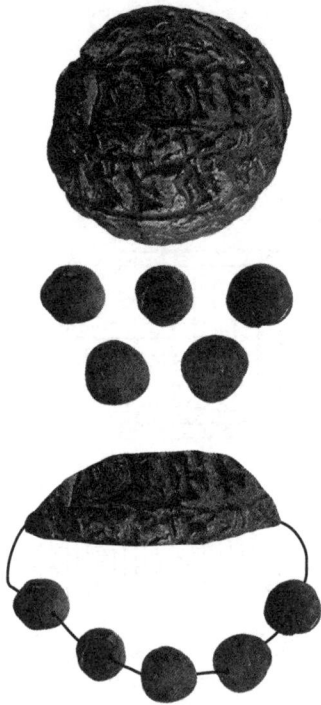

JEFFERSONIAN CRYPTOGRAPH

While stationed in Paris serving as Minister to France (1784–89), Thomas Jefferson developed a cryptographic system for encoding messages. As an ally of the French Revolution, he befriended the Marquis de Condorcet↓96↓105 and consulted with republican agitators. He discovered that his correspondences back to the United States were routinely inspected by French censors, so he developed an encryption device to foil them. The so-called Jefferson Disk uses a system of discs with holes drilled in the center to align them along an axle in an order agreed upon by the sender and receiver of the encrypted message. The sender spells out a plaintext key by rotating the wheels accordingly. A string of letters from any other row is then recorded to create a cryptographic key.↓6↓108

What this and the clay bulla and tokens↖111 make apparent is the way that encryption, in an expanded sense that includes everything from clay to code, functions as a key technique in securitizing the validity of a document.

111   Above, a clay envelope from present day Susa, Iran, ca. 4th millennium BCE with the calculi that would be encrypted therein. These are thought to function as a kind of contract to hire, for instance, a shepherd to tend five sheep. The owner of the sheep would hold the envelope with five tokens, and the shepherd would carry a corresponding set of tokens threaded onto some kind cord (below).

This illustrated reconstruction imagines that the larger clay surface (the *bulla*) wrapped around the cord is impressed with the same cylinder seal used to sign the envelope in order to reinforce their correspondence. When the contract is concluded, the number of sheep to be returned can be checked by "decrypting" the owner's envelope to corroborate the claim made by the shepherd's cord document.

110   Above, a modern U.S. Navy version of Jefferson's cipher disk. Below, a steganographic cipher for decoding Jefferson's original cipher disc.

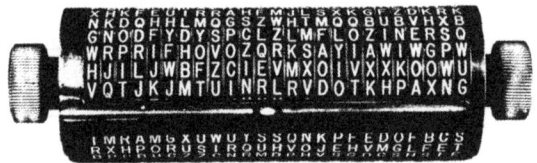

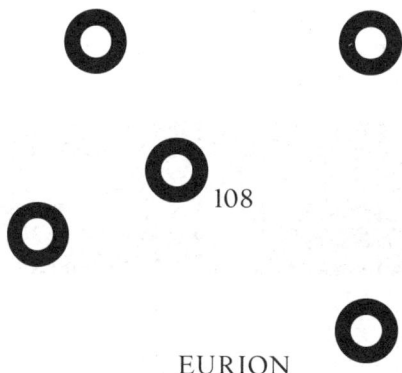
SHA-0, SHA-1

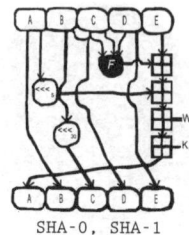
SHA-2

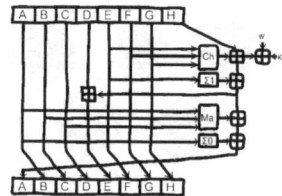
SHA-3

SECURE HASH ALGORITHM (SHA)

SHAS are a series of cryptographic hash functions developed primarily by the National Institute of Standards and Technology (NIST), which essentially produce unique signatures of a fixed length for the purposes of encrypting digital documents. The algorithm has undergone multiple innovations (SHA-3 being the latest) in response to vulnerabilities exposed by hackers. Hash values are a key element of technologies like blockchain and function like seals that certify data inscribed on a distributed ledger. The composition of functions that constitutes the blockchain is the proverbial stone upon which the records of some transaction are set, precluding the need for an institutional third-party authority to govern the validation and secure transmission/ exchange of documents like cryptocurrencies.↓4

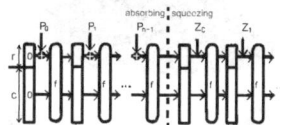
108

EURION

The EURion Constellation↑108 is a steganographic symbol that appears on banknote designs from around the world. Functionally legible to an algorithmic, sentinel gaze, the constellation protects the document from counterfeiters and reinforces its authenticity. Controversy arose when it was discovered that Adobe® Systems had voluntarily colluded with the Central Bank Counterfeit Deterrence Group (a consortium of twenty-seven central banks in the US, Canada, Japan, and Europe) to adopt their Counterfeit Deterrence System (CDS) as a security standard. Critics were concerned about the possible implications for further government intervention in a popular commercial software. Color photocopiers and graphics programs like Adobe® Photoshop® can detect the symbol and prevent scanning and printing banknotes on which it appears.↑119

109 Schematic diagrams show the algorithmic processes for generating a cryptographic hash using SHA-0 through SHA-3. Here, they are styled as if derived from glyptic drawings carved out of stone.↑154 ↓73

108 Organizations like the CDS, NIST, and BIPM promote adoption and police compliance of the standards and protocols they govern. Non-compliance can be penalized in a variety of ways: Direct coercion or the threat of social exclusion (*Speak [insert imperial language]!*). The adoption of a standard can also be formally voluntary but structurally coerced—conditioned by the lack or suppression, of viable alternatives (Singh Grewal 2009), or reasoned as a convenience, while leaving out an analysis of the power dynamics at play. (*It makes more sense [read: it is more economical] for the international students to learn English, than for the teacher to learn all their languages.*)↓106

107 Detail of Jan Dibetts' 1994 public art installation entitled *Hommage à Arago*. 135 medallions were set into the pavement along the Paris meridian with the letters "N" and "S" to indicate north and south.↓105

III   Measurement & Standardization

107

Conflict and negotiation around exchange are endemic to the development of the state. To manage this, the state mobilizes graphic design in its attempts to objectify—that is, displace from the illegibility (illegitimacy) of the subjective—the guaranteed foundations of meaning and value upon which exchange might be rationally and peaceably conducted. Where the assurances of substrates like clay and metal fail to secure the validity of an inscription, policy steps in to repel the breach.

Seeking to secure a standard's validity, their progenitors strive to win for their way of measuring (and knowing) the status of universality and inevitability. Efforts at standardization, undertaken to rationalize administration, aim to obliterate an outside—alternative units for counting, other techniques for measuring, charting/mapping, vernacular ways of knowing and managing—that elude or are simply incommensurable with those that are amenable to an administration's capacity to know, and to command what they know.

LE MÈTRE ÉTALON

The French Revolutionary government took up programs to rationalize exchange standards for things like money, time, spatial measures, and weight, both to harmonize disparate regional differences and remedy the various forms of abusive arbitrage, manipulations, and arbitrary taxations exercised throughout the Ancien Régime. For instance, prior to this process of metrication, the definition of a unit of textiles in one part of France might not be the same as in another part of the country. Or, what a peasant farmer thought of as a barrel, and what their landlord defined as a barrel might be two completely different things. This uncertainty and instability of definitions created disputes in commerce and onerous impositions in taxation. Metrication was a process of standardization designed to facilitate the rational governance of exchange across a national territory (and eventually the world), based on stable and putatively objective norms of measurement and value. Establishing a universal standard ostensibly grounded in a natural phenomenon (i.e., the size of an observable section of the planet ↗105), and ensuring its legal recognition by the state, constitute efforts to place the metric system beyond political contestation—to sediment it firmly as fact. ↑147 Teaching citizens through universal education to calculate and keep records is beneficial to the state because it makes economic exchange more legible and thus more available to taxation. ↓95

PARIS OBSERVATORY

As secretary of the Paris Observatory, François Arago undertook the completion of the meridian arc measurements in the first years of the nineteenth century in order to determine the exact length of a meter. This

105

106 A 3D scan of one of the last remaining public standard meter panels (*mètre étalon*) in Paris, still in its original location. This marble monument was mounted to serve, like a clock tower, as a public utility for commercial coordination.

105 Paris meridian line set in paving stones on the grounds of the Paris Observatory. Ken Alder has found evidence that the *savants* who originally determined the length of the meter made a calculation error and covered it up. Jean-Baptiste Joseph Delambre writes of his collaborator, Pierre Méchain: "I have carefully silenced anything which might alter in the least the good reputation which M. Méchain rightly enjoyed for the care he put into all his observations and calculations" (Alder 2014, 331).

104 The legitimacy of the metric system would be premised not on the arbitrary, subjective, or traditionally established claims and definitions—the kind that sometimes assert themselves through public monuments. Rather, its foundation is displaced onto the objective, empirical, and positive, though practically unfathomable, phenomenon of the globe. The length of the meter would come to be defined as 1/10,000,000th of the distance between the equator and the North Pole along the Paris meridian. As a fraction of a longitudinal line, it postulates the globe as perfectly spherical, and affirms that this definition could be derived from any other longitudinal line: it would have no political bias nor would it privilege any particular subject position, and would therefore be irreproachable. In the spirit of Republican universalism, the definition would be derived from nature (φύση) and not be declared by fiat (nómos). The proposal pictured below would have memorialized on a monumental scale a declaration to the public that "the Revolution has given the people the meter!" (Scott 1998, 32; cf. Hellman 1931, 271)

continued the work he had begun with Jean-Baptiste Biot, when they were charged with making the measurement by a commission of the French Academy of Sciences. This commission included the Marquis de Condorcet, a mathematician and philosopher who advocated for free universal education and is alleged to have said: "Le peuple ne sera jamais libre tant que les gens ne pourront calculer." (The people will never be free until they can calculate.) ↓78 ↓46

BASTILLE

The Bastille Prison was famously stormed and overtaken by a Parisian mob on July 14, 1789, inaugurating the French Revolution. It had been a symbol of a tyrannical monarchy, in spite of only having seven prisoners at the time, four of whom were held for forgery. ↓2 A cadre of so-called "revolutionary architects" produced a speculative proposal to replace the monumental symbols of the Ancien Régime. Though it was never actualized, one of these was the proposal to renovate the Bastille Prison into a monument for the new metric system. ↓104 The generalization of metrication through a social-compact-as-monument, constructed upon education, discipline, and printing, obviated this proposed renovation of the Bastille. Napoleon praised the savants (roughly, someone who studies nature) Jean-Baptiste Delambre and Pierre Méchain, ←105 who presented to him their basis for the meter, saying: "Conquests will come and go, but this work will endure" (Alder 2014, 325).

FOIDS   MESURES

LA LIBERTÉ
SORT DU SEIN DE L'ESCLAVAGE

KILOGRAM

The unfathomability of the calculation from which
the meter was derived functions as a kind of "god
trick" (Haraway 1988) that effectively places the
definition outside of localized scrutiny and contestation. The Republican standard would be established
by decree in 1795. Another standard base unit, the
kilogram, was tautologically derived. A gram was
defined as water contained within a 1 cm cube at
the melting point of ice.↑113 1,000 of these equals
a kilogram. This definition was mineralized in the
Kilogramme des Archives.↗103 A replica of this artifact
standard is on display in the meeting room of the
Comité international de poids et mesures (CIPM). The
meter has since been redefined seven times, and the
Kilogramme des Archives was retired as a definition only
in 2019, when it was replaced by a definition using the
Planck constant—a universal mathematical expression
that helps describe mass in terms of energy, observed
using a complex apparatus called a Kibble balance.

103 (above) Standard kilogram cer-
     tified by the National Institute
     of Standards and Technology.
     According to their website,
     "NIST's portfolio of services
     for measurements, standards,
     and legal metrology provide[s]
     solutions that ensure measure-
     ment traceability, enable
     quality assurance, and harmo-
     nize documentary standards
     and regulatory practices."
     (below) Section view of a new
     generation Kibble balance.

102 « Les nouvelles mesures seront
     distinguées dorénavant par
     le surnom de républicaines;
     leur nomenclature est
     définitivement adoptée comme
     il suit:
On appellera: Mètre, la mesure de
     longueur égale à la dix-million-
     ième partie de l'arc du méridien
     terrestre compris entre le
     pôle boréal et l'équateur. »
     (Grandes lois, Digithèque MJP)
     ↓96 ↓94
101 NIST certificate stating the
     accuracy of the kilogram
     weight it accompanies.

STATEMENT OF ACCURACY

This statement guarantees that the product has been manufactured to meet the tolerance specifications for its class.

Note: The Statement of Accuracy Does Not Provide Traceability and is Not Suitable for Quality or Regulatory Requirements.

Troemner ID: _101618_

Class:

UltraClass:
- ☐ UltraClass Platinum
- ☐ UltraClass Gold
- ☐ UltraClass

ANSI/ASTM:
- ☐ 000
- ☐ 00
- ☐ 0
- ☐ 1
- ☐ 2
- ☐ 3
- ☐ 4
- ☐ 5
- ☐ 6
- ☑ 7

OIML:
- ☑ E0
- ☐ E1
- ☑ E2
- ☐ F1
- ☐ F2
- ☐ M1
- ☐ M2

NIST:
- ☐ Class F

Troemner, LLC

201 Wolf Drive • Thorofare, NJ • 08086-0087 • USA
Phone: (856) 686-1600 • Fax: (856) 686-1601
troemner@troemner.com • www.troemner.com

Joseph Moran
Joseph Moran
QC Metrology Manager

* NVLAP Laboratory Code 105013-0

6-069-BF
59B011-00 (Rev 7 8/16)

LITHO IN U.S.A.

© QDES 64-1

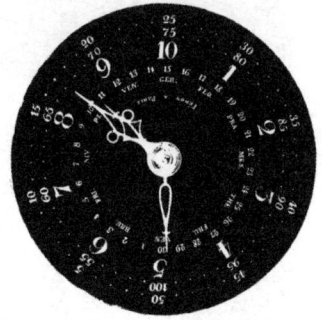

POSITIVIST CHURCH

Metric rationalization was proposed throughout Revolutionary France, and for a brief period, it seemed like anything countable, even time, would also be decimalized. →100 The *Encyclopédie*'s entry for "*Décimal*" advocates for decimalization as it "would be very desirable [so] that all divisions, for example of the *livre*, the *sou*, the *toise*, the day, the hour, etc., would be from tens into tens. This division would result in much easier and more convenient calculations" (Boucher et al., 1751). The keeping of Revolutionary time—a ten hour day, with each hour lasting one hundred minutes, and each minute lasting one hundred seconds—was abandoned after about a decade due to the impracticality of policing timekeeping and overcoming the force of historical convention. ↓78

Some decades later, the dream of a modern universalism premised on the rationalized standardization of counting and measuring (quantification) was taken up and expanded upon by the Religion de l'Humanité (Religion of Humanity) or the *église positiviste* (the positivist church), cohered by the philosopher of science Auguste Comte. Comte's doctrine of positivism holds that sensory experience interpreted through reason and logic are to be the exclusive basis of legitimate knowledge. The church's rituals venerated humanity and the belief in a universe explainable only through "positive" science. Comte and his adherents sought to generate a guarantee of meaning that was not premised on the superstitious belief in an irreproachable deity or the absolute, coercive power of kings, but on reason and enlightened thought. This was the proselytizing mission of the church. Outside of France, this religion was most successful in gaining popularity in the Brazilian Empire among Republican agitators.

100 André Féron's 1795 clock face design using the Republican decimalized units for hours, days, and weeks. Proponents of metrication argued that making time knowable in a way that is commensurate and calculable with other kinds of decimalized measurement could stabilize the validity of this modern counting system on a foundation outside of traditional forms of authority. ↓7

Simon Stevin, author of the book popularizing decimalization in the West, also introduces the Latin term for mathematics to Dutch—*wiskunde*—literally "knowledge of what is certain," meaning what is countable is the premise of what is reliably knowable. *Wiskunde* is a preference for a foreclosure on doubt and dispute. ↓77

Positivism and graphic design are largely sympathetic to this preference. Design students are often admonished to keep things uncomplicated, legible, and uninflected by passionate affect, ethnic particularity, and anything superfluous—more reason, less intuition—suppressing that which is outside of accountability and is impiously non-universal.

99 A sketch by Oscar Niemeyer schematizing the urban plan of Brasília. A landscape prepared as tabula rasa for the magisterial perspective and speculative power of the colonial imagination. The elemental graphical gesture—an intersection of axes extending outwards (indefinitely to all horizons) as the basis for coordination, signification, ordering, and command. ↓84

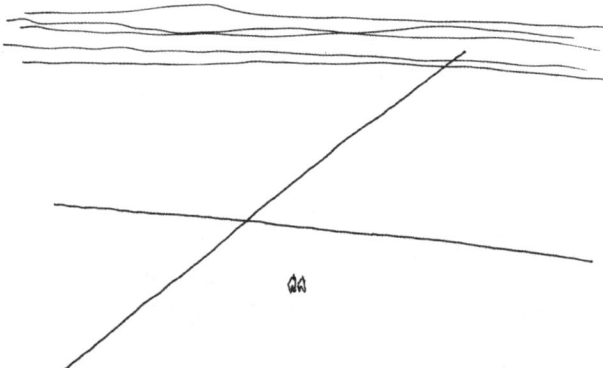

MODERNIST BRAZIL
Raimundo Teixera Mendes, a philosopher, mathematician, high-priest of the positivist church in Brazil, and designer of the modern Brazilian flag (1889, with the overthrow of the monarchy), "advocated" for the (paternalistic) protection of Indigenous people, especially from Christian missions, which he criticized as the incorrect path for Indigenous assimilation into modern society. He believed that the errors of the imperial state and conservative elites and the evils of politics could be undone by a form of governance premised on the inevitability of scientific rationality.

97

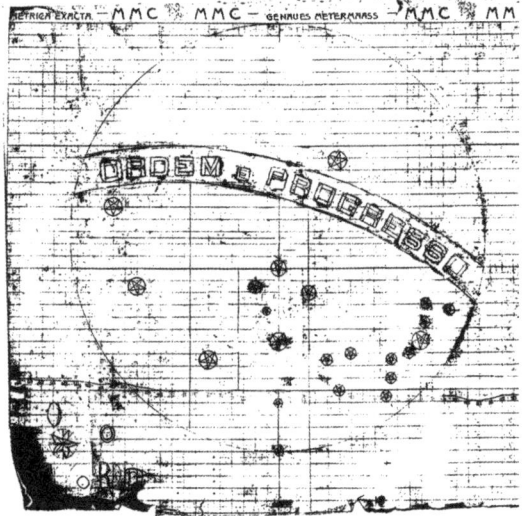

98   Rondon standing next to a monumental survey marker facilitating the coordinated incursion of an army of communications engineers and the Brazilian Republic.
↑141 ↑137

97   Mendes was the designer of the current Brazilian flag, emblazoned with the slogan "*Ordem e Progresso*" (Order and Progress) derived from doctrines of the positivist religion.

Note the similarity of Mendes' mechanical lettering with the typeface **EUROSTILE**, designed by Aldo Novarese in 1962, and popularized in sci-fi films and TV programs as a sign of techno-progressive modernization (Addy).

ORDER AND PROGRESS
The Rondon Commission (1900–1930), lead by the positivist Brazilian army officer Cândido Rondon, undertook the deployment of a telegraph network into the Amazon. Its mission was ultimately to spur economic development, scientific study, and Indigenous assimilation, activities characterized as "protection" and "progress" (de Sá, et al.). Rondon's admirers praised him for shifting the onus of "pacifying" and "civilizing" the Indigenous people from the Christian missions to the secular Republican state (Langfur). Rondon, who was himself part Indigenous—Bororo and Terena—and Mendes shared a preference for "non-coercive," long-term "acculturation" of Indigenous people, which revisionist histories would characterize

as genocidal nonetheless (Diacon 2002, 164). Rondon essentially recognizes this himself when he writes, "it is we who are the invader, but this time we are inspired by the principles of Justice that a new civilization [positivism] has inculcated in us" (172). Whether it is the advancement of positivist ideals, or a greater economic and political integration of the colonial hinterland, the development of communications infrastructure and extension of the colonial state is facilitated by the transmission of documents like orders, reports, and currency, and the metropolitan ways of knowing and seeing they represent and project. ↓24

96

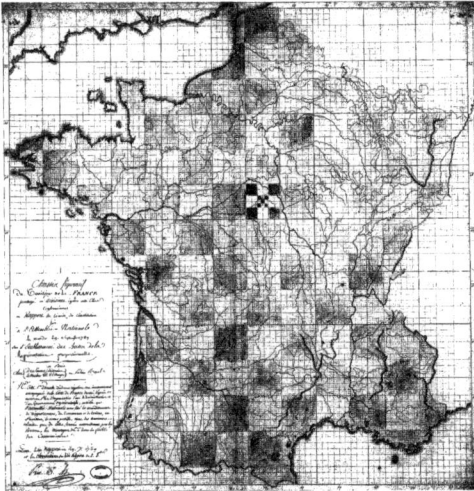

CHÂSSIS FIGURATIF

July 1789, the National Constitutional Assembly, just before the fall of the Bastille Prison, took up the idea of a geometrical revision of traditional administrative boundaries, as had been undertaken in the United States by Thomas Jefferson. ↑137 This map, the *Châssis Figuratif*, ↑96 was plotted by the geographer Mathias Robert de Hesseln, subdividing France into 81 square "counties," each 18 leagues square (roughly 100 square kilometers), each of which was divided into 9 districts of 9 cantons each. Thus, every canton had two leagues to each side, and an area such that, as the Marquis de Condorcet had desired, "in the space of a day, the citizens furthest from the center could go to the chief town for business within several hours and return home" (Souchon and Antoine, 2003). It was an expression of

96 What many teleological techno-progressive histories fail to address is that what was regarded as rational, progressive modernization in the West—premised on positivist scientism as a remedy to the crimes of the old, arbitrary order—was imposed in the colonies as a violent, quasi-apocalyptic reordering of the world. The things that tend to be reified and valorized in such a world, are the things that are made legible from the synoptic viewpoint of the administrator's desk—an essentializing, schematic transliteration of the world's thickness to the scale of typographic marks, flat surfaces representing coordinates, costs, laborers, hours, and other quantities relevant to the colonial/capitalist administrator/designer. ↓74

95 An educational pamphlet issued in 1800 by the the French government to announce the new legal standards for weights and measures. Its aim is essentially to reduce and align the welter of vernacular practices of exchange and standards of measurement to those that are recognized—that is, legible, legal, and legitimate—by the state. ↑153

Usage des Nouvelles Mesures.

J.P. Delson G..... inv.   Labrousse Sculp

1. le Livre (*Pour la* Pinte)
2. le Gramme (*Pour la* Livre)
3. le Metre (*Pour* l'Aune)

4. l'Are (*Pour la* Toise)
5. le Franc (*Pour une* Livre Tournois)
6. le Stere (*Pour la* Denie Voie de Bois)

Déposé a la Bibl.que N.le le 24 Ventose An 3. | A Paris chez Delon Rue Montmartre N.º 142 pres le Boulev.d the universalizing desire to make all things, lands, people, etc. into knowable, mappable resources, available to management, appropriation, and governance. Throughout the eighteenth century there were debates about the problems of overlapping jurisdictions of the institutions of the Ancien Régime (including the courts, the church, the landlords). However, this discussion lacked a vision for reform that would not upset the various hierarchies structuring French society. On August 4, 1789, the old feudal system was formally abolished, along with its rules, taxation and privileges, to preemptively appease the peasantry in the provinces whom the government feared would imitate the uprising in and around Paris.†↑[104]

† The rationalization of measurement standards and the privileging of legibility as an element of modern statecraft models ethical discourses in graphic design. In statecraft, it signals the emergence of a bourgeois liberal order and emancipation from unjust systems structured by ancient and arbitrary standards. This is echoed in the ostensibly populist ethics of formal rationalization in design, often cast as a struggle against the regressive illegibility and irrationality of traditional form *tout court*, without recognizing these as possibly attending to other, radically different, and perhaps emancipated ways of knowing and being.

POLITICAL ARITHMETICK

The English economist and philosopher William Petty promoted empiricism as the epistemological foundation of what he called "political arithmetick"—a tool of governance that sees and manages the world through its quantifiable, typographical dimension. Without expecting much from the the *Encyclopedia Britannica*'s entry on Petty, one notes that it includes a rather passive characterization of *Political Arithmetick* "as the art of reasoning by figures upon things relating to government," and offers that "His *Essays in Political Arithmetick and Political Survey or Anatomy of Ireland* (1672) presented rough but ingeniously calculated estimates of population and of social income" (Britannica), as if the colonization of Ireland merely entailed surveying, observation, and accounting as *neutral* information gathering activities.↑[138]

On the ground, such surveying is not possible without the establishment of some kind of stable administrative standard for how land, people, and things are to be counted. James C. Scott suggests a critical tool for querying the political dimension of measurement standards (that is, the ways these are contingent). He writes: "Every act of measurement was an act marked by the play of power relations. To understand measurement practices in early modern Europe... one must relate them to the contending interests of the major estates: aristocrats, clergy, merchants, artisans, and serfs" (Scott 1998, 27). The query: To ask whose ground, that is, whose standard, is cast as normal and established—placed outside of contingency?

94

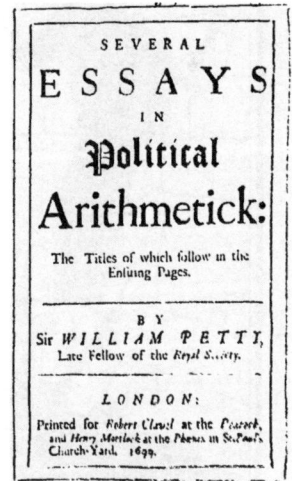

94   Title page for *Political Arithmetick*, a collection of essays by William Petty published in 1687. As a refugee fleeing civil war in England, he spent time in the Netherlands and France, where he would become the personal secretary and protegé of Thomas Hobbes.↑[133]

Recall the role of state money as a tool for measuring one's contribution to the sovereign's agenda. ↑133 To the extent that the state issues money to incentivize the production of the things it needs (in effect, the state can create/issue money through spending ↓34/33), the amount that one has, come tax time, indexes one's contribution (read: value) to the "commonwealth." The question of which coin—that is to say, whose memorializing token—is used to measure value can be understood as a matter of contestation. Imagine matching 2022 childcare funding in the US (~$18 billion) with the military budget (~$730 billion) ↓8 by memorializing the debt to child caregivers with a parallel currency. It is barely plausible today that care could *count* as much as "defence." In matters of "political arithmetick," then, one ought to ask: Who's counting, and why?

93   Portrait by Philippe de Champaigne of Jean-Baptiste Colbert holding a paper document dated the year the portrait was completed, 1655.

From the *Châssis Figuratif* to Petty's *Political Arithmetick*, we have some grounds for discerning an interest in empiricism and quantification as frameworks for management and the imposition of claims articulated as quantities, making them available to management, extraction, and for the state, taxation.

Scott argues that the benefit of rendering legible stuff according to a standard determined by some centralized authority is that it endows this authority with a capacity to govern by effecting a schematization of the world that privileges its synoptic perspective. Jean-Baptiste Colbert, ↑93 Finance Minister to Louis XIV (the Sun King) exemplifies this when he allegedly says: ─────────────────→

... In other words, too light an imposition, and your appropriations are suboptimal (you're leaving money on the table). Too onerous an imposition, on the other hand, would trigger either rebellion (which came with the risk of toppling the regime), or flight (which threatens the disappearance of the tax base). The careful calibration of tax policy to avoid these possibilities is enabled by making those things that are subject to expropriation more legible to a managerial perspective premised on contestable, schematic onto-epsitemological designations of things in the world as numbers. ↓76

92 A diagram of Blaise Pascal's calculator (1645, the print is from *L'Encylopedie*, 1751). This device was designed to aid his father, a tax official in Rouen. Several iterations were later developed and purchased by accountants, scientists, and surveyors. The appeal of the calculator is the displacement of reckoning (vulnerable to error and manipulation) to the mechanical, (ostensibly) dispassionate rationality of metal gears.↑133 ↑119

"L'art de l'imposition consiste a plumer l'oie pour obtenir le plus possible de plumes avant d'obtenir le moins possible de cris." (The art of taxation consists of obtaining the most possible feathers from the duck while obtaining the fewest possible cries.)

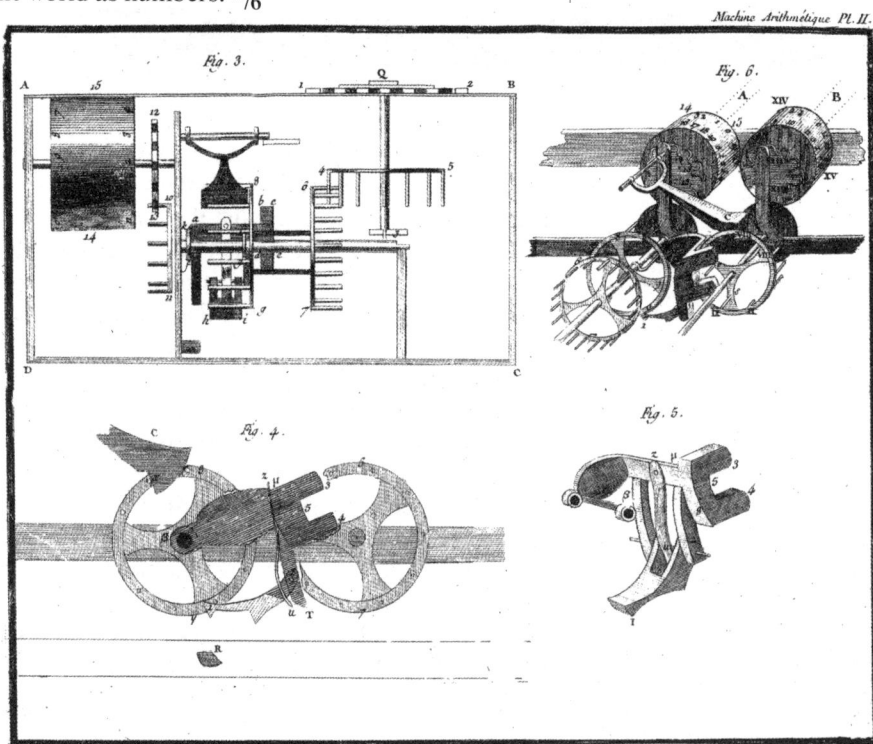

Machine Arithmétique Pl. II.

Fig. 3.

Fig. 6.

Fig. 4.

Fig. 5.

P. M. Bradel del et Sculp.
3.

Tom. IV.

91 Digital rendition of the earliest simple calculi typical of the ninth millenium BCE. ↑III

"[T]he story of information is the story of the financialization of the formerly extra-economic domains including culture, communication and cognition. Information becomes the privileged medium of capital's message... Digitization as we know it and live it is inseparable from financialization, information-alization and statistical analysis, and inseparable again from the imposition of standards of normativity and deviance that encode and thus over-determine the semiotic parameters of bodily phenotype, geo-location, gender and sexuality; among many other variables." (Beller 2017, 8-10).

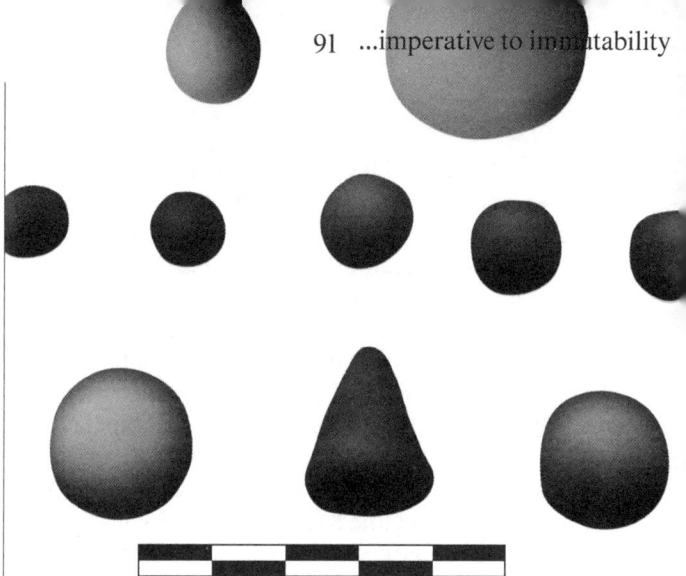

90

90 Official Mesopotamian weights shaped like sleeping ducks were sometimes inscribed with the name of the king or the legitimate authority who authorized its production. Their polish suggests accurate crafting and possibly an air of authority in contrast to more crudely fashioned weights (Hafford 2005). ↑144/143

DIGITIZATION

Information is often regarded as ontologically neutral. Digitization—the (in)*form*ation of things as countable (Hobart and Schiffmann 1998)—is its principle as enacted in administration and management. For Michael Hobart and Zachary Schiffman, one of the key elements of information's status as such is the relative immutability of its form. That is, the question of how to design a document is actually the question of how information is given form and how this is preserved (and Latour, 1986, would add as a corollary, made mobile). They make their point by contrasting information with, for instance, the commemoration of a military victory: While commemoration does transmit memory, it is not constitutive of information because its form, say, a ritual performance, is mutable. Slight alterations from one iteration to another disqualify such knowledge as information. So the status of a thing as a document—"any concrete or symbolic indexical sign, preserved or recorded toward the ends of representing, of reconstituting, or of proving a physical or intellectual phenomenon" (Briet 1951, 10)—and the status of information as such both rely on a capacity to maintain some kind of formal immutability. The desire for information figures here as a desire for a means of facilitating a rational administration of the world—documentary forms generated as a matter of course in the administration of the colonial state and the capitalist enterprise. All things that concern the prince/manager are thus calcified, made calculable—commensurate and current—enveloped and contained, thus tradable, combinable, fungible, and ultimately, governable. ↓71

STATE (Digital) TYPEFACE

The 1693–1718 Bignon Commission, directed by the French Minister of Finance Jean-Baptiste Colbert, charged the abbot Jean-Paul Bignon with describing all the arts and industrial processes applied in France at the time. He begins with a study of printing and typography—"that art which will preserve all others." His efforts lead to the first typographic point system, and inspired the creation of an official royal typeface.

Colbert directed the royal typographer Jacques Jaugeon and the priest Jean Truchet to develop the *Romain du Roi* (the King's Roman). Majuscules were constructed on a grid of 2,304 small square cells, minuscules on 2,688 cells, effectively making it the first digital typeface (Devroye). The precise specifications exceeded the skill with which metal punches could actually be cut at the time, but the geometric and mathematical principles used to rationalize its design suggested, at least conceptually, the possibility of a precise command of its reproduction. Sophie Beier (2012) notes that the commission never intended for their exacting guidelines to be applied with absolute fidelity at the scale of the punch. Phillipe Grandjean, the punchcutter tasked with cutting the *Romain du Roi*, deviated from the drawings to correct for the cold rigidity of the committee's design.↓88 Nevertheless, by establishing a prescriptive standard, the timbre of the King's typographic voice and a capacity to project the sovereign's (soft) power were produced while providing a basis for policing usurpatory bastardizations. The typeface was originally applied to a book of comemmorative medals narrating the life of the "Sun King," Louis XIV.

89   Since 1635 the Académie Française has been the authority on matters of the French language. It was established by Cardinal Richelieu as part of an effort to centralize French state authority. Its members are invested as *les immortels* (the immortals) and charged with publishing the official French dictionary.↓49

88   Pierre-Simon Fournier, whose own work is inspired by the *Romain*, adapting his work from the drawings below, had a similar resistance as Grandjean to the typeface's mechanical conceit (Beier 2012, 54).†

Incidentally, the only place left in the world to receive formal training in punchcutting is the Imprimerie Nationale in Paris (its founding instigated by Richelieu in 1640), from Mme. Nelly Gable, the first and only woman known to be a punchcutter. The Imprimerie specializes, at the time of this writing, in the printing of security documents, like passports.

† Working with composer and typographer Johann G.I. Breitkopf, Fournier developed the first modern, moveable typeface for musical notation in 1754. ↓cf.29

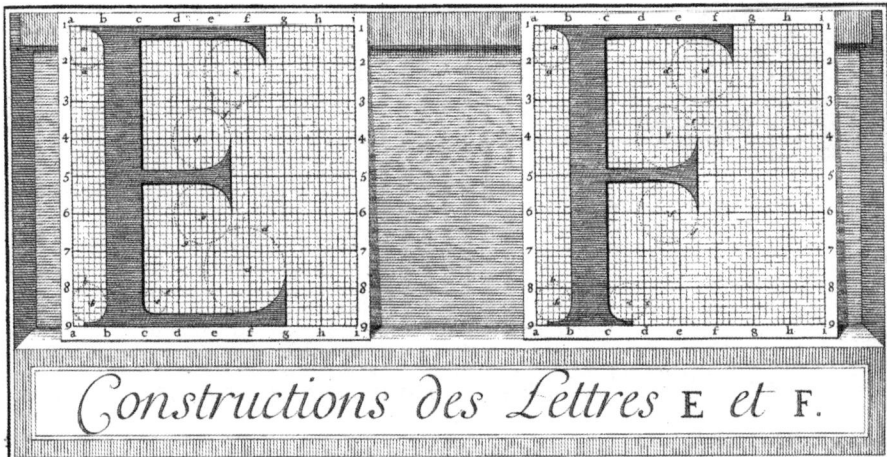

Constructions des Lettres E *et* F.

Dessiné et gravé par L.Simonneau 1716.

87   Barcelona's Eixample neighbor-
hood was planned by Ildefons
Cerdà, who coined the term
urbanización. The urban
grid was counterposed as
a modernist remedy to the
irrationality of the medieval
city. The old form festers with
ancient disorders—it is illegible, unsanitary, and it breeds
insurrectionists. The new
form privileges circulation,
commerce, and legibility—
it facilitates urban bourgeois
progress through the parceli-
zation of land, and middle-
class property ownership
by people subjectivized as
standardized particles.‡ Cerdà
believed that his proposal, by
virtue of its rather mechanical
rationality "would render the
state and politics redundant
vestiges of the past" (Exo
Adams in Soule 2020). ↑137↓6

‡ "From the heights of the state,
the society below increasingly
appeared as an endless series of
nationally equal *particuliers* with
whom it dealt in their capacity
as subjects, taxpayers, and
potential military draftees."
(Poggi 1978, 78, as paraphrased
in Scott 1998, 365.)

86   U.S. Army forklift and warehouse illustrating the imperial/
managerial principle of universal standardization. Such grids
project and prescribe—they are
written before other writing.
The coloniality of the grid is found
in the presupposition that it
can be extended and divided
indefinitely, that everything
can be rendered on its terms.

STANDARDIZATION (Quantification)

The measurement of matter and time, as well as the
establishment of language and money, are fields of
struggle in which standards compete for dominance,
privileging those for whom the standard is native, and
penalizing those for whom adoption of the standard
comes at a cost (Singh Grewal 2008). This requires
little explanation for readers whose mother tongue
is not English—there is/was a cost for you to comply
with the standard that I have not had to incur in our
exchange through this book.

Dominant standards for counting and
measurement—which approach the status of general
equivalent (*Equi-*, as in an all-encompassing sameness;
valent as in value, strength, power)—partly gain their
status through their capacity to reduce and represent
things as elemental and fungible. One of its tactics
is to make marks at the scale of the cellular grid, the
point, the pixel, and so on. Doing so renders all things
recognizable in terms of the putative universalism of
the particle, making all things knowable through the
banal epistemology of calculation. ↑162

The true power of standardization is discernible when units in one domain of quantitative representation, say money, can be translated into units
from another domain, say, hectares of land, or kilos of
coltan, and vice versa. Standards become enmeshed
with multiple domains of knowledge and practice, securing their validity and positioning their progenitors
advantageously. Colonial expansion (spatial) and
capitalist speculation (temporal) are made banal by
the kind of *invest*ment that dresses the world in a bourgeois cognitive grid—how the world has largely come
to value time, space, labor, knowledge, etc., almost
entirely in quantitative terms and compact numerical
representations. ↓74

TRANSPOSITION (Projection)

Such reductive quantification is seen here as a typographical phenomenon, a flattening miniaturization of the world made available to a commanding, synoptic gaze, that enables a capacity to transpose the measurements, calculations, and plans of one world upon another.† Digitization, standardization, drawing, and other techniques of visualization ⌄85 facilitate practices of command and capture—the articulation of metropolitan orders, the projection of colonial utopias. Standardized orthography and free public education for citizens enables the transmission of such impositions by affording the author of an order a reasonable degree of confidence that their information will be received as intended, facilitating the projection of power. Techniques of observation →84 and the rational schematization of vision‡ are applied to the transposition of an ideal image—claims of what ought to be—"civilization" made mobile and immutable (Latour, 1986) by virtue of an assemblage of ink, paper, bookbinding, shipbuilding, perspectival drawing,

85 An adaptation of Plate XII from James Malton's *A Young Painter's Maulstick* (1800), a treatise on perspective drawing for students.

---

† "The genius of capitalism's cheap nature strategy was to represent time as linear, space as flat, and nature as external. It was a civilizational inflection of the 'God-trick,' with bourgeois knowledge representing its special brand of quantifying and scientific reason as a mirror of the world— the same world then being reshaped by early modernity's scientific revolutions in alliance with empires and capitals." (Moore 2014, 286)

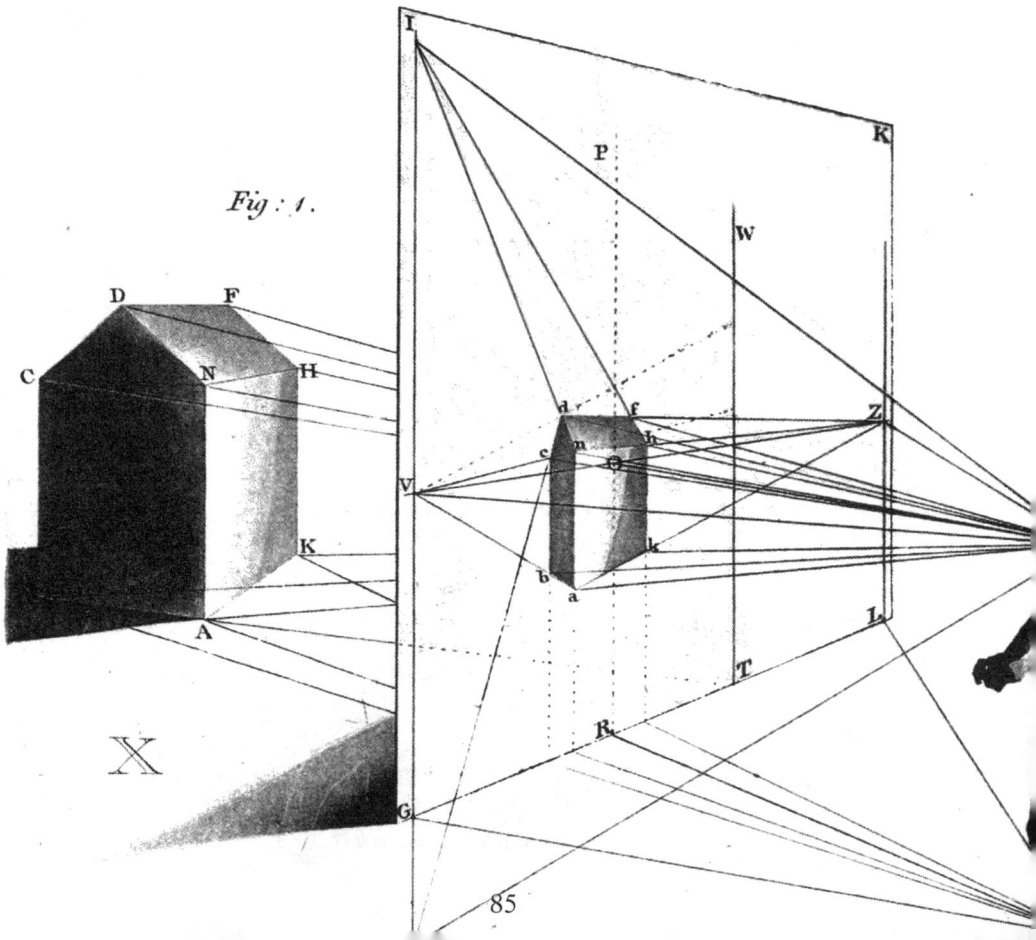

Fig : 1.

85

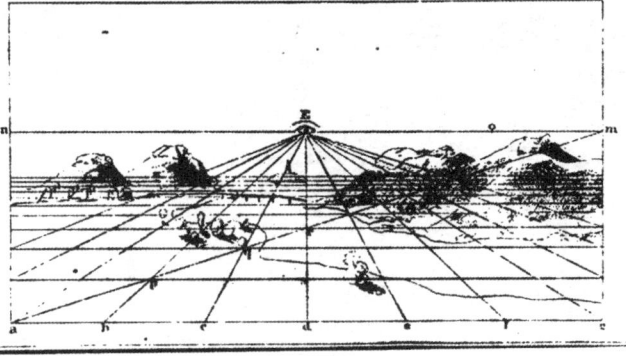

84   Plate 6 from Lt. Seth Eastman's *Treatise on Topographical Drawing* (1837), which was a standard text at the U.S. Military Academy. The preface states that the book's intent is to "to aid in establishing a uniform and permanent system of topography in this country, as well as to render some assistance to the cadets."

‡ "An interesting feature of treatises written on physiological optics is that they were illustrated with grids. Because it was a matter of demonstrating the interaction of specific particles throughout a continuous field, that field was analyzed into the modular and repetitive structure of the grid. So for the artist who wished to enlarge his understanding of vision in the direction of science, the grid was there as a matrix of knowledge. By its very abstraction, the grid conveyed one of the basic laws of knowledge—the separation of the perceptual screen from that of the 'real' world... as an emblem of the infrastructure of vision." (Krauss 1979, 57)

cartography, warmaking, and so on. Actual territorial colonialism and the coloniality of graphical ways of knowing are co-extensive. [86] Bruno Latour advises:

There is nothing you can dominate as easily as a flat surface of a few square meters... In politics as in science, when someone is said to "master" a question or to "dominate" a subject, you should normally look for the flat surface that enables mastery (a map, a list, a file, a census, the wall of a gallery, a card-index, a repertory); and you will find it. (Latour 1986, 19)

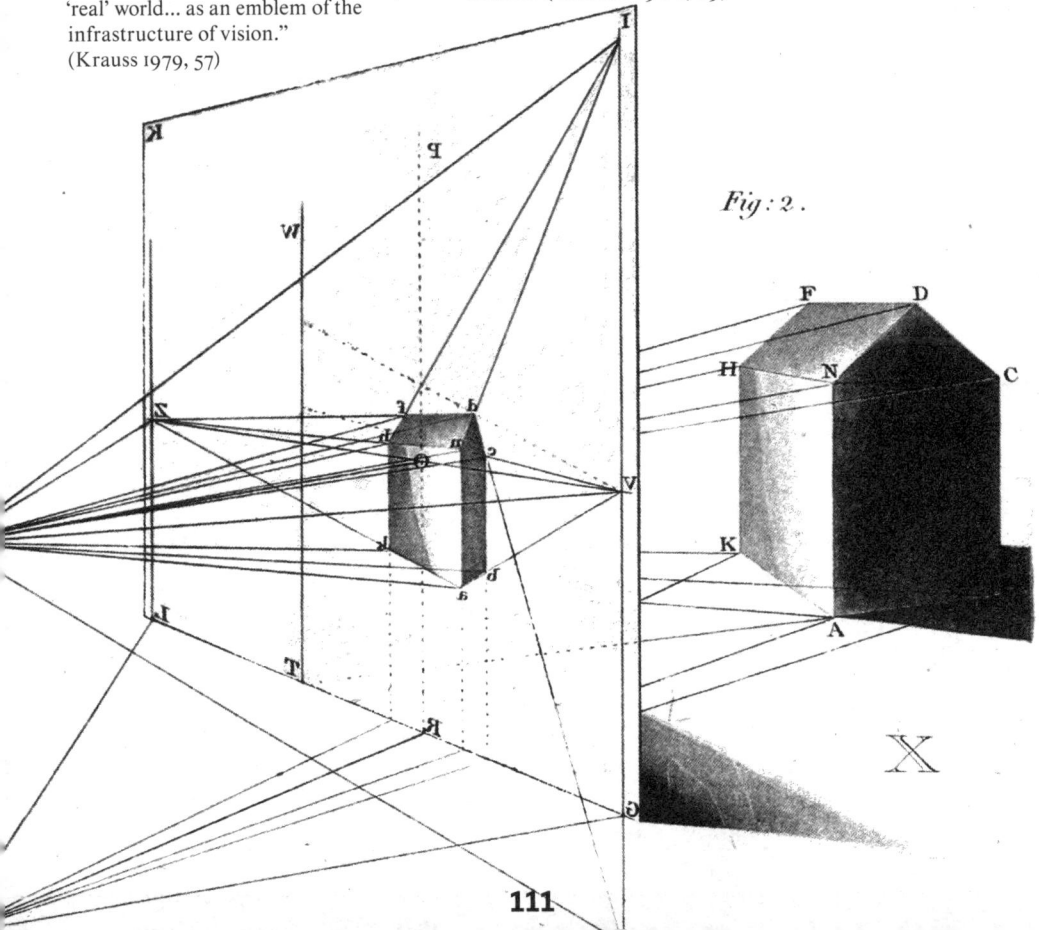

Fig: 2.

OCEANVS SCYTHICVS qui & inter Tabin

OCEANVS
THIOPICVS

PARS CON   TINENTIS AV
                STRALIS

MERCATOR, THE MERCHANT

Franco Farinelli notes the elective affinity between cartographic symbols and money in capitalist societies.... [T]he first work on the map and the second works in the market, they both perform the role of 'general equivalents,' making space and commodities commensurable.... Gerardus Mercator may be the Latin translation of the Flemish name Gerhard de Kremer, but the fact remains that mercator means "the merchant."
—Société Réaliste, *Empire, State, Building*

The printing house of Christophe Plantin, founded in 1555 and based primarily in Antwerp, was responsible for the publication and dissemination of the Mercator projection during the earlier decades of the euphemistically named "Age of Discovery." The Oficina Plantiniana, often credited with accelerating the development of science, published many seminal books that contributed to fields like mathematics, philosophy, theology, and others, forming the intellectual foundation for capitalist/colonial praxis and the production of coloniality.

For "Bifo" Berardi, the core of modern science is found in the commensurability of knowledge seeded in printing houses like Plantin's—a precondition for capitalism, which he sees as:

[A] social system that is based on the conventional equalization of all produced goods, both material and semiotic.¶ Since the common measure of value is based on socially necessary labor time, ↑119 time itself has been reduced to computation. The objectivation of time as a computable extension is the foundation of the social, economic, and cultural dynamics of capitalism.¶ Thanks to the mathematization of the world and to the computabilization of time, the mental sphere emancipates itself from the dimension of perishability. Abstraction is not subject to the rule of death. (Berardi)

In relation to the above, it is worth remembering George Caffentzis' (1989) insight that "oblivion is the great enemy of property" and that property, by virtue of the immutability of documents like maps and bureaucracies like land registries, is an angels of colonial/capitalist apocalypse.†

83 Mercator's 1569 world map: *Nova et Aucta Orbis Terrae Descriptio ad Usum Navigantium Emendate Accommodata* (New and more complete representation of the terrestrial globe properly adapted for use in navigation) centered on the North Atlantic, providing loxodromic rules for surer navigation.↓77

82 Portrait of Gerard de Kremer, Mercator, with an inscription that reads: "Above all you, Gerard, will be seen in our book, who make peoples, cities, realms visible. There is no need to journey to those realms out of a longing to see them, for on your maps you let them be seen."

81 Inner courtyard of the Plantin-Moretus Huis, Antwerp, Belgium. It now functions as a museum and facilitates an advanced program in typographic design.

† The following excerpt from Diana Taylor's *The Archive and the Repertoire* is just as apt for cartography: "Writing now assured that Power, with a capital P, as Rama puts it, could be developed and enforced without the input of the great majority of the population, the [I]ndigenous and marginal populations of the colonial period without access to systemic writing.... Writing is about distance, as de Certeau notes: 'The power that writing's expansionism leaves intact is colonial in principle. It is extended without being changed.... immunized against both any alterity that might transform it and whatever dares to resist it'" (Taylor 2003, 18).

GERARDVS MERCATOR.
Imprimis nostro, Gerarde, videbere libro,
Qui populos, urbes, regna videre facit
Non opus est studio proficisci ad regna videdi
Scilicet in TABULIS regna videre facis.

IV Printing & Typography

81

Money and typography overlap again in early instantiations of the printing press and moveable metal typography. Deepening the occlusion of graphic design's fraught relationship to administrative power, this period of the incunabula is typically considered to be the moment when graphic design as such properly emerged. The field's normative foundations and its self-image ever since (as well as claims about what is or isn't graphic design) have invoked mechanical reproduction, expanding mass markets, and an amorphous entity called the *public*.

As a counterpoint, the following section grafts elements from the histories of mathematics, accounting, economics, colonialism, and music to outline relationships between those fields' graphical artifacts and the development of capitalism, nationalism, and colonialism. It explores the limitations of thinking graphical objects as discrete artifacts produced by individual authors (a method borrowed from the historiography of visual art), and instead tries to understand them as mutually constitutive of the (often violent) systems in which they are circulated.

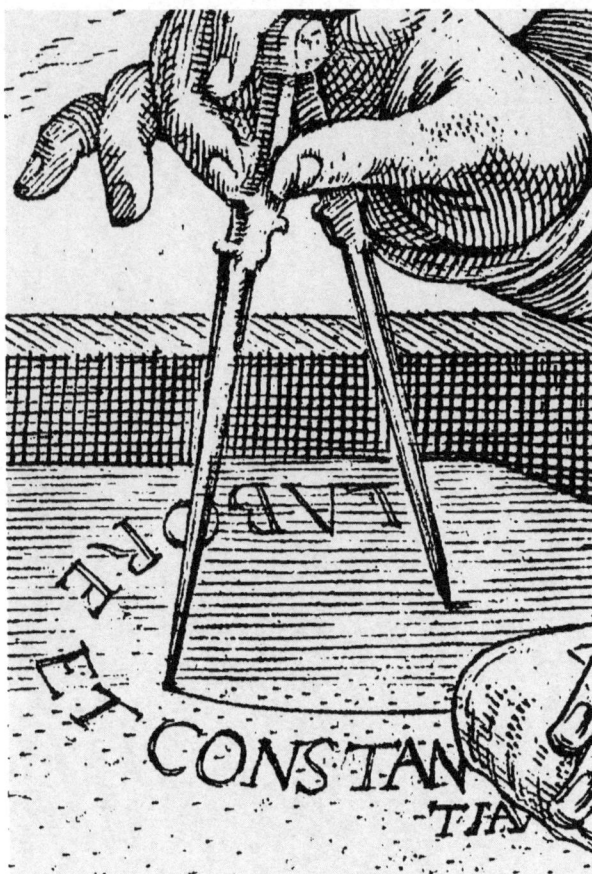

80   Detail from *Portret van Christoffel Plantijn* (ca.1581–85) by Hendrick Goltzius. The compass and the slogan "Labor and Consistency" were the main elements of Plantin's printer's mark.

79   The opening passages of Genesis, set in Hebrew, Latin, and Greek columns from Plantin's *Biblia Polyglotta*.

LABORE & CONSTANTIA

Historian Léon Voet exhaustively chronicled the significance of the publisher Christophe Plantin's printing house in Antwerp, a major commercial center in the sixteenth century, as a site for some of the most influential humanists of the time to converge not only through his publishing, but also through his routing of correspondence among the Pan-European intelligentsia. Plantin's famous *Polyglot Bible*, →79 produced between 1568 and 1573 and including text in Hebrew, Latin, Greek, Syriac, and Aramaic, sprung from this diverse cross-pollination—the most comprehensive and rigorous rendering of the Bible in its day. The appendices, which would reinforce Plantin's claim that his Bible was scientifically grounded, provided elaboration on nearly anything a reader wished to learn more about. They included contributions by experts ranging from linguists to cartographers, indexing the dynamic encounters between Renaissance thinkers across the West. Among these was Simon Stevin, author of *De Thiende*.

×100 Seconds/Minute

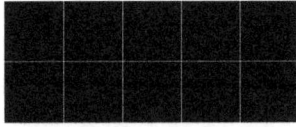

×100 Minutes/ Hour   ×10 Hours/Day

×10 Days/Week

×3 Weeks/Month

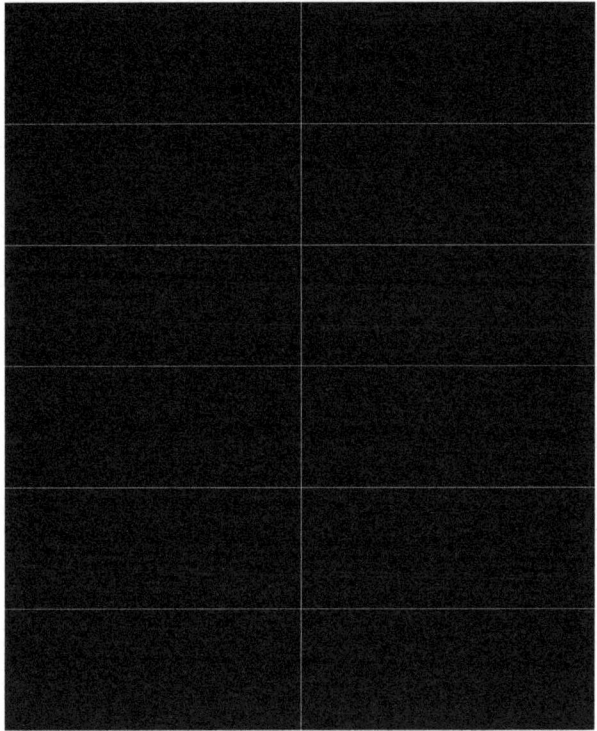

×12 Months/Year (above, 4 months)

78   Decimalized time units represented as volumes.

---

77   The frontispiece for Stevin's *De Thiende*. Stevin is also known for: publishing the first *Tables of Interest* books, which helped merchants in borrowing and lending money; applying double-entry bookkeeping↓67 to the management of the army of the Seven United Provinces; and advocating for the use of loxodromic navigation (charted on Mercator's maps)↑83 so that the VOC fleet would have a safer method for traversing vast oceans without having to continuously adjust course.

DE
THIENDE

Leerende door onghehoorde lichticheyt allen rekeningen onder den Menschen noodich vallende, afveerdighen door heele ghetalen sonder ghebrokenen.

Beschreven door SIMON STEVIN van Brugghe.

TOT LEYDEN,
By Christoffel Plantijn.
M. D. LXXXV.

DE THIENDE

The American statesman Thomas Jefferson, inspired by Stevin's *De Thiende* (Decimals), advocated for the decimalization of the American money system for the first emission of the United States dollar in 1792. This would help normalize a base-10 number system, making land, labor, and goods more easily commensurable and available to rational administration should the standard units for the measure of these be decimalized as well. Flattened to the dimensions and scale of an administrator's desk, the comparison and calculation (the commodification) of anything reducible to numerical representation is made more feasible.↑105 Statesmen like Jefferson saw in decimalization a tool for bourgeois democratization because it would mean, according to the historian Clarisse Doris Hellman (1931), that "all calculations of interest, exchange, insurance, and the like, are rendered much more simple and accurate... more within the power of the great mass of people. [Because] wherever such things require much labor, time, and reflection, the greater number who do not know, are made the dupes of the smaller number who do" (268).

HAEC CONTEMPLANDIS   NVMERIS   ARS   GAVDET   EORVM
OCCVLTA   SOLLERS   ERVENS   MYSTERIA.

ACCOUNTING (Listing)

The etching above is part of a series called the *Seven
Liberal Arts*, each of which is personified by a muse-
like figure. Arithmetica sits at a table in an office and
writes out numerals, perhaps performing a calculation. Her three assistants support her by counting,
studying, and checking. Note the hem of Arithmetica's
dress, decorated with numerals. Michael Hobart and
Zachary Schiffman, in their book *Information Ages*,
tell us that the word *list* comes from the Old English
liste—a hem, a border, a delineation—a strip of cloth
bounding, finishing, stabilizing or enclosing the edges
of fabric to prevent it from unravelling. They suggest
that the hemming-in of a list creates classification
boundaries that implicitly encourage scrutiny about
how they are composed—what is included, what is
excluded, and why—enabling the formulation of
new categories. The elemental graphical gestures of
alignment and segmentation actuate categorization
visually (Hobart & Schiffman 1998, 46).[↑162]

76 The French term, *police* trans-
lates in English to typeface, but
its meaning is more particular
to metal typography. According to the TLFi dictionary, or
*Trésor de la Langue Française
informatisé* (Digital treasure
of the French Language), the
term suggests an evidentiary
document, like a loading
policy, an insurance policy,
or a checklist. The *Encyclopédie*,
refers to a *police* as a contract
memorializing the order of
certain styles and quantities
of characters of a typeface.
Its etymology may also be derived from the Latin *pollicitatio*
(promise), the Greek ἀπόδειξη
(*apodeixis*, proof), or the Spanish *póliza* (schedule).[↓29]

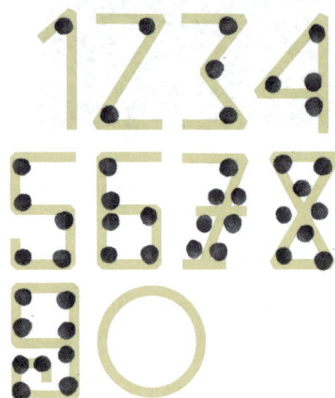

74

75 The grid of Hammurabi's stele
with the cuneiform inscriptions
(a schedule of crimes and their
penalties) omitted, leaving only
the syntactic column/row
structure.[↑148][↑151]

74 From a scientific perspective,
it is controversial to claim that
Hindu-Arabic numerals are set
around the number of angles
it contains. From a designerly/
scribal perspective, this is not
implausible, even as a post-
rationalization of irrational
antecedent forms. It is a compact, modular, visualization
system that enables positional
notation and advanced forms
of graphical calculation.

73

ПОЧТА СССР
1983
1200
ЛЕТ
Мухаммед
аль·Хорезми

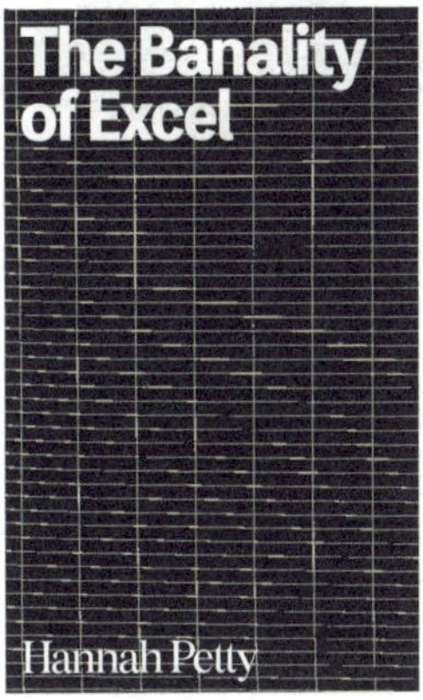
The Banality of Excel
Hannah Petty

72

73 A 1983 postage stamp issued in the USSR commemorating the 1200th anniversary of al-Khwārizmī.

72 Cover design for a fictitious book about the violence of managerial schematization.

↑137/136

71 Luca Pacioli, depicted on a 500 lire coin (1994), commemorating the 500th anniversary of the publication of the *Summa de arithmetica, geometria, proportioni et proportionalita*.

70 Detail of a COVID-19 American economic stimulus check, 2020. While individual numerals hold value, their position relative to the rightmost digit expresses the magnitude of the integer.

71

CALCULATION

The first edition of Luca Pacioli's *Summa de arithmetica, geometria, proportioni et proportionalita* was printed on a Gutenberg press in Venice in 1494. It was an update of Leonardo of Pisa's (Fibonacci), which was itself a Latin translation of ninth-century treatise on algebra (or, *al-jabr*, which means completion, reckoning, perhaps settling [i.e., ($a = x - 6$) = ($a + 6 = x$)]) by the Persian mathematician Abū Ja'far Muhammad ibn Mūsā al-Khwārizmī (محمد بن موسى الخوارزمي, Latinized as *Algorithmi*).↖73 This treatise is significant for its introduction of Hindu/Arabic decimal-positional numeral system to the West. Pacioli's contribution of a chapter on accounting includes a comprehensive explanation of double-entry book-keeping. By dint of the book's application of positional numerals,←74 and the fact that it is perhaps the first major volume on mathematics to be printed, Pacioli's *Summa* takes on added significance as a graphical artifact.

×1000
×100
×10
$*1200*00
OID AFTER ONE YEAR

70

DOUBLE-ENTRY BOOKKEEPING

Josiah Wedgwood is canonized in design history for his sophisticated application of industrial techniques to the manufacture of tableware and pottery. In accounting history, he is lauded as a pioneer in the use of double-entry bookkeeping—where income and expenses are noted in relation to each other, making accounting errors much more apparent— to analyze the business practices and financial health of industrial capitalist enterprises. He ensured the survival of his company by rationalizing his methods of accounting. For example, by applying double-entry bookkeeping, he was able to discover that a manager had been embezzling funds. More importantly, however, Wedgwood could produce analyses to streamline expenses and project profits. Advanced accounting helped him stave off ruin during the economic depression of the 1770s, which took down many of his competitors (McKendrick 1970).

Bruce Carruthers and Wendy Nelson Espeland (1991) demonstrate that the success attributed to Wedgwood's application of this technique is due more to the reputation of trustworthiness and credibility that accounting endowed the bookkeeping entrepreneur. They demonstrate that his books possessed a more performative force—they were not, in fact, all that accurate or comprehensive. His command of this accounting technique was still nascent. Rather, what worked for him, they argue, was that the effort to keep transparent records gave confidence to investors that he was a diligent, transparent, and thus credit-worthy businessman.[148]

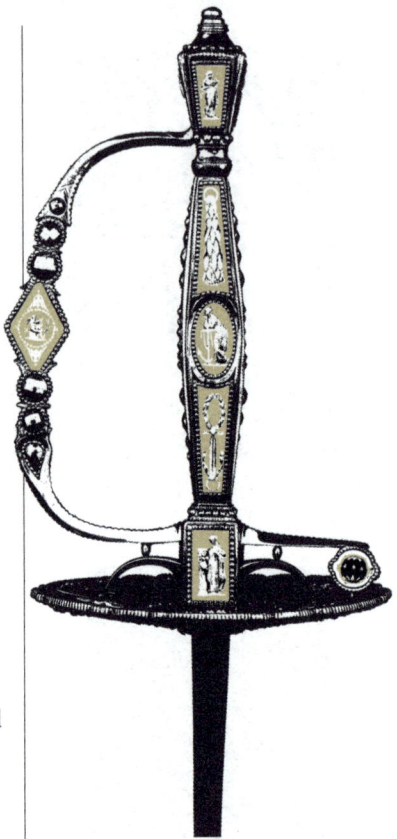

69 Sword hilt combining the cut steel expertise of Matthew Boulton and the distinct blue and white cameos of Josiah Wedgwood.

---

68 A little over sixty years after the publication of Pacioli's *Summa*, the Welsh mathematician Robert Recorde's book *The Whetstone of Witte* (1557) would contain the first known printing of the modern mathematical notation system using the "=====" or simply, "=" sign. Such typographic tools and techniques like double-entry bookkeeping aid graphical calculation.

Prior to the book's publication, Recorde had served as Comptroller of the Bristol Mint, then took up a post as Surveyor of the Mines and Monies, in Ireland. He died in a debtor's prison about a year after the *Whetstone* was published.

67 Detail of the typeset facsimile of a page from one of Wedgwood's account books (McKendrick 1970, 60).

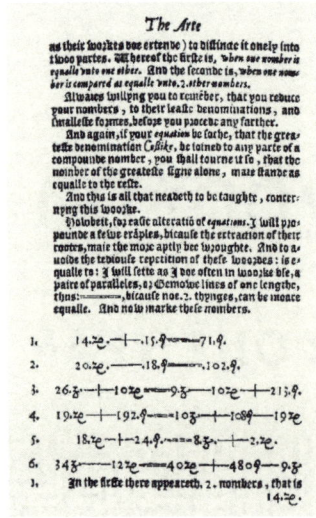

770 to 10th Aug. 1771. Viz –

y	...	...	...	...	...	238.16.
ges	...	...	...	...	...	798. 2.
idental Expences, viz Coals, Carr. } ent, use of Utensils & fixtures &c }					...	345.11.
f Gold paid for in London			...		...	50. 3.
dries paid for in London			...		...	84. 8.
ot &c & Goods retd		...	...		...	69.18.
l for Models & Model Molds		...			...	106.11.
pounds P. Ct. Int. on Capital.		...			...	108.12.

Chelsea Works

ter's Wages	...	...	...	...	381. 4.
idental Wages	...	...	47.5.9½		
er incidental expenses	...	36.4.4			
t 50£ Gilding 22.9	...	72.9.0			
					155.19.

ence of Sales at Warehouse in London ... 321.12.

ss Sales

Etruria and in Liverpool	...		...		...	134. 4.
London	...	...	...	...	...	3078. 6.
London to Messrs Jackson & Co	...			...	785.13.

rease in Stock

Etruria	...	...	...	...	...	530.17.
Liverpool	...	...	...	...	...	65. 3.

London Exclusive of the Increase by painting at
Chelsea ... ... 1161. 8.

Total of the years

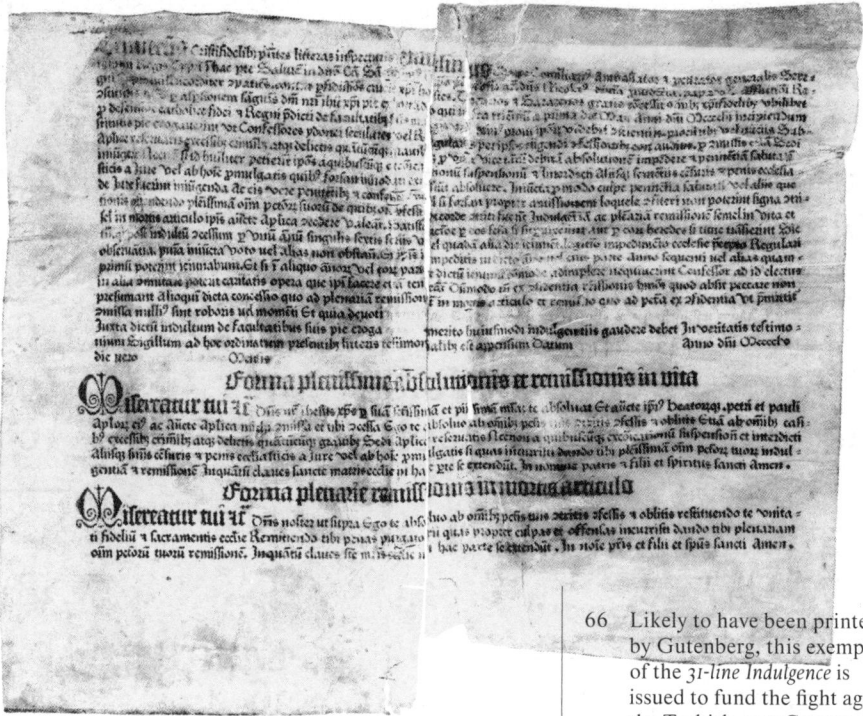

66 Likely to have been printed by Gutenberg, this exemplar of the *31-line Indulgence* is issued to fund the fight against the Turkish over Cyprus. It is the first dated instance of a document printed using moveable metal typography.

PAPAL INDULGENCE

Above, an example from the mid-fifteenth century, issued by the Archibishop of Mainz. Blank spaces on lines 18-21 are for the date of sale and the name of the purchaser to be entered manually. On the following spread ↓61 are the recto and verso of the second oldest extant stock certificate, representing a share in the United Dutch East India Company (De Verenigde Oostindische Compagnie, or, VOC) and recording the payment of dividends in 1606. Note the formatting similarities, which are banal yet significant: the blank spaces amongst the typesetting make themselves available for an inscription specific to the holder of the document, actualizing an industrial capacity to figure individual, yet interchangeable (private property owning) subjects. Pressing and printing are conventionally brought into relation with the democratization of literacy and the conjuring into being of a "public" audience. More interestingly, the printing of such documents fortifies the concept of private ownership, and the legal (legible) identity of the bourgeois individual. What the dividend payments listed on the obverse actually obscure is the violent colonial activity that went into the extraction of wealth being disbursed to shareholders. ↓20

65 As the European economy began to recover in the wake of the Black Death, two conditions set the stage for another imbrication of money and writing that we have already seen emerge with clay and early coinage—printed paper money. The first was the popularization of linen undergarments as a relatively affordable way to practice and maintain personal hygiene and mitigate the spread of infectious disease. As the undergarments were worn out and discarded as rags, they were collected by *chiffoniers*, or "bone and rag men," who would then sell them to mills, which would turn them into pulp for making paper. With this abundant and

regular supply of material, the mills were able to produce and sell their wares at increasingly cheaper rates.

The second condition was that gradual economic recovery from the plague had also generated a frenzy for documents. Scribal labor was in high demand as survivors sought ways to reinforce, for instance, their inheritance claims on the property of deceased kin. Medieval stationers also furnished a more general increase in the need for documents used in business administration—contracts, bills, calendars, and such. But there was a shortage of skilled labor to fulfill this demand—scribes, whose numbers were reduced as a result of the plague were finding that their labor had become relatively scarce and quite valuable. The resulting production bottleneck—a high demand for documents, lots of cheap substrate, and few qualified to do the required work—created an entrepreneurial opportunity for the development of capitalist printing (Burke 2009).

STOCK MARKETS

While the VOC is widely considered the world's first multi-national corporation, its significance in this narrative has more to do with its status as the world's first publicly listed company. Moveable typography and the printing press enabled the VOC to issue stocks and bonds in unprecedented quantities, ↓61 making investment in the company newly and widely accessible. The printing press essentially chartered the formation of a general public, consolidating it within a commercial framework, and distributing across a national polity the economic risk of its colonial ventures. Amsterdam's stock exchange opened in the very early years of the seventeenth century, ↓62 and the full scope of modern investment vehicles and tactics (short selling, forward contracts, derivatives) were all well underway by the 1650s.

63

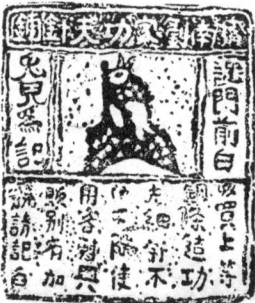

64   First printed company logo, Song Dynasty (960–1279 CE). One of paper's initial uses in China was for packaging and padding.

63   Drawings of private coinage issued by the VOC, with its monogram pressed therein, sexagesimal denominations.

62   Hendrick de Keyser, *De Beurse der Stadt Amsteldam is begonnen inden jaere 1608, ende volbouwt Anno 1611*, 1668.

VVY onderghefchreven van weghen de Camere der Ooft-Indifche Compaignie tot Enckhuyfen, bekennen by defen ontfanghen te hebben vanden E. *Pieter Hermanß*

Soone de fomme van *twaelf gulden*

Hier Guynder ende dat voor refte van *el honderd vyftich gulß* daer mede de voornoemde *Pieter Hermanß soon* inde voorfz. Compaignie gheregiftreert ftaet te herideren opt Groot-boeck vande voorfz. Camere folio *254*. Synde hier mede de voorfchreven *honderd vyftich gulden* — daer mede de voornoemde *Pieter de Herman* inde voorfz. Compaignie voorde eer-fte Thien-Iarighe Rekeninghe participeert, ten vollen opghebracht ende be-taelt: Ende voorts gheannulleert ende te niete ghedaen alle de Recipiffen, over de betalinghen opde ghemelde partye ghedaen, voos defen ghegheven. Actum den *9 September* Anno 1606 *Fy Enckhuyfe*

Dozits

Key Chays donde 1606

Anno 1612 aeñ 6 Novembre betaelt voor Aftdelinge a 5 7/12 #to
onder 150 gl Capl _____ ſ 86 . 5 . 0

1615 aeñ 26 septembr betaelt voor Aftdel a 42 1/2 #to _____ 63 . 15 . 0

1610 aeñ 21 aprill betaelt voor Aftdelinge
a 62 #to _____ 93 . 15 —

1620 . 20 may betaelt voor Aftdelinge a 37 1/2 #to _____ 56 . 5 —
4o.

1625 . 6 october voor Aftdelinge a 20 #to _____ 30 —
1627 . 12 april Dits voor Aftdelinge a 12 1/2 #to _____ 18 . 15 —
1629 . 28 februari Dits voor Aftdelinge a 25 #to _____ 37 . 10 —
1631 . 11 febr Dits voor Aftdel a 17 1/2 #to _____ 26 . 5 —
1633 . 9 marty betb voor Aftdel a 12 1/2 #to _____ 18 . 15 —
1634 . 13 febr betb voor 20 absoluto _____ 30 —
1635 . 15 april voor Aftdel 20 #to _____ 30 —
       11 july voor Aftdenige was 12 #to in nagl _____ 18 . 15 —
       11 septembr voor tot der 12 1/2 #to nagl _____ 18 . 15 —
1637 . 27 marty 27 1/2 #to in nagl _____ 41 . 5 —
1638 . 8 novembr Aftdel a 25 #to in nagl _____ 37 . 10 —
1639 . ady 13 dedud voor wld a 10 gl capl delingen ____
1640 . aeñ 24 marty voor Aftdel 15 #to absoluto gl ____ 22 . 10 —
       voor Aftdel a 25 #to _____ 37 . 10 —
1642 . 26 august voor Aftdel 25 #to in gl _____ 37 . 10 —
       voor Aftdel a 15 #to in nagl _____ 22 . 10 —
1642 . 26 voor Aftdel 25 #to absoluto _____ 37 . 10 —
1643 . 20 January 50 gl _____ 75 —
       aeñ 29 septembr voor 15 #to nagl sort _____ 22 . 10 —
1645 febr _____ april 20 #to 25 #to _____ 63 . 10 —
1646 . 8 octob 22 1/2 #to _____ 33 . 15 —
1647 . 15 april 25 #to _____ 20 _____ 37 . 10 —
1649 . 18 January 30 #to 25 #to _____
       januari 1648 30 gl _____ 02 . 10 .
1649 .
1650 6 marty 20 _____ 30 —

SHIPBUILDING/PAPER

Jason W. Moore casts capitalism as a geological agent with his concept of the "capitalocene." The expanding frontier to procure cheaper timber for the construction of a growing seventeenth-century Dutch trade fleet produced massive deforestation, particularly in the Baltic region, contributing to ecological collapse and famine (Moore 2010). This became the impetus not only for further colonial expansion and the incorporation of ever more lands into the capitalist map (Java in particular),↓20 but it also prompted the development of scientific forestry. Dutch timber exploitation had afflicted Java for more than two centuries when, in the mid-to-late nineteenth century, Dutch colonial administrators enacted forestry laws declaring vast areas "unused" and therefore subject to direct state (scientific) management and policing (Gunawan 2004, 68–69).

60 3D scan of the inner courtyard of the Amsterdam chamber of the VOC. Today it is part of the Universiteit van Amsterdam.

59 *Spiegelretourschip* replica, flying a flag augmented with a VOC mark of the company's Amsterdam chamber.

58 1:1 section of a standard 8.5″ × 11″ sheet.† Although American standards for paper are the exception to those set by the ISO (International Standards Organization), Shannon Mattern reminds us that the German architect Ernst Neufert argued for the standardization of paper formats as a way to facilitate the circulation of ideas. As an architect, his concern was with the design of furniture and spaces for writing and record keeping—there is scalar resonance between the standard sheet, the filing cabinet, and the corporate skyscraper—that pinnacle of bureaucratic architecture.‡ (2017, 163)↑136

Today, 30–40% of the production of industrial forests goes towards paper manufacturing. The United States accounts for about 18% of the world's production of paper and paperboard products, while China accounts for about 35%. (Statista)

‡ With all this investment, there emerged a greater desire for information and accountability to shareholders. Reporting and record keeping, while somewhat developed in commercial centers like Florence and Venice, tended to be spotty in the more nascent markets.

The corporate annual report is a modern instantiation of this desire. In 1929 the United States made it a legal requirement that publicly traded corporations produce annual reports, after the stock market crash that lead to the Great Depression. One of these reports' key elements was the presentation of data that enabled accountability and analysis.↑67 ↓15

† The banality of paper makes it easy to overlook the lesson it contains: A surface must be *prescribed* for anything to become legible and facilitate the reader/writer's distinction between inscription and the asemic vagaries of other surface features. The substrate is disciplined as a *tabula rasa*. A clay tablet must be smoothed, a landscape schematized, protocols observed, assumptions and defaults set—white paper privileges black ink, or perhaps it's the other way around. Nonetheless, it is this act of clearing that constitutes the primary imposing mark.↑145

---

57   Left, an "illegible" wild forest where the trees can be understood as a source of firewood and kindling for warmth and cooking, a place to forage, hunt, etc.↑139; Right, a "legible" scientific forest where trees are known primarily by their number—in other words, their market value.

56   An 8th c. BCE cylinder seal depicting a scene from the *Epic of Gilgamesh*. The cedar forest giant Humbaba is vanquished by Gilgamesh and Enkidu— a wild man who is tamed, clothed, and submits to Gilgamesh after losing a fight. They become friends, and are inspired by the sun god Shamash to steal a sacred cedar tree and kill Humbaba, a monster associated with darkness. With a raiding party of fifty men, they also strip the cedar forest for lumber to be brought back to Gilgamesh's kingdom in the valley.

HUMBABA/THE LEGIBLE FOREST

In the legendary *Epic of Gilgamesh*, Shamash helps Gilgamesh defeat the giant Humbaba. The conflict symbolizes the opposition of light and dark, civic and ethnic, central and peripheral, legible and illegible.

James C. Scott's notion of *legibility* is illustrated by counterposing the "illegible" natural forest to the "legible" scientific forest—a landscape that has been domesticated, commodified, and made available to the rationality of commercial management. The landscape is shaped to fit techniques of observation that privilege the synoptic perspective of the administrator and the graphical logic of their charts (Scott 1998). Although no such utopian scheme is absolute, Scott contends that these forests were at least partly effective "in stamping the actual forest with the imprint of its designs" (19). Rendering things legible, at a minimum, means articulating names and quantities, which then become available to ordering and command (de Certeau 1984) by virtue of their reduction from existing things to ciphers, arranged in tables that support combinatory (combination and calculation) activity (Drucker 2014).

8.5″ × 11″

This still from a video showing a moment of conflict between some tech bros and local youth in Ramaytush land (San Francisco's Mission District) illustrates the distinction between a mode of governance mediated by documents, and one more embodied by custom. In the video, a group of mostly white and East Asian tech bros argue that they are entitled to the use of the soccer field by virtue of their possession of a permit. The local youth (mostly Brown and Black) counter that the space is governed by the principle of pick-up ball—you have seven players, we have seven players, winner stays on. One form of governance is mediated by an archival, documentary artifact, a banal 8.5″ × 11″ sheet, legible within the bureaucratic system that is the San Francisco Recreation and Parks Department, and therefore legitimate and legal; while the other is actualized in the performative contest that is soccer—it leaves no documental trace, is illegible to any kind of administrative authority, and therefore illegitimate by that authority's standards.

     This still captures the moment one of the tech bros admonishes the young man on the left to "read it" (his permit), as if the problem of recognizing the "legitimacy" of his claim were simply a matter of literacy. This conflict maps onto the distinction Diana Taylor makes between the "archive and the repertoire," where the "archive" represents forms of knowledge production and transmission actuated in documental forms, and the "repertoire" represents forms of knowledge production and transmission embodied in what she calls "performatic" practices (i.e., a dance is reified as a form of knowledge in its performance—it is transmitted, learned by another dancer through direct experience/observation and not necessarily through any sort of choreographic notation).

55 In Marshall McLuhan's *The Medium Is the Massage*, one hears a snippet that goes: "there ain't no grammatical errors in a non-literate society!" This may be a way of saying that without the archive and its documental forms, there is no stable law, no reliable notion of what a "crime" is, let alone a just way to discipline those outside of legality.

The Italian legal scholar, Cesare Beccaria argues for the mass publication of the state's laws so that: "everyone has access to them; what is needed is not oral traditions and customs, but a written legislation which can be 'the *stable monument* of the social pact.... Only printing can make the public as a whole and not just a few persons depositories of the sacred code of laws" (Beccaria 1764, 26, quoted in Foucault 1995, 96. Emphasis mine). What Beccaria seems to be talking about is the role of education and literacy in disciplining a state's subjects.

54 Beccaria's criticism of retributive punishments like the death penalty (adopted by the likes of Thomas Jefferson) held that the application of such punishments was not only unjust, but impractical and, according to utilitarian philosophy, not beneficial to the greater public good. On the other hand, universal public *education* (and forced labor, represented by the work tools entangled with the scales of justice, bottom-left corner),

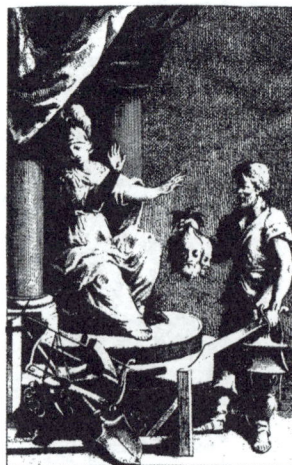

modernized and made more accessible, would instead satisfy the role that more regressive, violent forms of punishment played in disciplining the members of a society.

From Thomas Hobbes' *Leviathan*:

LAW MADE, IF NOT ALSO MADE
KNOWN, IS NO LAW

8. From this, that the Law is a Command, and a Command consisteth in declaration, or manifestation of the will of him that commandeth, by voyce, writing, or some other sufficient argument of the same, we may understand, that the Command of the Common-wealth, is Law onely to those, that have means to take notice of it. Over naturall fooles, children, or mad-men there is no Law, no more than over brute beasts; nor are they capable of the title of just, or unjust; because they had never power to make any covenant, or to understand the consequences thereof; and consequently never took upon them to authorise the actions of any Soveraign, as they must do that make to themselves a Common-wealth. And as those from whom Nature, or Accident hath taken away the notice of all Lawes in generall; so also every man, from whom any accident, not proceeding from his own default, hath taken away the means to take notice of any particular Law, is excused, if he observe it not; And to speak properly, that Law is no Law to him. It is therefore necessary, to consider in this place, what arguments, and signes be sufficient for the knowledge of what is the Law; that is to say, what is the will of the Soveraign, as well in Monarchies, as in other formes of government. (Hobbes 1651, ch. 26)

Interpellation by, and subordination to the state, in Hobbes' formula is thus effectuated by the literacy of a subject population, educated by the state, and informed, ideally, through printing. ↓46

---

53   A printed etching by Pieter Bruegel the Elder lamenting greed and money as the causes of war. *The Battle about Money* depicts treasure chests and barrels and bags full of coins as soldiers engaged in an a great battle.

The tech bro can't believe that his permit doesn't legitimize his claim in the eyes of his fellow citizen—the problem must be that this youth is illiterate! One imagines here the mental play-by-play of his incredulity: "This kid must not understand that this permit has *my* name on it, and that I could corroborate this by showing him a photo ID, and that I'm not making this up because all these documents correspond to a file in some government database! If only these kids could read!" Were the situation to escalate and an officer of the state called in to mediate the situation, one can be fairly certain that they would be biased, or perhaps simply obliged to recognize the archival, rather than the performatic basis of the claim.

While the image above seems to be about money, ↑53 we could also say that it is about what Bruno Latour calls "mustering allies"—the mobilization of documental evidence to support contestable statements about what is correct and incorrect, what is valid and invalid, and ultimately, in this case, to mark a distinction between the civic and the ethnic—the legitimate and illegitimate. ↓46

Who will win in an agonistic encounter between two authors, and between them and all the others they need to build up a statement? Answer: *the one able to muster on the spot the largest number of well aligned and faithful allies.* This definition of victory is common to war, politics, [and] law. (Latour 1986, 5)

It is crucial to remember that what makes "mustering" possible are the graphical techniques for rendering an inscription immutable and mobile (7). ↓1

PRINTING, NATIONALISM

The growing public trade of corporate stocks and the explosion of print communications as a new social field and market frontier ushered in an ascendant urban bourgeoisie with ambition and disposable income. Commerce rules, but financial success doesn't yet afford the full access, privilege, and power still held by the traditional aristocratic elite. To muster more popular force, the bourgeoisie align themselves with the less privileged multitudes whom they can come to think of as compatriots. Despite the fact that these groups had previously considered themselves to have little in common, the printing press (and its popular formats including the newsletter, gazette, pamphlet, or broadsheet) enabled the generation of new forms of political collectivity (Anderson 1983).

Historians and grammarians would be the ones to lead the charge with printed media as their weapons. The vagaries of what was once a jumble of geographically divergent dialects and other social differences became consolidated as nations, or what the historian Benedict Anderson calls "imagined communities." In his 1983 book of the same name, Anderson argued that for a nation to be actualized (as a thing, he most poignantly posits, for which one would kill and die), people must be made to believe that they have compatriots with whom they share a common origin, a common language, and collective geopolitical interests, first among them the defense of the nation against its enemies. ↑133

A key phenomenon in the development of the nation was a force that Anderson calls "print-capitalism." The large amounts of capital required to establish a press is one of the factors that casts printing, in the European context, as a properly capitalist enterprise. After saturating the early print market with books written in Latin, early printers sought to create new frontiers for their investments to conquer by promoting publications in vernacular languages. Indeed, capitalism's growth imperative compelled printers/publishers to seek and cultivate the largest market possible by printing in what they bet on as being the most commonly understood dialect of a given vernacular language. ↑Standardization, 55 Whereas before print, there were several Englishes, Germans, Portugueses, and so on, printing steered these languages towards greater standardization around the

52 Symbols printed on early continental paper currency by the new American government. The all-seeing eye and the 13-stepped pyramid would be combined into the more familiar seal seen on contemporary US currency. ↓8 ↓34/33

132

Courante uyt Italien, Duytslandt, &c.

51,
50
Various antecedents for the newspaper existed before Gutenberg's press. Particularly of note are the "advices": handfuls of manuscript copies distributed to exclusive networks of the gentry—those with an interest in information that might have a bearing on their investments and opportunities. These "advices" addressed topics like wars, natural disasters, political marriages, shipping news, and so on. ↓19

Above, the title page of the *Relation: Aller Fürnemmen und gedenckwürdigen Historien* (1609)—generally considered to be the world's first printed newspaper. Above-right, *Courante uyt Italien, Duytslandt, &c* (1618), considered by British historian of printing Stanley Morison to be the first proper newspaper by dint of its being printed on a broadsheet format, thus establishing the conventional column structure familiar to readers today.

administrative dialects used in political and commercial centers. To a large extent, that's where the presses were, and that's who the publications were for: an emergent class of bourgeois merchants and administrators who could afford to buy printed matter. This represented a larger market than the Latin-speaking elite. This goes some way to explain why today we have Standard English, Hochdeutsch, and Português padrão, and why these dialects map to capital regions. These were reconciled in print languages that existed "above" the various, sometimes mutually unintelligible dialects, and below Latin—the common transnational language of the Catholic church. Such was the "embryo" for the national community (Anderson 1983, 46).

One of print's most crucial effects is its production of what Anderson calls "simultaneity," which he illustrates by describing the design of a new publication genre—the newspaper. The newspaper's masthead, with the latest printed date, is set at the top of a page with multiple columns of text reporting on disparate events that occured prior to that date (i.e., news of a political marriage, reports of a shipwreck carrying cargo from the East, rumors of war, etc.) (Anderson). By dint of the fact that a newspaper is printed in multiple, one is conscious of a world full of people that one may never meet, but with whom one may share concerns. Lisa Gitelman explains: "When two people read 'the same' book, they can each read different copies and be sure—even unthinkingly so— that they can compare notes" (2014, 113).

Anderson qualifies this explanation. Although a newspaper could conceivably travel all over the world, it doesn't generate a transnational global consciousness, because, at least in the earliest instances, the emergence of the imagined community as a symptom of printing is partly constrained by vernacular language networks. This early formula is destabilized when settler-colonial independence wars are fought between groups sharing a language (i.e., English/American Revolution, or Spanish/ Bolivarian Revolution), and national consciousness is generated along other, often more economic/ administrative schismatic distinctions.↘48

Furthermore, printing impels the fixity of language and informs the construction of a nation's mythical origins by establishing a *now* and a *then*. For instance, an English speaker from the fourteenth century might have quite a difficult time comprehending an English speaker from the eighteenth century, yet the latter may be quite well understood by an English speaker from today because of the effect that printing has had on settling manners of speech. A language community thus has a way of saying "this is what *we* used to talk like—this is how *we* talk now." This habit of linear-progressive narration aids in the work of building "[an] image of antiquity so central to the subjective idea of the nation" (Anderson, 44). The monumental archive that is language, instantiated through print, works to memorialize and sediment an idea as imaginary and contingent as the nation.↑89 ↑62

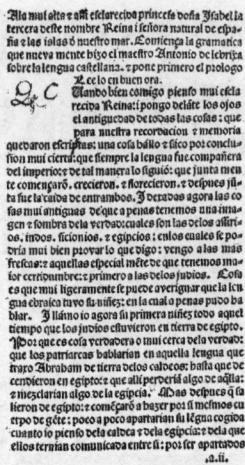

49   Page from Antonio de Nebrija's *Gramática de la lengua castellana* (1492), the first grammar book to be written for a Western European language besides Latin.

"*when you take away the punctuation* he says of lines lifted from the documents about military-occupied land its acreage and location *you take away its finality opening the possibility of other futures*"

(Excerpt from a poem by Craig Santos Perez, quoted in Tuck & Yang, 2012, 36). ↑151

48   Detail of *Het printatelier (1580– ca. 1605)* by Jan van der Straet, showing a sword leaning on a column in a print shop behind a type case being organized by an armed man. It was included in a print series celebrating the inventions and "discoveries" of the modern world, starting with Amerigo Vespucci's invasion of Turtle Island.

CODE DE HAMMURABI
Recto Col 9_16

68

I. ILLICH

47 Hammurabi's stele, flattened
detail. For the state, what is at
stake in establishing orthographic convention is the
correct interpretation of the
authorship/authority of the
sovereign's judgement. This
was the concern of Antonio de
Nebrija (1444-1522) the Spanish
grammarian and lexicographer
whose project—the establishment of a standard grammar
for the Spanish language, the
first published in any European
language—approached the disciplining of letters as a matter
of statecraft, and was putatively
motivated by the belief that
language is the consort of
empire. ↑55/54

46 Excerpts from Ivan Illich's
"Vernacular Values" (1980).
An appreciation of the political
dimension of early printing
is clearly articulated in the
appeal made by Antonio de
Nebrija to the Queen Isabella I
in seeking support and funding
for his research into grammar.

My Illustrious Queen. Whenever I ponder over the tokens of the
past that have been preserved in writing, I am forced to the
very same conclusion. Language has always been the consort
of empire, and forever shall remain its mate. Together they
come into being, together they grow and flower, and together
they decline.

70   I. ILLICH

Nebrija here reminds the queen of the new pact possible
between sword and book. He proposes a covenant between two
spheres, both within the secular realm of the Crown, a covenant
distinct from the medieval pact between Emperor and Pope, which
had been a covenant bridging the secular and the sacred. He proposes
a pact, not of sword and cloth — each sovereign in its own sphere —
but of sword and expertise, encompassing the engine of conquest
abroad and a system of scientific control of diversity within the
entire kingdom.

Nebrija calls to their minds a concept
that, to this day, is powerful in Spanish — armas y letras. He speaks
about the marriage of empire and language

VERNACULAR VALUES   73

Nebrija argues for standardizing a living language for the benefit
of its printed form. This argument is also made in our generation,
but the end now is different. Our contemporaries believe that standardized language is a necessary condition to teach people to read,
indispensable for the distribution of printed books.

He wants to replace the people's vernacular by
the grammarian's language. The humanist proposes the standardization of colloquial language to remove the new technology of
printing from the vernacular domain — to prevent people from
printing and reading in the various languages that, up to that time,
they had only spoken. By this monopoly over an official and taught
language, he proposes to suppress wild, untaught vernacular reading.

CHINESE PAPER MONEY

The earliest surviving instances of paper money are found in China. They were issued under 明太祖 (Ming Taizu, 1368–98 CE), founder of the Ming Dynasty. There are earlier mentions of paper money going back to 1024 CE. These were designed as claims on deposited metallic coins. This late fourteenth-century example →₄₃ shows the quantity of coins the note can be used to redeem. It also states that the Emperor punishes counterfeiters and rewards informants.↑₁₁₃

While it is significant that the combination of the printing press and moveable typography was first developed in Asia and not Europe, histories that recuperate the Asian precedent risk the traps of tokenization and eliding a more substantive scrutiny of design historiography. Besides emphasizing print's literary impacts over a consideration of its administrative ones, this deference to precedent is itself a bias consonant with the way that private property ownership privileges provenance.↑₆₅ The popular science broadcaster James Burke has noted that the first half-century of proliferation of the Gutenberg press in Europe took it to commercial centers, royal courts, and banking cities, rather than university towns. Histories of printing also rarely mention the printing of money and government documents. This elision serves a techno-progressive narration of design's development and fails to convey its entanglement with the emergence and expansion of the modern state, its supranational capitalist enterprises, and the colonialist extraction and violence those phenomena have wrought. In *Before European Hegemony* (1989), Janet Abu-Lughod makes a point of the non-development of an industrial capitalist economy in China, in spite of the earlier development of gunpowder and the printing press. For her, the ascent of capitalism in Europe is less a factor of Western ingenuity and entrepreneurialism than it is a matter of the immense wealth extracted through primitive accumulation, slavery, and colonization.

45 Man with ~13,000 coins strung together in units of 1,000 coins called *chuàn* (串) (or *diào* [吊]). Confirming the actual content of *chuàn* was impractical and inconvenient. They were often short a dozens to a few hundred coins. The strings would nevertheless be exchanged, like a fiat currency, based on their nominal value. While teleological histories of paper money affirm its convenience and portability, the main advantage of paper notes is rather that its nominal value, like clay calculi, corresponds directly to its actual form. It simply is what it says it is.

44 *Wuzhu* (五銖) coin matrix mold for coins to be issued by the Western Han Dynasty. No other coin in history has circulated for as long as these with a more or less continuous emission between 118 BCE and 621 CE.

43 Paper was treated with skepticism, as foreign and unreliable, when first introduced to Europe by Arab traders. Roger II of Sicily (1145) and Frederick II of Germany (1221), for instance, prohibitied its official use. Ernst Kantorowicz identifies these monarchs as adherents of the doctrine of the "mystery of the state"—an ancient Roman legal idea that to dispute the Prince's "divine" judgement would amount to "sacrilege" (1955, 69). ↓₆ ↑₁₄₅ While gauging the possible significance of this legal doctrine to a prohibition on the use of paper requires more study, it is conceivable that objectifying the proverbial prince's judgments with documents endows them with evidentiary validity. Perhaps the concern was that the prince's sovereignty would be usurped by its displacement from his body onto an object vulnerable to forgery, obliteration, and scrutiny.↑₅₆

大明通行寶鈔

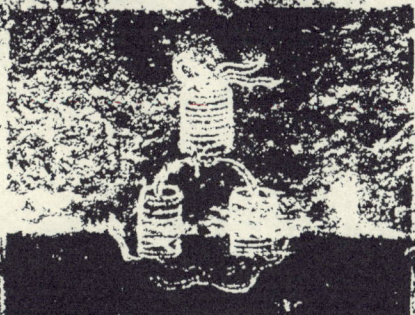

叁佰文

中書省
奏准印造
大明寶鈔與銅錢通行
使用偽造者斬告
捕者賞銀貳佰伍拾兩
仍給犯人家產
洪武　年　月　日

BANKNOTES

Early European banknotes were issued as direct claims on metal deposits held in banks, as Ming Dynasty notes had been centuries earlier. While paper immediately opened up new avenues of trade and exchange, its ability to hold value was premised on tight administrative control. Paper money risked devaluation if printed excessively or arbitrarily—for instance if a bank issued more claims on the money it held than it could actually honor. The advent of paper money in the European context in the mid-seventeenth century,↑40 Sweden in particular, was itself a response to the rapid devaluation of copper and the impracticality of circulating the large copper plate coinage that had come into existence. This new, light, and portable form of money had vulnerabilities that were addressed with a variety of graphical security features. For instance, the inclusion of the bank administrators' signatures and the embossing of their corresponding seals both aimed to foil forgery and name those responsible for issuing the notes. Johan Palmstruch (1611–71), Europe's first central banker for the Stockholms Banco, is credited as the publisher of Europe's first paper money. However, he was sentenced to death (though this was later commuted to a prison sentence) for printing more claims to deposits than were held in the bank. The severity of the punishment gives a sense of the gravity of the crime.

42 Detail of a Swedish copper plate money (*plåtmynt*) stamped with an 8 daler face value.

41 A 4 daler plate with a square excised (perhaps an adjustment for inflation?). At the start of the seventeenth century, Sweden was rich in copper and deployed this wealth to mint coinage used to pay soldiers and finance rising military expenses. The inflationary overproduction of this coin meant that its face value far exceeded the metal's commodity value. *Plåtmynt* was issued in an attempt to bring these back in line.

39 An eighteenth-century etching by Daniel Chodowiecki showing a public flogging with boughs.↑139

'Tis DEATH to Counterfeit. PRINTED BY A. C. and W. GREEN.

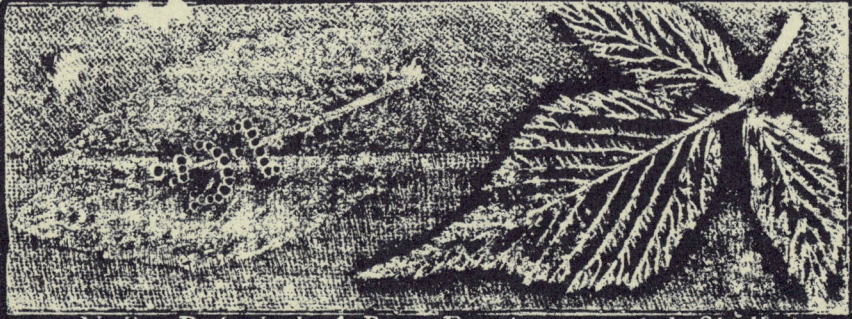

ONE DOLLAR. Equal to 4s. 6d. Sterling.

Twelve Shillings.

To counterfeit is Death.

Burlington in New-Jersey,
Printed by I. Collins, 1776.

FOUR SHILLINGS.

To Counterfeit is Death

Printed by JAMES ADAMS, 1776.

38 The protection of these bills by the threat of capital punishment adheres to the point of view that privileges retributive correctives and contends that crime might be deterred by a punishment equal in severity to the egregiousness of the offense.↑55

37

37 An illustration depicting the counterfeit wampum manufactory of John W. Campbell, celebrated in local lore as an entrepreneur who "revolutionized wampum production by inventing a hydraulic drilling machine." Originally published in *American Magazine* in 1888.

36 The Wikimedia Commons page for this Spanish doubloon alleges that it is a counterfeit. "If you're being linked to this page from an eBay auction that is trying to sell the coin imaged above as authentic—PLEASE BEWARE that it is NOT,[dubious–discuss] in fact, AUTHENTIC." — Coinman62

35 "Dr. Benj. Franklin now in France" (listed #42) and others lose money speculating on an investment in a proprietary colony west of the Allegheny Mountains. Their claim was purchased at roughly 1 pound per 1,000 acres (10,000 pounds for 1,000,000 acres), in a venture called the Vandalia Company. The Quebec Act of 1774, decreed by the government in London, which extended Quebec's boundaries into this territory, effectively prohibited colonists from settling there, and scuttled the venture.

COLONIAL ECONOMY

Trade in the early American colonies was hindered by the lack of a standard, legitimate currency. While the Spanish doubloon ↑36 was prized for its morphological regularity, its supply, along with other forms of reliable coin, were insufficient for facilitating everyday exchange. Other kinds of commodities and objects, such as nails, were treated as legal tender for extinguishing tax obligations to some colonial administrations. *Wampumpeag* (wampum), which was used by the Northeastern Woodlands Tribes for making documents like land claims or adornment signifying political status, was misunderstood and misappropriated by the colonists as a form of currency. Subsequently, the value and significance of wampum was inflated by settler-made counterfeit beads in "New England" manufactories. These were sold to settler-capitalist wholesale merchants who subsequently sold them to traders and to US American officials to be deployed as tools of destabilization and dispossession in what has been termed "wampum diplomacy." ↖37

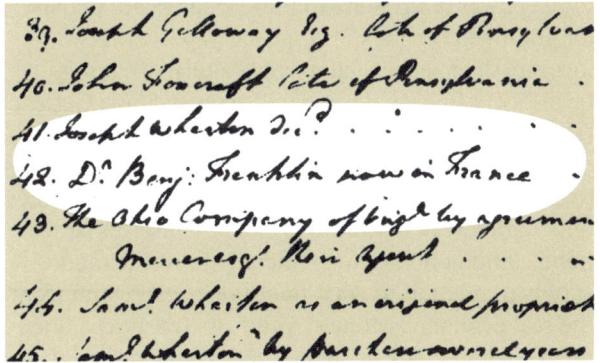

35

Compounding colonial US American economic instability were trade monopolies that privileged English imports, taxes rendered back to the British metropole, and other policies regarded as unjust impositions. This helped to intensify American revolutionary angst. The Stamp Act of 1765—a demand to use imported and stamped British paper for any document requiring certification (from tea packages and newspapers to maps and legal documents), while exclusively accepting British currency for its purchase—was seen as an egregious imposition. This spawned the revolutionary group the "Sons of Liberty," who protested the Act in major cities across the colonies. With few recognized, legitimate forms of currency available, colonial administrations were compelled to print their own. The American Revolutionary War became the first ever to be financed almost entirely by paper money, paying soliders, mercenaries, and purchasing material with colonial paper notes. →34/33

TO COUNTERFEIT IS DEATH

Printing money was seen as an act of defiance and an instrument of propaganda. It speculated on the actualization of a national imaginary called the United States of America, and was also, of course, economically speculative. As the war continued, printing exponentially larger quantities of notes was authorized, causing inflation and decreasing the currency's exchange value. Colonial-era notes included vein pattern motifs and other security ornaments to function as anti-counterfeiting measures. Philadelphia printer Benjamin Franklin's technique for pressing tree-leaf molds into the banknotes, as well as the invocation of the power of the state to impose the death penalty for graphical "crimes," ↑38 armed paper with two forms of deterrence against any "alterity that might transform it and whatever dares to resist it" (de Certeau 1988, 216).

    However, the graphical/political (administrative) techniques that help maintain the value of money only really work if administrators themselves set policy (and policing) to artificially limit the money supply in relation to what that money can claim from the real economy. Money's value, its status as a document—its ontology as such—exceeds the material and visual boundaries of its discrete instantiations. Documents like money are not self-contained artifacts, but are rather recognized as "legal tender" by the bureaucracies within which they circulate. In other words, without the other, neither money nor the bureaucracies that concern themselves with it have any reason to be—the document and its bureaucracy are co-constitutive (Gitelman 2014).

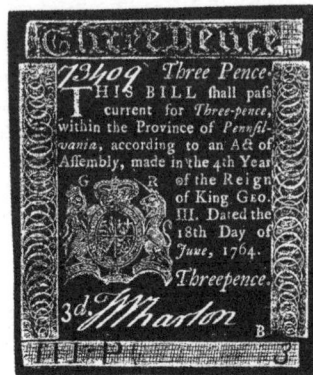

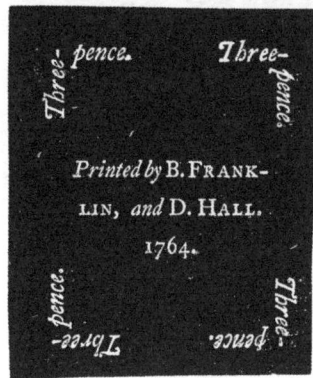

34, 33 Examples of so-called "continentals," produced nearly a century after the first European paper banknotes, were the first printed banknotes in the West to be issued directly by a government (Newman 1967, 7).

---

32 Detail of an American $10 bill depicting the US Treasury. The first version of this design appears in 1928. The overproduction (inflation) of "continentals" by the various colonial governments leads to rapid devaluation. The US Department of the Treasury is established in 1789 to centralize and coordinate the country's monetary and fiscal administration. The Treasury oversees the Bureau of Engraving and Printing, the Mint, and the Internal Revenue Service.

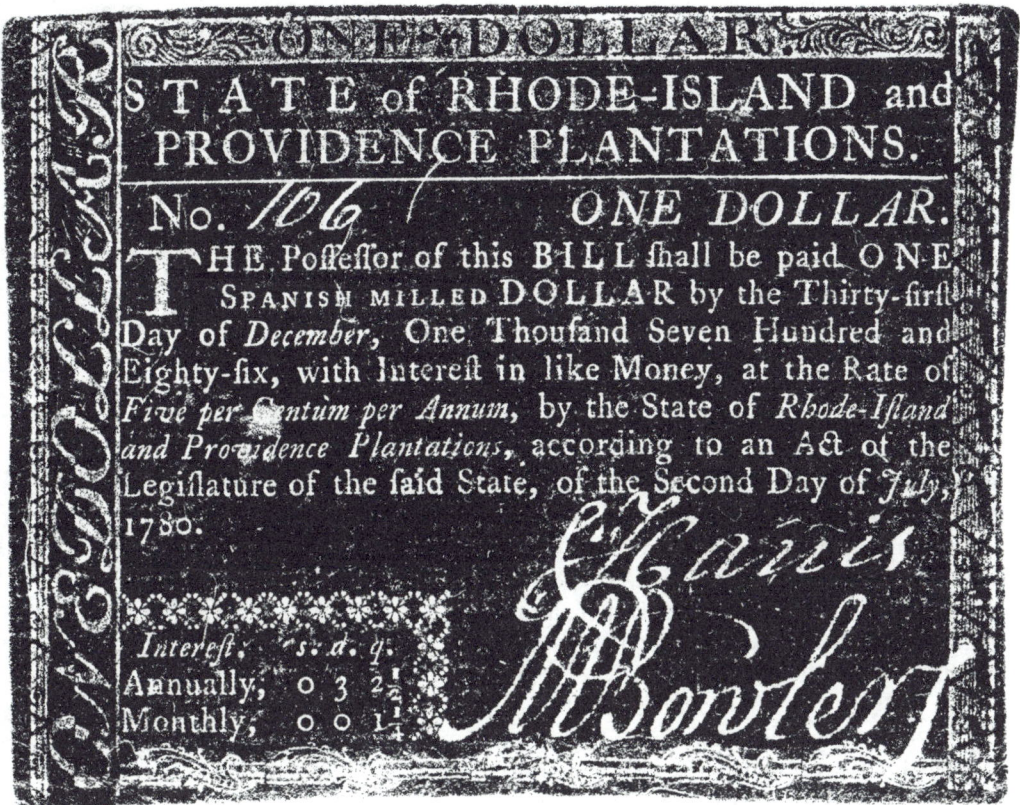

ONE DOLLAR

STATE of RHODE-ISLAND and PROVIDENCE PLANTATIONS.

No. 106   ONE DOLLAR.

THE Poſſeſſor of this BILL ſhall be paid ONE SPANISH MILLED DOLLAR by the Thirty-firſt Day of *December*, One Thouſand Seven Hundred and Eighty-ſix, with Intereſt in like Money, at the Rate of *Five per Centum per Annum*, by the State of *Rhode-Iſland and Providence Plantations*, according to an Act of the Legiſlature of the ſaid State, of the Second Day of *July*, 1780.

Intereſt.   s. d. q.
Annually;   0 3 2¼
Monthly;   0 0 1¼

32

U·S·TREASURY

TYPOGRAPHY FOR MUSIC

The second musical typeface to ever be designed was completed in 1760 by the punchcutter Joan Michaël Fleischman at the Royal Joh. Enschedé & Zn securities printer in Haarlem in the Netherlands. It failed commercially as composers found it too unwieldy and rigid for composition. The typeface was unused and unseen, collecting dust until just after the end of the French occupation of the Netherlands (1795–1813).

It was during this period that *assignats* (designed by Jean-Pierre Droz [113] [121])—promissory notes issued by the French government—were used to pay the wages of the occupying French soldiers. Although excessive printing rapidly destabilized their value, the local populace was forced to accept them in everyday transactions. Fleischman's typeface would be revived to securitize the first Dutch national banknotes (1814) issued to stabilize the monetary system when a new independent Republic was established.

"Patriot brokers," Dutch Republicans, and bourgeois professionals had amassed great wealth through bold investments in pre-Revolutionary France. Abundant capital in Amsterdam's stock market sought new frontiers of investment as Britain became an unfavorable bet due to the animosity of the Anglo-Dutch War of 1780–84. France became attractive for Dutch capital seeking opportunities to support republicanism contra monarchism (Riley 1973).

Decades later, these investors would invest in the United States through loans negotiated with John Adams in 1782 (then US envoy to the Seven United Netherlands). In 1792–93, the Holland Purchase [28] was made through a syndicate called the Holland Land Company. New York prohibited aliens from owning land at the time, so a local agent was hired and a US American board of trustees was set up to oversee purchases and dispatch reports (Chazanof). Typically, these communiqués would take several weeks to cross the Atlantic.

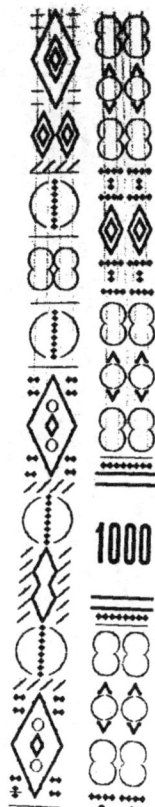

30

31 Printing proof from Joh. Enschedé & Zn. for the Dutch National Bank's first printed banknotes shows Fleischman's tyepface used to create security ornamentation.

30 Sample security ornaments using Fleischman's type for musical notation.

29½ Proposed album cover design (actual size) template for the 595 notes from Ryuichi Sakamoto's NFT sale. [6]

On December 20, 2021, Ryuichi Sakamoto launches an NFT sale of 595 individual notes from the melody to "Merry Christmas Mr. Lawrence," the title track composed for the eponymous WWII film set in a Japanese POW camp for Allied prisoners in Java. Capital's poietic capacity has not only generated new frontiers in the realm of the virtual, but also found them on the scale of molecular musical time. [20]

29 A sample sheet for Fleischman's musical tyepface. [76]

Register van de Musie

	100	+	2400	3	16		90		250	‖	20	(	14
	420	+	100	3	16		60		220		20		14
	2000	⌐	200	1.	8		65		110		20		14
	5600	⌐	80	2	10		70		70				14
		—	160	3.	12		45		60				10
	16		320	4.	12		40		45		8		10
		—	200	5.	10		25				12		10
	18	◦	30	6.	12		30		270		26		
	24	◦	24	7.	12		20		210		12		20
	8		16	8.	12		20		110		26	—	20
			16	2	10				70		12		15
	8		35	4	10		120		250		12		
	8		35	6	10		23		220		12		
	24		880	✕	40		48		50	✓	10		
	16		500	✳	30		18		60		10		
	45		300	✕	22		40		45		12		
	6		220		35		35				12		
	6		40		35		12		8		8		
	6		18		20		15		10		8		
	0		12		26				10		10		
	0		16		26		18		10		10		
	20		8		22		18				12		16
	30		12		10		30		20		12		16
	18	+	30		10		20		30		10		16
	18	⫶	25		8		16		30		10		30
	40	⫶	20				20		12		10		80
	40		20		90		16		35				
	00		45		45		20		22				
	80		18		45		16		22	(	12		12
	20		30		70				20		16		
	30		12		50		220		20		20		12
	25		12		40		270		20		10		10
	35		16		60		50				12		8
	20		20		60		115		15		15		
	60		10		20		100		20		15		
			12		32		80		20		14		
					20		65				14		

NB in de bindings die malkander te lyken dag in de lezen verschillen...

V   Cables & Crypto
(or Speed & Displacement)

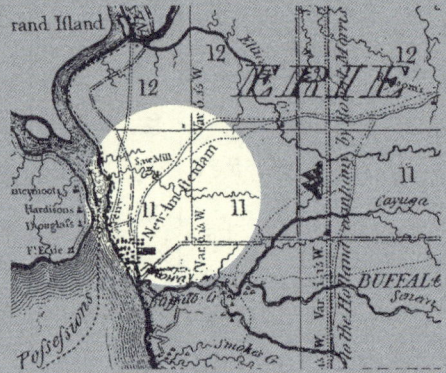

28

Digitization and telecommunication infrastructures sediment atop old imperial flows of information and command. The arrival of telegraphy and telephony ushered in an age of instantaneous communication, whereby the compression of time and space became another front in the ongoing struggle against entropy, decay, friction, dispute, fraud, and anything else that would interrupt the faithful transmission of information and command or the projection of power and colonial violence.

The actors that emerged to actualize a global layer of governance built upon imperialist scaffolding, provoke both armed resistance and elicit the disdain of a nominally subaltern class of non-state actors. Cyber-libertarian projects exemplify a systemic attempt to subvert the old centralized networks and techniques of immutability located within human, political institutions. Enter the blockchain: the utopian promise of disintermediated, decentralized, and "trustless" transactions—a documental technology that bypasses the traditional guarantees of knowledge and value by offering a stable, universal, and objective constant. Crypto is not the telos of the kinds of promissory inscriptions rendered on clay tablets—it is rather a manifestation of the persistent problem of contingency forged by thousands of years of dialectical innovation and subversion. Here, instead of the sovereign authority of kings and gods, we are left with the pithy theology of "code is law."

CREDIT CARDS

William Fargo and Henry Wells were among the founders of the American Express Company in 1850, in Buffalo, New York (initially New Amsterdam, crown of the Holland Purchase). In 1852, when other directors of the company objected to expanding operations to California, then in the midst of a gold rush, the two men ventured to form Wells Fargo & Company to convey travelers, documents, money, and other valuables securely across the continent. Often dangerous, and requiring its employees (so-called "expressmen") to be armed, Wells Fargo's secure transfer services enabled enterprises to operate at regional and national scales.

    Today's telecommunication networks have different vulnerabilities, but they have resolved many of the historic risks that troubled earlier forms of material transmission: the securitizing labor, the potential violence, the time-lag of travel, the counter-claims of robbery ("that's mine now!"). Barring outright fraud, the integrity of an inscription is now practically guaranteed to arrive at its receiver as the sender had intended, making the old dream of secure financial transactions now banal and quotidian. But the speed and opacity of credit card systems mask their origins in wooden wagons and shotguns.

28   Map of the Holland Purchase (detail). New Amsterdam (today known as Buffalo, New York, is circled). Commissioned by the Holland Land Company to lead the survey the Holland Purchase (of vast areas of Haudenosaunee land), Joseph Ellicott averaged each of his surveyor's rulers to derive a standard brass ruler that could be reissued to his staff, due to the United States' lack of national standard for measure-ment. According to the Holland Land Office Museum, Ellicott thus established the standard 12-inch ruler used in the United States today.

27   (above) A *guilloché* etching—machined, algorithmic, secure. (below) A US patent for a *guil-loché* machine, submitted by Wilhelm Brandstätter.[119]

26   Express services like those of-fered by Wells Fargo capitalized on *speed* as a security feature. The company's classic logomark depicts a stagecoach being drawn by six horses.

25   American Express Centurion Bank card with skeuomorphic security features (i.e., micro-printing and *guilloché* ornament-ation), indications of trademark registration and copyright protection, and an atavistic logo depicting a Roman centurion—an unfortunate symbol of impe-rialist security.[122]

INFRASTRUCTURE

The twilight of the stagecoach and express services would come with the dawn of transcontinental tele-graphy. The Western Union Telegraph Company won the contract to construct its last great segment between Missouri and California, and a continuous line spanned all American occupied territory in 1861.

The venture was highly risky and would not have been undertaken without government subsidies. A civil war had just erupted, and the cable network would be vulnerable to sabotage by Confederate forces and Indigenous resistance, as both understood the wire as an instrument of American military expansion. Inclement weather and natural wear also threatened to dim the prospects of this infrastructural invest-ment. The near extinction of the American bison is attributed to the apocalyptic reaction of railroad and telegraph companies to the damage roaming herds caused to new cable infrastructure (Peters 1996). While the line's completion was widely celebrated, its customers would soon protest Western Union's ruthless price gouging. Having sanctioned the project, the federal government could now only admonish its builders for unscrupulous practices. Thanks to the telegraph, not only was the frontier now incorporated into the settler-colonial/national imaginary, it also spawned its first national monopoly.

Upon California finally being connected to the rest of the United States, the pilot message came from Stephen J. Field (brother of Cyrus Field ↓12), Chief Justice of California, assuring Abraham Lincoln of his state's loyalty to the Union. ↑133

24 The Pony Express was another mail delivery company that sent horseback riders through a series of relay stations, mov-ing parcels between riders in a vast system that shortened coast-to-coast transmission time from several weeks to ten days. Speed offered a degree of security against interception and robbery. In April of 1861, its Western half was folded into Wells Fargo. The remain-der of company went out of business almost immediately after the establishment of the transcontinental telegraph.

23

23 The notorious stagecoach robber "Black Bart" and others like him represent one form of antagonism that financial/communication technology sought to over-come. However, crimes like robbery and forgery, as forms of resistance, can't help but affirm the systems they set out to subvert—after all, the robber steals money so they can do their shopping, pay their rent, etc.

As we'll soon see, cyber-libertarians, like the progenitors of crypto-currencies, exceed the political limits of crime and circum-vent the privileged capacity to conduct financial transactions held by Wells Fargo, American Express, etc. ↓11

20 Gutta-percha gum being ex-tracted from a tree trunk by Javanese laborers overseen by a Dutch administrator. The earliest telegraph wires, vulnerable to inefficient signal transmission and damage from exposure to the elements, called for an abundant, durable, and

flexible material for insulation. The gutta-percha trade filled the need for nearly a century through massive extraction causing unsustainable deforestation.[119] The gum would fall out of mass use with the advent of wireless communications (Tully, 2009).

22

22　A botanical illustration of a gutta-percha plant. As the coltan of the nineteenth-century global economy, its ruthless extraction enabled the construction of vast, global communications networks/empires.

TJIPETIR (Cipetir)

Tjipetir is the Dutch romanization using the Van Ophuijsen Spelling System of Cipetir, the name of a village in West Java, Indonesia. Gutta-percha plantations were developed there and across the colonies of Southeast Asia held by the British, French, and the Dutch to extract a rubbery sap used, among other things, for insulating copper telegraphic wires, such as those laid by the HMS Agamemnon and the USS Niagara.[12] The sap was formed into fungible tablets like the one pictured below for transportation and processing. Almost completely unknown now, from the mid-nineteenth to the mid-twentieth centuries, gutta-percha was a ubiquitous industrial and domestic commodity like plastic is today.[8]

21

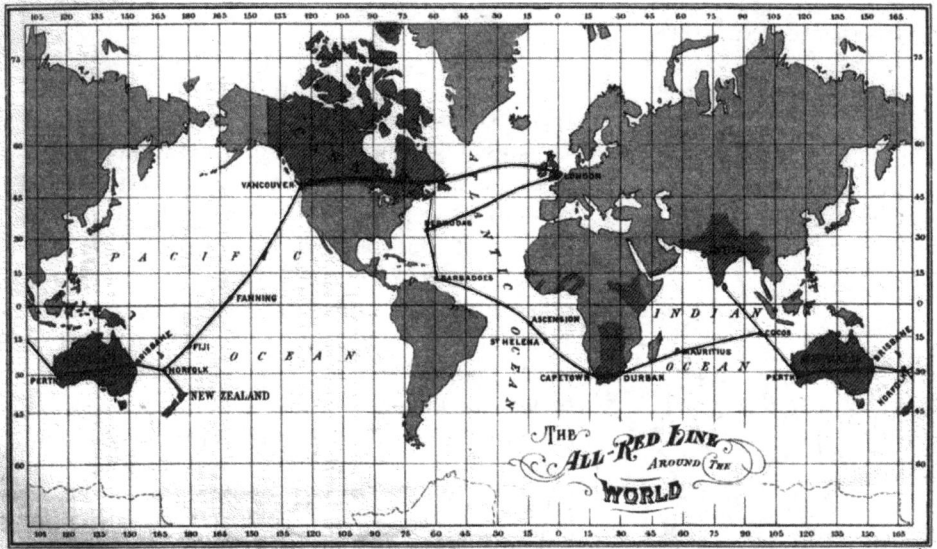

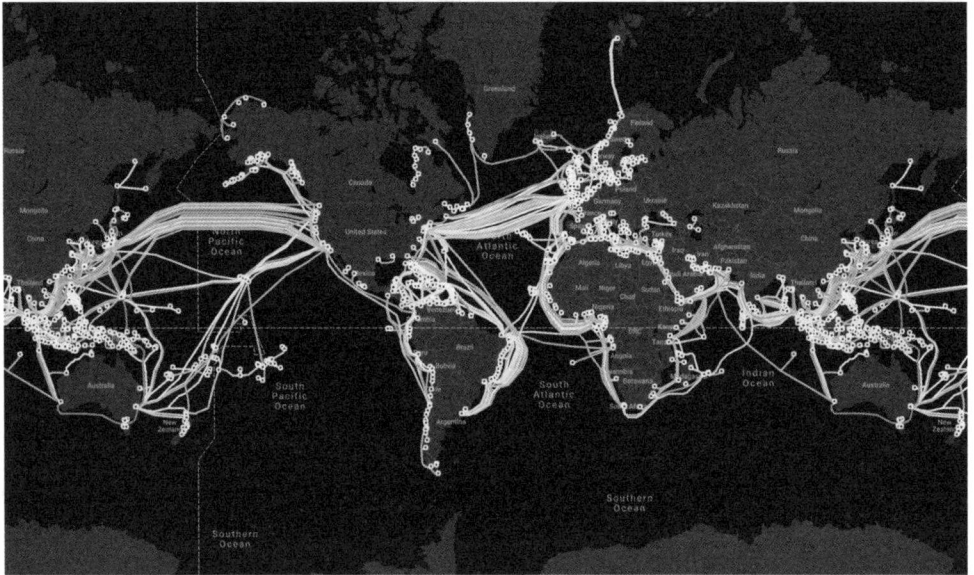

19 (above) A map of the imperial
   "All Red Line." (below)
   The contemporary submarine
   cable network constituting the
   physical infrastructure of the
   internet.
The cable, if nothing else, symbolizes
   the "rapid displacement"
   (Latour, 1986) of inscriptions,
   in that their speed subverts
   the entropy of movement in
   time and space.
18 Lydian coin depicting a horse
   memorializing the Greek victory over Troy and indicating
   its emission by the House of
   Agamemnon.
17 SS Great Eastern, lithographic
   print by Charles Parsons, 1858.
16 A commemorative segment
   of the first Atlantic cable.

CABLES AND CARTOGRAPHY

At a time when messages traveling between the metropole and the colonies could take up to six months by ship, both expanding global empires and capitalist interests invested heavily in developing technology and infrastructure for rapid, global communication. The first successfully laid transatlantic telegraph cable ↙16 ↓14 would not last a month, but efforts continued for another eight years until a stable line was set in 1866 by the steamship SS Great Eastern,↑17 whose conversion to a cable-laying ship was overseen by Isambard Kingdom Brunel, a leading engineer of British industrial infrastructure. Running from Valentia Island off the Irish coast to the small Newfoundland town of Heart's Content, this telegraphic network would enable the transmission of information across the Atlantic in minutes rather than weeks or months, allowing investors on either side of the ocean to stay current with their interests. By the turn of the twentieth century, the telegraphic cable network that connected the colonies of an empire (upon which the "sun never set") to its metropole (London) was called the "All Red Line." ↖19 Such communication lines served as the basic physical, financial, and political scaffolding of today's network of submarine cables— the physical infrastructure of the internet.

16

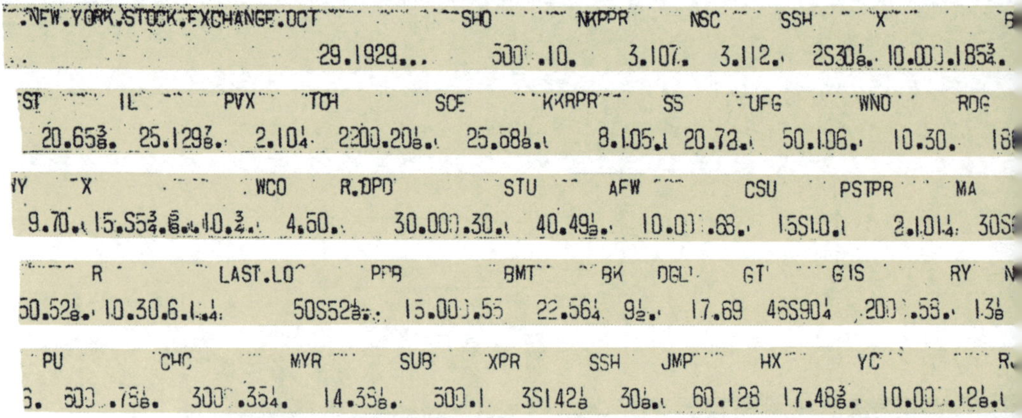

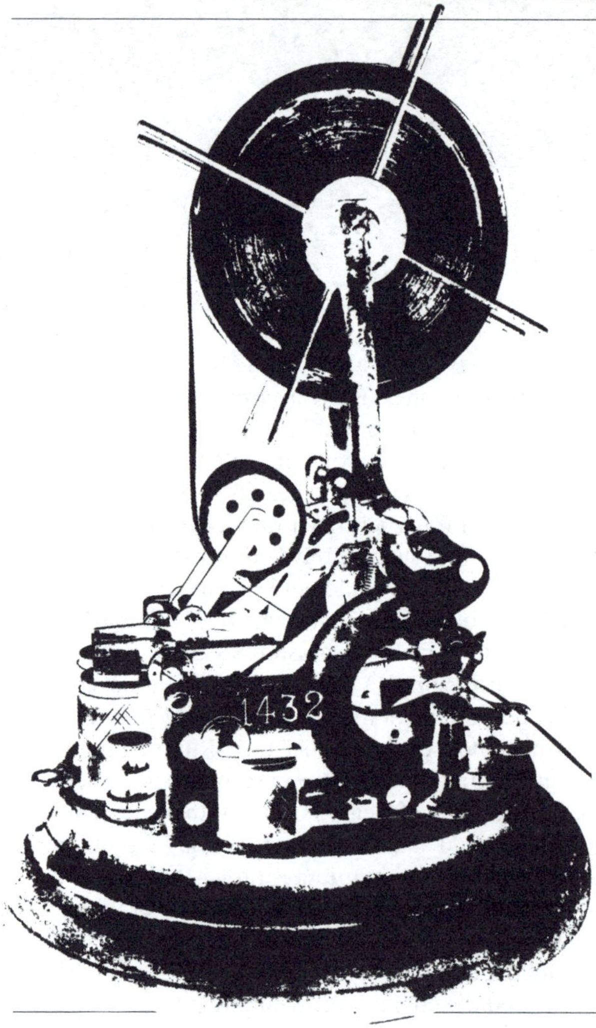

```
NEW.YORK.STOCK.EXCHANGE.OCT            SHO       NKPPR     NSC       SSH       X              R
            29.1929...          500 .10.     3.107.   3.112.,    2S30⅛. 10.00⅜.185¾.

ST        IL        PVX      TCH        SOE       KXRPR       SS      UFG       WND       RDG
20.65⅜.  25.129⅞.   2.10¼  22D0.20⅛.,  25.68⅛.,   8.105.₁ 20.7₂.,  50.106.,  10.30.    18

NY     X              WCO     R.DPD            STU       AFW        CSU      PSTPR     MA
9.70.,  15.5S⅝.₆..10.⅞.,   4.50.,   30.00⅜.30.,  40.49½.,  10.0⅜.68.,  15S1.0.₁   2.1.01¼.  30S

           R           LAST.LO^     PPB        BMT      BK    DGL'   GT      GIS      RY    N
50.52⅛.,  10.30.6.₁.₄.     50S52⅜.,,   15.00⅜.55   22.56¼   9½.,   17.69   46S90¼  .200 .58.,  1.3⅛

PU       CHC         MYR      SUB    XPR     SSH    JMP      HX       YC          R
6.  5D0 .78⅛.   300 .35¼.   14.38⅛.,   500.1.   3S142½   30⅛.₁   60.128  17.48¾.,  10.00 .12⅛.₁
```

14

15 Ticker tape from the New York
    Stock Exchange from the date
    of the 1929 market crash.↑58(‡)

14 A medal commemorating the
    first successful transatlantic
    cable. Bolts of electricity extend
    from John Bull's and an Uncle
    Sam-like figure's hands:
    "HOW ARE YOU JONATHAN"
    "PURTY WELL OLD FELLER
     HEOW'S YERSELF."

13 (above) A Universal Stock
    Ticker designed by Thomas
    Edison to include a mechanism
    that enabled multiple printers
    to output in unison and avoid
    errors in the transmission of
    information for brokers and
    investors. This model was
    developed for a subsidiary of
    the Western Union Telegraph
    Company; (below) Excerpt
    from John Tully, "A Victorian
    Ecological Disaster," *Journal
    of World History* (2009, 562).

"The need of a constantly expanding market for its
products chases the bourgeoisie over the whole surface of the globe,"
observed Marx and Engels in 1848. "It must nestle everywhere, settle
everywhere, establish connections everywhere."[5] With the creation of
an increasingly integrated world market in what some may see as an
earlier phase of globalization, the captains of the new industries could
not base their calculations of profit and loss and the creation of new
factories and markets on long-distance communications technology
that had changed little in essence since ancient times.

12 From the notes of Cyrus Field,
    a map (detail) charting the
    meeting of the USS Niagara and
    the HMS Agamemnon to splice
    the first transatlantic cable in
    1858. It includes a diagram of
    the cable, insulated by tar and
    gutta-percha. ↓11

13   **152**

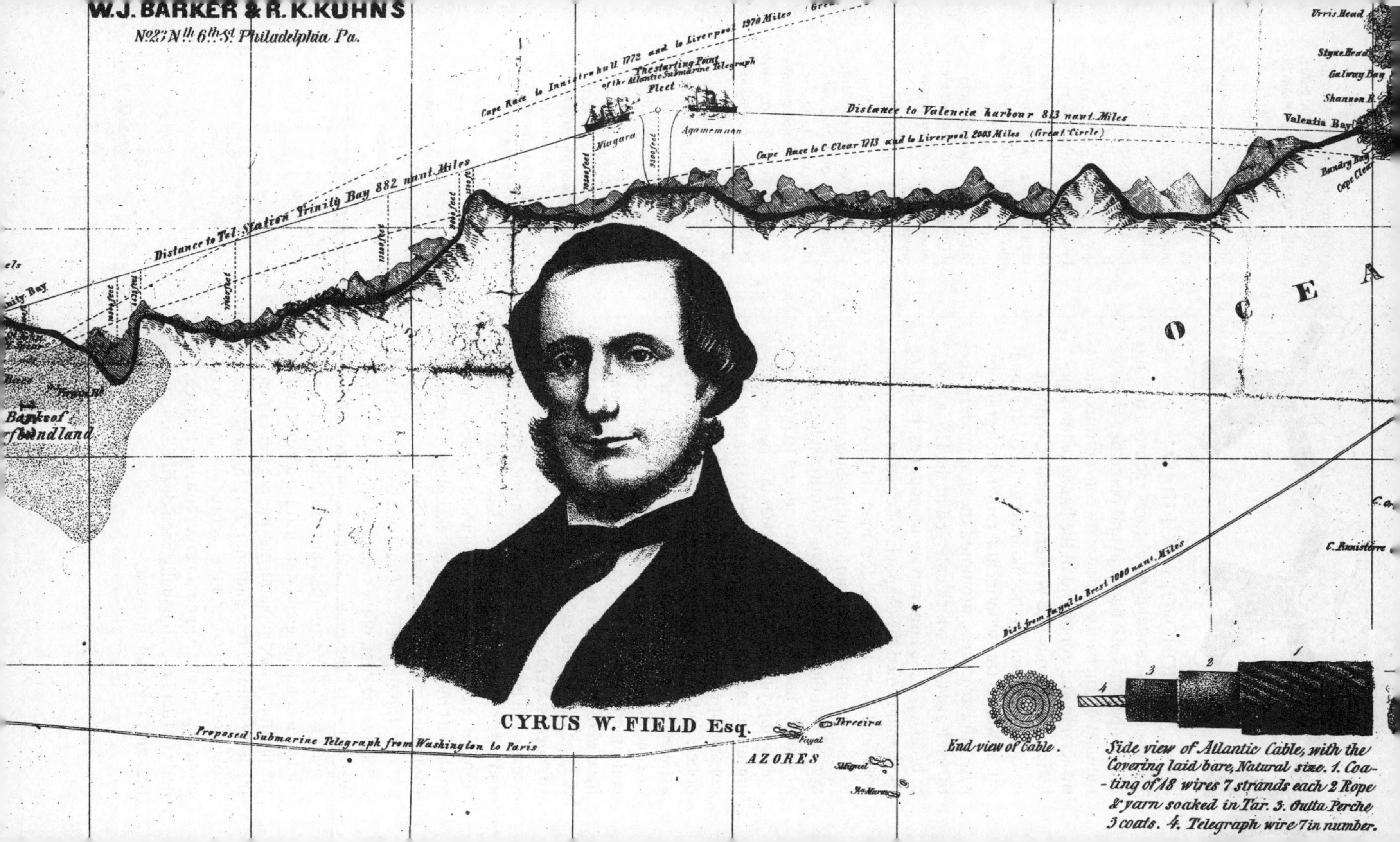

W.J. BARKER & R.K.KUHNS

No 37 N 11th 6th St Philadelphia Pa.

CYRUS W. FIELD Esq.

Proposed Submarine Telegraph from Washington to Paris

AZORES

Side view of Atlantic Cable, with the Covering laid bare, Natural size. A Coating of 18 wires 7 strands each 2 Rope & yarn soaked in Tar: 3. Gutta Percha 3 coats. 4. Telegraph wire 7 in number.

End view of Cable.

Distance to Valencia Harbour 813 naut. Miles

Distance to Valencia Harbour and to Liverpool 2065 Miles (Great Circle)

Cape Race to C. Clear 1713 and to Liverpool 2065 Miles

Distance to Tel. Station Trinity Bay 882 naut. Miles

1970 Miles east to Liverpool

Cape Race to Liverpool

Valentia Bay

Galway Bay

Shannon

Cape Clear

Banks of Newfoundland

MONOPOLY/POPULISM

The enormous capital expenditures required to build the components of a national and planetary communications network necessarily concentrated their ownership and command in the hands of monopolistic corporations like Western Union. Corporate consolidation across the manufacturing of steel and oil, as well as transcontinental rail and telegraphic wire infrastructures, prompted the first modern antitrust legislation, which emerged in the US in 1890, to break up these large private monopolies, including those that owned the channels for circulating information and money (that is, documents) (Sawyer 2019).

Legal scholar Laura Phillips Sawyer has argued that the original intent of antitrust legislation was somewhat populist, in that it aimed to prevent anti-competitive business practices that bypassed presumed market pressures exerted to prevent massive upward wealth redistribution. Trusts, monopolies, and other effectively conspiratorial business arrangements—that had, say, colluded to fix prices or control barriers to entering the market—forced consumers to pay more than they otherwise would have were the market operating "rationally." Distrust of large centralized corporate (and state) institutions, she suggests, emerged from this time, persisting as a feature of both contemporary American populism and cyber-libertarianism—a tendency from which things like blockchain and cryptocurrencies emerge to subvert the monopolistic gatekeeping of credit card companies and banking systems (Sawyer 2019).

But the politics of antitrust law have lost sight, at least somewhat, of the reality of what McKenzie Wark in calls "the vectoralist class" in her 2019 book *Capital Is Dead*. Vectoralists are the industrial captains who own computing and data infrastructure, and/or the profitable media platforms that are built upon them. Vectoralist transnationals run the network choke points and control the secure flow of information at a point when commerce, culture, finance, and conflict have all equally been distilled into forms that only they can transmit.

11 A Monopoly character for an adaptation of the classic game, called **POLITICAL ECONOMY**.

10 Omron Tateisi (developer of the EURION constellation ↑108) invents, according to the patent record, the first *online* "automatic credit loan machine" (later, automatic teller machine, or ATM), filed 1967, published 1969. It was first installed in 1971 at the central office of the Mitsubishi Bank in Tokyo. What distinguished it from earlier cash dispensers was that it could directly verify account holders' balances stored in a central database and identify them through information encoded into a magnetized strip in a plastic card.

The rise of the ATM shifts bank employees away from teller services towards sales of auto insurance, mortgages, and other high-margin products. Automation also allows banks to reduce their workforce while broadening access to checking accounts and credit cards (Bátiz-Lazo 2015). Over the next few decades the increasingly pervasive electronic banking infrastructure helped to popularize debit and credit cards and drive consumers towards a "cashless society" where higher proportions of everyday transactions are intermediated digitally by commercial banks.

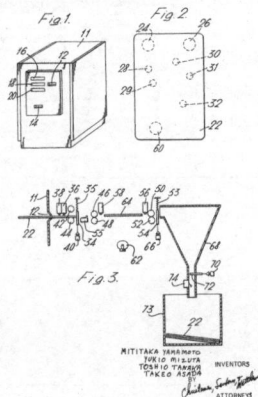

9   The "Eye of Providence"
     represents divine intervention
     in the affairs of the world. It
     sits in a radiating triangle
     floating above a pyramid built
     in thirteen layers, representing
     the original thirteen colonies
     of the settler-state known as
     the United States of Amer-
     ica. The position of the eye
     corresponds to the synoptic
     vantage point of the colonial
     administrator (or the gunship
     administering policy)—styled
     by the art historian Albert
     Boime as the "magisterial gaze"
     (1991). The gaze—how the
     world is looked upon—might
     be understood as a matter
     of *design*ation. It imposes a
     reductive schematization of the
     world through categorization.
     Things and people are rendered
     graphically as signs (values)
     that fit on a page or a screen.
     The ontological force of these
     ciphers enables murderous
     calculation dressed as rational
     administration, and delineates
     that which can be from that
     which cannot—one column for
     who lives and another for who
     dies. The capacity to make
     such designations and to act
     affirmatively upon them must
     then be seen as an element
     of the administrator's *design*
     process.

8   Still from "Collateral Murder."
     ↑85

THE OIL WAR AND BITCOIN

American Express was one of the major credit card
companies (including Visa, Mastercard, and PayPal)
to halt donations to the WikiLeaks Foundation
following the release of the illicit Iraq war footage
entitled "Collateral Murder."↓8 The video, leaked
by Chelsea Manning in April of 2010, shows a
heinous attack dating from 2007 which resulted in
the murder of civilians, including two journalists,
and the wounding of two children, at the hands
of a US American gunship in Baghdad. The credit
payment embargo—an apparent act of solidarity
between global financial institutions and the imperial
American state—inadvertently helped to popularize
cryptocurrencies like Bitcoin, which was swiftly
adopted as a means to circumvent the blockade and
send financial support to WikiLeaks.

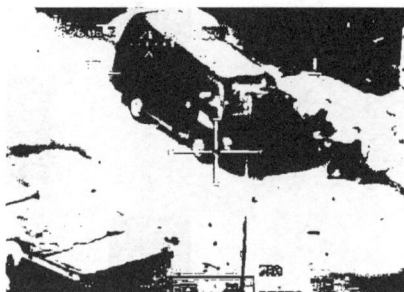

8

Bitcoin transfers move through a global server network outside of established financial institutions,
and cryptocurrencies like them represent one of the
newest techniques of immutability. A Bitcoin token's
securitization is enacted through advanced crypto-
graphy, where chunks of transaction data ("blocks")
are hashed with unique character strings (generated
using the SHA-256 algorithm), and a widely distributed
and collectively approved ledger maintains their
ordered sequence (their "chain"↑140) against any
efforts to tamper, adjust, or falsify it.↑111 ↑109

     We have thus arrived where we began: not
only to Mesopotamia and its ancient civilizational
cradle, but to the most contemporary instantiation of
the iterative, recursive, and dialectical development
of efforts to depoliticize inscription, driven by efforts
to design immutable documents and the new kinds of
transgressive resistance they inevitably generate.

155

BLOCKCHAIN

The blockchain maintains the immutability of inscriptions by distributing instantiations of a record across a network of computers that can essentially corroborate the validity of each others' copies.↑67 Unilaterally altering an inscription or claim from the blockchain—say, to erase a record of debt or change the amount of a transaction—is effectively impossible, because it would require a magnitude of computational power and speed that could rewrite all the previous transactions stored in the current

7 The "distributed ledger" is a form of decentralized multi-entry recordkeeping according to which the immutability of an inscription is grounded not in the legitimacy of a traditional institutional authority like a bank, but in the fact that the ledger is held across a network of independent computers. In other words, it is practically impossible to authorize a unilateral change to the ledger unless, as in the case of cryptocurrencies like bitcoin, 51% of all copies of the ledger agree.

7

Centralized Ledger

Distributed Ledger

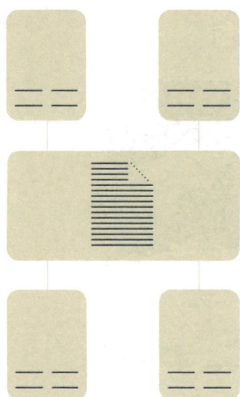
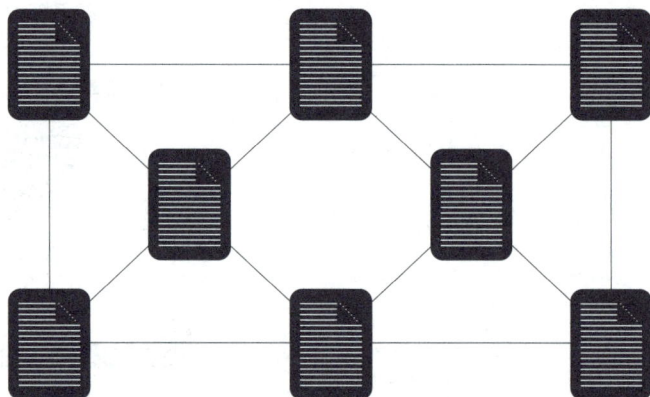

Transactions | A | B | C | D

SHA-256

Ledger

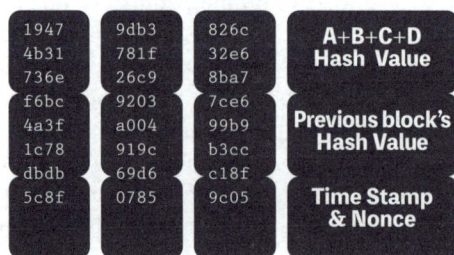

1947	9db3	826c	A+B+C+D Hash Value
4b31	781f	32e6	
736e	26c9	8ba7	
f6bc	9203	7ce6	Previous block's Hash Value
4a3f	a004	99b9	
1c78	919c	b3cc	
dbdb	69d6	c18f	Time Stamp & Nonce
5c8f	0785	9c05	

Four kinds of identifying signature

Blocks | **334** | **335** | **336** | ...

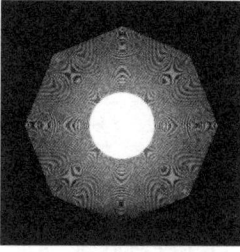

5 Still from *Quantum*, Kevin McCoy, 2014. The first known NFT artwork, registered on the Ethereum blockchain. The *moiré* effect is remeniscent of *guilloché* patterns.

6 A schematic diagram of a blockchain built by bundling hash strings representing unique transaction records; the blockchain then assigns itself a SHA-256 string that is time-stamped and given a random nonce—a unique number that helps to "seal" the block by ensuring its singularity. The key to the immutability of the blockchain itself is that each new block stores the value of previous blocks as a hash value. This means that in order for a change to any past block to be valid, all the blocks that come after it would have to be changed as well.

† Satoshi Nakamoto's second-to-last confirmed message laments the massive amounts of attention Bitcoin received following an editorial in *pcworld.com* titled "Could the Wikileaks Scandal Lead to New Virtual Currency?" (Thomas 2010). "He" writes: "It would have been nice to get this attention in any other context. Wikileaks has kicked the hornet's nest, and the swarm is headed towards us" (Satoshi 2010).

The adoption of a Japanese male's name as an alias reads as a performative "Fu Manchu"-inflected projection. The name reads as an orientalist affectation, where the oriental (yellow) peril is cast as a subversive, irrational ethnic adversary to the formal and institutional stability of the civic.

block before the creation of a new one. This would be like trying to catch up to the lead runner in a marathon having started ten minutes behind but running at roughly the same pace. What is more, the cryptographic hash signatures identifying unique transactions are like a *guilloché* design traditionally used to protect the integrity of physical documents with algorithmically-generated ornamentation.[27]

Blockchain registrations of cryptocurrency transactions and NFTs (non-fungible tokens, or pieces of code that have an absolutely unique identity) are understood as an assemblage of contemporary iterations of techniques for enacting documental securitization. The value of the document is premised on the mobilization of algorithmic protocols that repel human cognition: automated inscriptions are ostensibly uninflected by fallible human interests; records maintain their integrity in transmission by being converted to digital signals while traveling through cable networks at unfathomable speeds, resisting the entropy of movement through space and time; and value is premised on the artificial scarcity of unique digital tokens. Ownership claims and their transactions are inscribed upon a ledger distributed across a decentralized global network of computers that can only be voided following the so-called "51% rule"—a practical impossibility akin to the Biblical Jubilee. The mysterious mastermind behind Bitcoin and the first blockchain, Satoshi Nakamoto, is effectively cast beyond reproach.[†43] Nobody knows who Satoshi Nakamoto is or was. "His" last known communication appeared in December 12, 2010. "His" silence and anonymity reanimate ancient techniques of deification (and mystery [145]).

David Golumbia polemically attacks the blockchain as a fascist technology that forecloses the human contingency essential to politics. Proponents of the blockchain and cryptocurrencies fantasize about disintermediated, "trustless" exchange systems that obviate a reliance on centralized authority for adjudicating disputes and seek to function, like a standard, as a guarantee of value and meaning. Absolute immutability, where nothing can be *un-* or *re-*written, would mean the impossibility of disputing a wrong, altering a record, obliterating a colonial memory, or asserting countervalent claims to the ones prescribed on the common and contestable fields of knowledge and memory (Golumbia 2016). Where there is no dispute, there are no politics— that is, no other real possibility of (more just) alternatives, only the trap of meme coins.

The relentless linear sequentiality of the blockchain deepens a naturalization of prescriptive, linear-progressive time. The techno-libertarian ideology that colors the crypto utopia, not unlike Rondon's positivism, is one according to which the status of divine authority (the ultimate guarantee) is conferred upon the proof-of-work—a dispassionate string of machine-readable alphanumeric signs.

Insofar as blockchain ledgers represent the latest point in an asymptotic curve towards perfect immutability, the relative contingency and fallibility of graphic design could appear to have a renewed charge, both in rejecting the apolitical story of techno-progressive inevitability, and in challenging us to study and renew countervalent ways of remembering that embrace contingency, negotiation, and entropy. The affirmative features of blockchain and cryptocurrencies help remind us that their opposites—destruction, forgery, forking, counterfeiting, and non-linearity—could figure as frameworks for the antagonistic design student interested in the questions and problems of the document.

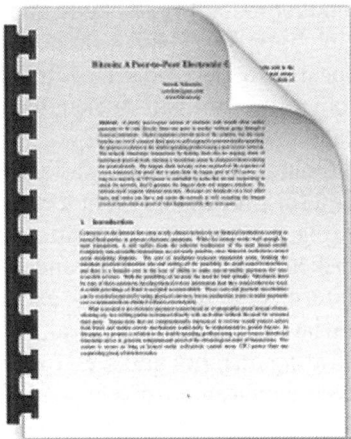

bitcoin.pdf

4   This skeuomorphic, commemorative coin misrepresents technologies like the blockchain—a thing which frustrates visualization—through the very attempt to give them form. The diagrams above also only give an illusory grasp of the blockchain's magnitude, yet this unfathomability is precisely that which deflects the kinds of intervention (i.e., forgery and destruction) available with other forms of documental inscription.↑118

3   This skeuomorphic document icon for osx depicts the file as a paper document, printed and bound by plastic comb-binding. This would seem to suggest that the primary metaphor for graphical user interfaces comes from the context of business administration. In other words, the visual language for the most common form of human-computer interaction is—as it was with clay and the European printing press— informed by the documental requirements of management and bureaucracy.

2   Although versions of the tale vary, Diogenes the Cynic was expelled from his hometown of Sinope for adulterating the currency his father minted. Asked of his purpose in life, he responded *"paracharaxis"*— to deface or restamp, to invert or reorient the terms of value. He is depicted here in a painting by Jean-Léon Gérôme, seated at the periphery of a marketplace, inside a discarded *pithos*— a large container for storing commodities.

1 (following page) This image of a lithographic stone includes snippets of designs—blank form elements—of printed checks for various companies and banks. It is proposed as a generic icon for the PDF, or portable document format, which was first developed by Adobe Systems in 1991, for the purposes of digital document production in the context of business administration.

The primary function of this banal format is evident in its name—to make portable digital layouts, fonts, pictures, etc., so that they appear the same on any screen or output from any printer, effectively handling as immutable (Gitelman 2014). Gitelman remarks that a PDF is better understood as a "page image" obtaining the "printedness" of print wether they appear on the screen or on paper. They are meant primarily to be read and not edited. Typographic form, images, and the way that these are set in a layout communicate meaning supplemental to the content of a text. The political stakes of this file format become more discernible in Gitelman's discussion of its original function: to facilitate corporate authorship of digital documents by "imagining [its use within] hierarchical labor relations [with] readers above, below, or beyond" the author (130). In hierarchical administrative structures, authorship "is less about (intellectual) property than it is about liability and responsibility" (124).↑58

CODA

> Challenging the colonial world is not a rational confrontation of viewpoints. It is not a discourse on the universal, but the impassioned claim by the colonized that their world is fundamentally different.
> —Frantz Fanon, *The Wretched of the Earth*

This book has rendered some outlines for naming the various techniques of the colonial and capitalist document—of immutability—to suggest that what is remembered obtains precisely from its being designed to be so. So then, it ought to be asked: Could history be designed otherwise? Can this be a question for design pedagogy and praxis? Could that entail studying how new and old techniques of immutability might be undone to destabilize colonial and capitalist prescriptions—to ask how naturalized claims might be opposed, obliterated, or overwritten? Could a deepening of the study of the document, of which this book is an initial foray, enact what Laura Nader calls "studying up" (1972) (on those in power) in order to charge design with the task of exploring other ways of claiming, remembering, and knowing? To the extent that history is designed—deploying the various techniques of the document—could historio*graphy* as a creative, poietic praxis be about designing history otherwise and involve different and new kinds of writing, transmission, storage/retrieval and performance? To what extent is it even useful to retain graphic design as a disciplinary framework, and at what point must its institutional and professional horizons be abandoned to meaningfully explore such questions? The namesake of my graduate school, the designer Willem Sandberg, was known to have helped plan the bombing of the Amsterdam civil registry office to foil the Gestapo's policing of forged documents he had also helped to produce. Perhaps these were his most consequential design interventions.↑118

Immutable.pdf

Figures

49 Antonio de Nebrija, page from the introduction to *Gramatica de la lengua castellana* (Salamanca: Juan de Poras, 1492), print. Library of Congress, Washington, DC, lccn.loc.gov/2021667003. Public domain.

50 Ioris Vesler and Caspar van Hilten, page from *Courante uyt Italien, Duytslandt, &c., uitgeverij*, 1618, print. Koninklijke Bibliotheek, Den Haag. Wikimedia Commons (CC0).

51 Johann Carolus, title page from *Relation aller Fürnemmen und gedenckwürdigen Historien*, 1609. print. Universitätsbibliothek Heidelberg. Wikimedia Commons (CC-PD-Mark).

52 (above) United States of America, $50 Continental currency (reverse, detail) showing the stepped pyramid symbol, printed by Hall and Sellers, 1778; (below) $40 Continental currency (detail), showing the eye of providence symbol, 1778. Both Wikimedia Commons (PD US money).

53 Pieter van der Heyden after Pieter Bruegel the Elder, *The Battle of the Moneybags and the Strong Boxes*, after 1570, engraving, 23.5 × 30.7 cm. Baker Library, Harvard Business School, Boston. Wikimedia Commons (CC-PD-Mark).

54 Cesare Beccaria, *Dei delitti e delle pene*, 1766, engraving. Biblioteca europea di informazione e cultura. Wikimedia Commons (CC-PD-Mark).

55 MissionCreekVideo, "Mission Playground Is Not for Sale," uploaded September 25, 2014, YouTube video, 4:34, youtube.com/watch?v=awPVY1DcupE.

56 Neo-Assyrian cylinder seal, ca. 700–800 BCE, cornelian, 1.20 cm (diameter), 2.40 cm (height). British Museum, London, britishmuseum.org/collection/object/W_SOC-143. Public domain.

57 Chris Lee, *Illegible/legible Forest*, 2018, digital.

58 Chris Lee, *8.5″ × 11″*, 2021, digital, 21.6 × 27.9 cm.

59 McKarri, *Flag of the VOC (Dutch East India Company) on the Replica of the East Indiaman Amsterdam in Amsterdam*, 2009, photograph. Wikimedia Commons (CC-BY-SA-3.0).

60 Chris Lee, *Bushuis* 3D Scan, 2017, photogrammetry.

61 Verenigde Oostindische Compagnie, VOC AANDEEL, September 9, 1606, print and manuscript. Wikimedia Commons (CC-PD-Mark). This certificate was issued by the VOC- chamber Enkhuizen to Pieter Hermanszoon Boode. The verso lists dividend payments.

62 Pieter Hendricksz Schut, *Vogelvluchtgezicht op de Beurs van Hendrik de Keyser te Amsterdam, voor 1668*, 1662–68, etching, 24.8 × 29 cm. Rijksmuseum, Amsterdam, rijksmuseum.nl/en/collection/RP-P-AO-25-3-2. Public domain.

63 Anonymous, *Vier munten van de VOC*, 1700–1799, etching, 6.6 × 15.5 cm. Rijksmuseum, Amsterdam, rijksmuseum.nl/en/collection/RP-P-OB-75.320. Public domain.

64 Oldest printed company logo, Northern Song Dynasty (960–1279 CE), print. Gutenberg Museum, Mainz. Public domain.

65 Anonymous, *Le Chiffonnier-ferrailleur*, from the portfolio *Anciens cris de Paris*, 1500–50, woodblock print. Département Arsenal, Bibliothèque nationale de France, Paris. Public domain.

66 Catholic Church, Pope (Nicholas V, 1447–55), Cyprus Indulgence, 31 lines, print on vellum leaf, 21 × 26 cm, printed by Johannes Gutenberg (Mainz), 1455. Princeton University Library, dpul.princeton.edu/catalog/d217qp581. Public domain.

67 Neil McKendrick, originally Josiah Wedgwood, detail of "Table 2. Expenses, Sales and Stock," 1770–71, facsimile typeset in *The Economic History Review* 23, no. 1 (April 1970): 45–67.

68 Robert Recorde, excerpt from *Whetstone of Witte* (London: John Kyngstone, 1557), print. Wikimedia Commons (CC-PD-Mark).

69 Matthew Boulton and Josiah Wedgwood, *Smallsword Hilt*, ca. 1790, steel, Wedgwood jasperware, 17.5 × 11.4 cm. Metropolitan Museum of Art, New York, metmuseum.org/art/collection/search/24708. Public domain.

70 United States of America, stimulus check (detail), 2020, print.

71 Italy, commemorative 500 Lire coin, 1994, bronzital center in acmonital ring, 2.58 cm (diameter), minted by Istituto Poligrafico e Zecca dello Stato, Rome. Numista, en.numista.com/catalogue/pieces715.html.

72 Chris Lee, *The Banality of Excel*, 2017, digital.

73 Union of Soviet Socialist Republics, stamp commemorating the 1200th anniversary of Abu Ja'far Muḥammad ibn Mūsā al-Khwārizmī, 1983, print. Wikimedia Commons (CC0).

74 Hindu-Arabic numerals, ca. 1st–4th century CE.

75 Chris Lee, *Hammurabi's Stele Grid*, 2017, print, 24 × 36 inches.

Figures

102 Bureau international des poids et mesures (BIPM), Replica of the Kilogramme des Archives. Photograph by the author.

103 (above) National Institute of Standards and Technology (NIST), 1kg, 2018. Photograph by the author. (below) Kibble balance proposed design, 2014, 3D model. Institute for Manufacturing, University of Cambridge, ifm.eng.cam. ac.uk/research/cip/current-research-overview/realising-the-new-kilogram-a-linear-mechanism-to-for-the-next-generation-kibble-balance.

104 Jean-Jacques Lequeu, *Drawing, Design for a Monument Commemorating the Systematization of Weights and Measures in France, 1795–1800*, pen and black ink, brush and gray, red and blue wash on paper, 21.6 × 47.6 cm; Cooper Hewitt, Smithsonian Design Museum, Washington DC, collection. cooperhewitt.org/objects/18172131. Public domain.

105 Louis XIV, *Paris Meridian*, 1667. Photograph by the author.

106 Chris Lee, *Le mètre étalon (1796–97) 3D scan*, 2017, photogrammetry.

107 Jan Dibbets, *Hommage à Arago*, 1994, installation, 135 bronze medallions. Photograph by the author.

II Metals & Mechanization

108 Omron Corporation, *EURion constellation* (dubbed by Markus Kuhn), 1995.

109 National Institute of Standards and Technology (NIST), SHA 0–3 schematic diagrams, 1993–2012. Wikimedia Commons, SHA 0 by Matt Crypto (CC-BY-SA-2.5); SHA 2 by Kockmeyer (CC-BY-SA-3.0); SHA 3 by Armbrust (CC-BY-SA-3.0).

110 Thomas Jefferson, (above) Jeffersonian cryptograph, modern US Navy version, ciphermachines.com/Jefferson. Creative Commons (CC-BY-SA 4.0); (below) Thomas Jefferson to Meriwether Lewis, Cipher, 20 April 1803, Thomas Jefferson Papers, Manuscript Division, Library of Congress, Washington DC, loc.gov/item/mtjbib012330/. Public domain.

111 Unknown, Bulla with five calculi, late 4th millennium BCE, clay. Musée du Louvre, Paris. Public domain.

112 (above) United States of America, New Jersey, 1 cent, 1786, copper, 2.8 cm. National Museum of American History, Washington DC, americanhistory. si.edu/collections/search/object/nmah_1093549; (middle) US Mint, Philadelphia, Disme (dime), 1792,

copper, 2.7 cm. National Museum of American History, Washington DC, americanhistory.si.edu/collections/search/object/nmah_1099126 (below) US Mint, 10 dollar coin, 1797, gold, 3.31 cm. National Museum of American History. All public domain.

113 Domaines nationaux, France, designed by Jean-Pierre Droz, Assignat de vingt-cinq sols, 1790–96, print, 6 × 9.7 cm. Rijksmuseum, Amsterdam, rijksmuseum. nl/en/collection/RP-P-OB-86.594-5. Public domain.

114 Robert Bénard after Jacques-Raymond Lucotte, "Monnoyage, Balancier," etching with engraving, 36 × 23 cm platemark, Plate XV, in Denis Diderot and Jean le Rond d'Alembert, eds., *L'Encyclopédie, ou Dictionnaire raisonné des sciences, des arts et des métiers*, vol. 25, *Receuil de planches sur les sciences, les arts libéraux, et les arts méchaniques, avec leur explication* (Paris: Briasson/David/Le Breton/Durand, 1765). Public domain.

115 Soho Mint, designed by Conrad Heinrich Küchler, 1 penny "Cartwheel" (reverse), 1797, copper, 3.56 cm. Wikimedia Commons (CC-BY-SA-3.0).

116 Soho Mint, designed by Conrad Heinrich Küchler, Medal commemorating the execution of Marie Antoinette, October 16, 1793, bronze, 4.8 cm (diameter). Musée Carnavalet, Paris. Creative Commons (CC0).

117 Chris Lee, *Blank Coin (planchet)*, 2019, digital.

118 Unknown, Coin clippings, undated. Photograph by the author.

119 Bank of England, 50 Pound banknote, showing Elizabeth II, Matthew Boulton, and James Watt, printed by Thomas de la Rue & Company Ltd. (London), 2011, ink, paper, various security features, 15.6 × 8.5 cm. Museum of Applied Arts & Sciences, Sydney, ma.as/426371.

120 Chris Lee, *Reeded Edge*, 2020, digital. Wikimedia Commons. Public domain.

121 Jean-Pierre Droz, Segmental Collar, 1788. Digital illustration by the author.

122 Antoninus Pius, for Diva Faustina I, Senatus Consulto (decreed by the senate), after 141 CE. © Deutsche Bundesbank, Franfkurt am Main. Photograph by the author.

123 Adobe Photoshop™, EURion warning message.

124 Fritz Kredel, Illustrations adapted from Plates I, II, and III, from Paul Koch, "The Making of Printing Types," in *The Dolphin: A Journal of the Making of Books* (New York: Limited Editions Club, 1933): 26, 30.

Figures

144 Palace of Nabu-Shumu-lishir, son of the
Dakkuru tribe, One-third legitimate
mina [belonging to the] palace of
Nabu-Shumu-lishir, son of the Dakkuru
tribe..., late 8th–9th Century BCE,
carved and polished feldspar, 2.8 × 10.9
× 2.8 cm. Metropolitan Museum of Art,
New York, public domain.

145 *Stele with Law Code of Hammurabi*
(detail), c. 1792–1750 BCE, basalt,
225 x 79 x 47 cm. Musée du Louvre,
Paris, collections.louvre.fr/en/
ark:/53355/cl010174436. Photograph by
author.

146 British East India Company, William
Lambton, *Great Trigonometrical
Survey Peninsula of India Operations,
in "An Account of the Trigonometrical
Operations in Crossing the Peninsula of
India, and Connecting Fort St. George
with Mangalore," Asiatic Researchers; or
Transactions of the Society Instituted in
Bengal for Inquiring into the History and
Antiquities*, vol. 10 (1811). Wikimedia
Commons (CC-BY-SA-4.0).

147 Unknown, Si.427 Obverse, 1900–1600
BCE, clay, 10.5 × 10.3 cm.
Istanbul Arkeoloji Muzeleri. Wikimedia
Commons, contributed by Daniel
Mansfield (CC-BY-SA-4.0).

148 Carmen M. Reinhart and Kenneth S.
Rogoff, "Growth in a Time of Debt,"
*American Economic Review: Papers
& Proceedings* 100 (May 2010).

149 Unknown, late Uruk record of
Barley, 3300–3100 BCE, clay tablet,
8 × 5 cm. British Museum, London,
britishmuseum.org/collection/object/
W_1989-0130-2. 3D scan by author.

150 Proto-cuneiform to cuneiform transition,
ca. 3000–700 BCE. Adapted from
photograph by the author.

151 Unknown, late Uruk five-day ration list,
3000 BCE, clay tablet, 7.8 × 7.8 cm. British
Museum, London. Creative Commons
(CC-BY-NC-SA-4.0).

152 (above) Chris Lee, *826c32e68ba
77ce699b9b3ccc18f9co5eb8co1ca*, 2017,
clay, 7.4 × 10.6 cm. (below) Chris Lee,
*9db3781f26c99203a004919c69d6078
5a722555b*, 2017, clay, 6.8 × 10 cm.

153 Sexagesimal number system.

154 Chris Lee, SHA Cylinder (1 of 3), 2017,
3D print, 3.2 × 3.2 × 8.3 cm.

155 Chris Lee, *Hash Discs*, 2017, digital.

156 Unknown, Plate XXXVIII-8, drawing
of early Uruk period seal impression
from the Susa II period, 3800–3100
BCE, glyptic drawing, Firg. 646 in Pierre
Amiet, *Glyptique susienne des origines à
l'époque des perses achéménides: Cachets,
sceaux-cylindres et empreintes antiques
découverts à suse de 1913-1967* (Paris: P.
Geuthner, 1972).

157 Unknown, *Hexagone*, ca. 1894–1595 BCE,
clay, 12.1 × 1.9 cm. Musée du Louvre,
Paris.

158 Unknown, *Archaic Vessels and Garments*,
ca. 3200–3000 BCE, clay. Iraq Museum,
Baghdad.

159 Unknown, proto-cuneiform glyphs,
4th millenium BCE, stylus and clay.
Composite image from various sources
assembled by the author.

160 Unknown, tablet accounting for beer
products, grain groats, and malt,
3500–3100 BCE, clay, 8 × 7.4 cm.
Musée du Louvre, Paris.

161 Cuneiform writing with stylus on soft
clay, digital photograph, in Mathile
Touillon-Ricci, "Trade and Contraband
in Ancient Assyria," The British
Museum (blog), April 2, 2018, blog.
britishmuseum.org/trade-and-
contraband-in-ancient-assyria.

162 Unknown, *Complex calculi*, ca. 3300 BCE,
clay. Institut für Ur- und Frühgeschichte,
Heidelberg.

163 Unknown, Sumerian proto-cuneiform
tablet: administrative account of
barley distribution with cylinder seal
impression of a male figure, hunting
dogs, and boars, ca. 3100–2900 BCE,
clay, 5.5 × 6 × 4.15 cm. Metropolitan
Museum of Art, New York, metmuseum.
org/art/collection/search/32908.
Public domain.

Bibliography

A

Abu-Lughod, Janet. 1989. *Before European Hegemony*. Oxford University Press.

Addy, Dave. 2014. "Fontspots: Eurostile." *Typeset in the Future* (blog). November 29. typesetinthefuture. com/2014/11/29/fontspots-eurostile.

Alder, Ken. 2003. *The Measure of All Things: The Seven-Year Odyssey and Hidden Error That Transformed the World*. The Free Press.

Anderson, Benedict. 2006. *Imagined Communities: Reflections on the Origin and Spread of Nationalism*. 2nd ed. Verso.

André, Jacques, and Denis Girou. 1999. "Father Truchet, the Typographic Point, the Romain du Roi, and Tilings." *tugboat* 20 (1): 8–14.

Ansari, Ahmed. 2017. "The Work of Design in the Age of Cultural Simulation, or, Decoloniality as Empty Signifier in Design." *Medium*, January 4. medium. com/@aansari86/the-symbolic-is-just-a-symptom-ofthe- real-or-decoloniality-as-emptysignifier- in-design-60ba646d89e9.

Arcand, Joi T., Chris Lee, and Winona Wheeler. 2019. "I'm a Little Too Rebellious for That: A Conversation with Joi T. Arcand and Winona Wheeler." *C Magazine* 141. cmagazine. com/issues/141/ im-a-little-too-rebellious-for-that-aconversation-with-joi-t-ar.

Ascalone, Enrico, and Luca Peyronel. 2001. "Two Weights from Temple N at Tell Mardikh-Ebla, Syria: A Link between Metrology and Cultic Activities in the Second Millennium BC?" *Journal of Cuneiform Studies* 53: 1–12.

Azoulay, Ariella Aïsha. 2019. *Potential History: Unlearning Imperialism*. Verso.

———. 2019. "Undoing the Imperial Conception of Art." In *Crating the World*, edited by Jacqueline Hoàng Nguyên and Rado Ištok. Athenée Press.

B

Baraniuk, Chris. 2015. "The Secret Codes of British Banknotes." 2015. *BBC*, June 25. bbc.com/future/article/20150624-the-secret-codes-ofbritish-banknotes.

Barthes, Roland. 1977. "The Death of the Author." In *Image Music Text*. Translated by Stephen Heath. Fontana.

Bátiz-Lazo, Bernardo. 2015. "A Brief History of the atm." *The Atlantic*, March 26. theatlantic.com/technology/ archive/2015/03/a-brief-history-ofthe-atm/388547.

———. 2018. *Cash and Dash: How ATMs and Computers Changed Banking*. Oxford University Press.

Bauer, Gerda. 2016. "Women and Graphic Design in the History of Design and Design History." In *Graphic Design History and Practice*, edited by Antonio Benincasa, Giorgio Camuffo, Madalena Dalla Mura, Christian Upmeier, and Carlo Vinti. Bozen-Bolzano University Press.

Beier, Sophie. 2012. *Reading Letters: Designing for Legibility*. BIS.

Bedini, Silvio A. 2006. "Seth Pease." *The American Surveyor*, December. archive.amerisurv.com/pdf/ TheAmericanSurveyor_Bedini-SethPeasePart2_Mar-Apr2006.pdf.

Beuscher, Kristin. 2019. "From Pascack to the Plains: The Story of Campbell Wampum." *Pascack Press*, May 21. thepressgroup.net/frompascack-to-the-plains-the-story-ofcampbell-wampum.

Brekke, Jaya Klara. 2019. *The White Paper*, edited by Ben Vickers. Ignota.

Brown, J. Dakota. 2019. *Typography, Automation, and the Division of Labor: A Brief History*. Other Forms.

Beller, Jonathan. 2017. *The Message Is Murder: Substrates of Computational Capital*. Pluto Press.

Berardi, Franco "Bifo." 2019. "Game Over." *e-flux journal* (100). e-flux.com/ journal/100/268601/game-over.

Boime, Albert. 1991. *The Magisterial Gaze: Manifest Destiny and American Landscape Painting, c. 1830–1865.* Smithsonian Institution Press.

Bridis, Ted. 2004. "Adobe Says It Uses Anti-Counterfeiting Technology." *Washington Post*, January 10. washingtonpost.com/ archive/ business/2004/01/10/adobesays-it-uses-anti-counterfeitingtechnology/ 56cc8fc1-2357-40a4- b056-529f6d983103.

Briet, Suzanne. 2006. *What Is Documentation?*, edited by Ronald E. Day, Laurent Martinet, and Hermina G.B. Anghelescu. Scarecrow Press.

Burke, James. 2009. *The Day the Universe Changed.* Little Brown & Company.

Butler, Octavia E., and Samuel R. Delany. 1998. "Octavia Butler and Samuel Delany, 1998." MIT Media in Transition, August 29. web. mit.edu/m-i-t/science_ fiction/ transcripts/butler_delany_index. html.

C

Caffentzis, Constantine George. 1989. *Clipped Coins, Abused Words, and Civil Government: John Locke's Philosophy of Money.* Autonomedia.

Carruthers, Bruce G., and Wendy Nelson Espeland. 1991. "Accounting for Rationality: Double-Entry Bookkeeping and the Rhetoric of Economic Rationality." *The American Journal of Sociology* 9 (1): 31–69.

Castoriadis, Cornelius. 1991. "The Social-Historical: Mode of Being, Problems of Knowledge." In *Philosophy, Politics, Autonomy: Essays in Political Philosophy.* Oxford University Press.

Chak, Tings. "Poster Art, Internationalism and the Cuban Revolution." In *C Magazine* 141. Accessed December 4, 2024. cmagazine.com/articles/in-the-process-of-making-themselves-poster-art-internationalism

Chazanof, William. 1970. *Joseph Ellicott and the Holland Land Company: The Opening of Western New York.* Syracuse University Press.

Coomaraswamy, Ananda K. 1947. *Am I My Brother's Keeper?* John Day Company.

Corner, James. 1999. "The Agency of Mapping: Speculation, Critique, and Invention." In *Mapping*, edited by Denis Cosgrove. Reaktion Books.

Coulthard, Glen Sean. 2014. *Red Skin, White Masks: Rejecting the Colonial Politics of Recognition.* University of Minnesota Press.

D

Damerow, Peter. 1999. "The Origins of Writing as a Problem of Historical Epistemology." Lecture presented at "The Multiple Origins of Writing: Image, Symbol, and Script" Symposium, Center for Ancient Studies, University of Pennsylvania, Philadelphia, March 26–27. Published in Max-Planck-Institut für Wissenschaftsgeschichte's *Preprint* 114.

De Beccaria, Cesare. 1856. *Traité des délits et des peines*, edited by Faustin Hélie. Translated by Jacques Albin Simon Collin de Plancy. Guillaumin. First published in 1764.

De Certeau, Michel. 1984. *The Practice of Everyday Life.* Translated by Steven F. Rendall. University of California Press.

———. 1992. *The Writing of History.* Translated by Tom Conley. Columbia University Press.

De Sá, Dominichi Miranda, Magali Romero Sá, and Nísia Trinidade Lima. 2008. "Telegraphs and an Inventory of the Territory of Brazil: The Scientific Work of the Rondon Commission (1907–1915)." *História, Ciências, Saúde-Manguinhos* 15 (3). doi.org/10.1590/S0104-59702008000300011.

De Vinne, Theodore Low. 1876. *The Invention of Printing: A Collection of Facts and Opinions Descriptive of Early Prints and Playing Cards, the Block-Books of the Fifteenth Century, the Legends of Lourens Janszoon Coster, of Haarlem, and the Work of John Gutenberg and His Associates. Illustrated with Facsimiles of Early Types and Woodcuts.* F. Hart & Co.

Deaton, Clifford. 2013. "The Memory of May '68: The Ironic Interruption and Democratic Commitment of the Atelier Populaire." *Design Issues* 29 (2): 29–41.

Bibliography

Deutsche Nationalbibliothek. n.d. "Breitkopf, Johann Gottlob Immanuel: Result of the search for: idn = 118809873." Catalog of the German National Library. Accessed January 3, 2022. portal.dnb.de/opac.htm? method=simpleSearch&cqlMode=true& query=idn%3D118809873.

Devroye, Luc. n.d. "Johann Michael Fleischmann." Type Design Information Page. Accessed January 3, 2022. luc.devroye. org/fonts-24824.html.

———. "Philippe Grandjean de Fouchy." Type Design Information Page. Accessed January 3, 2022. luc.devroye.org/ fonts-43482.html.

———. "Romain du Roi." Type Design Information Page. Accessed January 3, 2022. luc.devroye.org/fonts-89919.html.

Diacon, Todd A. 2002. "Cândido Mariano da Silva Rondon and the Politics of Indian Protection in Brazil." *Past & Present* (177): 157-94.

Diderot, Denis, and Jean le Rond d'Alembert, eds. 1754. "Décimal." In *Encyclopédie, ou Dictionnaire raisonné des sciences, des arts et des métiers.* Vol. 4, 668-70. Briasson/ David/Le Breton/Durand.

Dilnot, Clive.1984. "The State of Design History, Part I: Mapping the Field." *Design Issues* 1 (1): 4-23.

Dilnot, Clive, Tony Fry, and Susan Stewart. 2015. *Design and the Question of History.* Bloomsbury.

Drucker, Johanna. 2009. "Philip Meggs and Richard Hollis: Models of Graphic Design History." *Design and Culture* 1 (1): 51-77.

———. 2014. *Graphesis: Visual Forms of Knowledge Production.* Harvard University Press.

Drucker, Johanna, and Emily McVarish. 2012. *Graphic Design History: A Critical Guide.* 2nd ed. Pearson.

E

"Editorial Note: Report on Copper Coinage." *Founders Online*, National Archives. Accessed December 24, 2021. founders. archives.gov/documents/ Jefferson/01-16-02-0200-0001. Originally published in 1961 *The Papers of Thomas Jefferson*, vol. 16, *30 November 1789-4 July 1790*, edited by Julian P. Boyd. Princeton University Press.

Emmerson, Donald K. 1984. "'Southeast Asia': What's in a Name?" *Journal of Southeast Asian Studies* 15 (1): 1-21.

Exo Adams, Ross. 2017. "Becoming-Infrastructural." *e-flux Architecture*, October. e-flux.com/architecture/ positions/149606/ becoming-infrastructural.

F

Fanon, Frantz. 2004. *The Wretched of the Earth.* Translated by Richard Philcox. Grove Press.

Fay, Nicolas, T. Mark Ellison, and Simon Garrod. 2014. "Iconicity: From Sign to System in Human Communication and Language." *Pragmatics & Cognition* (22): 243-62.

Fielder, Adrian V. 2000. "Historical Representation and the Scriptural Economy of Imperialism: Assia Djebar's 'L'Amour, la fantasia' and Cormac McCarthy's 'Blood Meridian.'" *Comparative Literature Studies* 37 (1): 18-44.

Fisher, Mark. 2009. *Capitalist Realism: Is There No Alternative?* Zero Books.

Fonseca, Gonçalo L. n.d. "Sir William Petty, 1623-1687." *History of Economic Thought.* hetwebsite.net/het/profiles/petty.htm.

Foucault, Michel. 1972. *The Archaeology of Knowledge; and The Discourse on Language.* Translated by A.M. Sheridan Smith. Pantheon Books.

———. 1995. *Discipline and Punish: The Birth of the Prison.* Translated by Alan Sheridan. Vintage Books.

Frankenberg, Ruth. 2001. "The Mirage of an Unmarked Whiteness." In *The Making and Unmaking of Whiteness*, edited by Birgit Rasmussen Brander, Eric Klineberg, Irene J. Nexica, and Matt Wray. Duke University Press.

Freire, Paulo. 2005. *Pedagogy of the Oppressed*. Translated by Myra Bergman Ramos. Continuum.

Fry, Tony. Design Futuring: Sustainability, Ethics and New Practice. Oxford: Berg Publishers, 2009.

G

Garland, Ken, et al. 1964. *The First Things First Manifesto*. Self-published. Republished on Design Is History. Accessed August 24, 2021. designishistory.com/1960/first-things-first.

Ghazaryan, Armina. 2018. "Impressions of the Atelier du livre d'art et de l'estampe." Association of European Printing Museums, May 17. aepm.eu/publications/focus-on-printingmuseums/impressions-of-the-atelierdu-livre-dart-et-de-lestampe.

Gitelman, Lisa. 2010. "Rethinking Attachment." *The New Everyday: A Media Commons Project*. MediaCommons, June 29. mediacommons.org/tne/pieces/rethinking-attachment.

———. 2014. *Paper Knowledge: Toward a Media History of Documents*. Duke University Press.

Goldberg, David Theo. 2001. *The Racial State*. Blackwell.

Golumbia, David. 2016. *The Politics of Bitcoin: Software as Right-Wing Extremism*. University of Minnesota Press.

Graeber, David. 2011. *Debt: The First 5,000 Years*. Melville House.

———. 2015. *The Utopia of Rules: On Technology, Stupidity, and the Secret Joys of Bureaucracy*. Melville House.

Graeber, David, and David Wengrow. 2021. *The Dawn of Everything: A New History of Humanity*. Allen Lane.

"Décret relatif aux poids et aux mesures du 18 germinal an 3 (7 avril 1795)." 1795. Republished in "Grandes lois de la République." Digithèque de matériaux juridiques et politiques. Accessed November 28, 2024. mjp.univ-perp.fr/france/1793mesures.htm.

Gunawan, I Ketut. 2004. *The Politics of the Indonesian Rainforest: A Rise of Forest Conflicts in East Kalimantan During Indonesia's Early Stage of Democratisation*. Cuvillier Verlag.

H

Hafford, W.B. 2005. "Mesopotamian Mensuration Balance Pan Weights from Nippur." *Journal of the Economic and Social History of the Orient* 48 (3): 345–87.

Haraway, Donna. 1988. "Situated Knowledges: The Science Question in Feminism and the Privilege of Partial Perspective." *Feminist Studies* 14 (3): 575–99.

Hart, Keith. 2020. *The Memory Bank: Money in an Unequal World*. Profile Books.

———. 2020. "Obituary: David Graeber (1961– 2020)." *Anthropology Today* 36 (6): 33–34.

Hartnett, J.P. 2021. "Ontological Design Has Become Influential in Design Academia—But What Is It?" Eye on Design (blog), *aiga*, June 14. eyeondesign. aiga.org/ontologicaldesign- is-popular-in-designacademia- but-what-is-it.

Heller, Steven. n.d. "Phillip B. Meggs." Accessed February 2, 2018. *aiga*. aiga.org/medalist-philipbmeggs.

Hellman, Clarisse Doris. 1931. "Jefferson's Efforts Towards the Decimalization of United States Weights and Measures." *Isis* 16 (2): 266–314.

Hobart, Michael E., and Zachary S. Schiffman. 1998. *Information Ages: Literacy, Numeracy, and the Computer Revolution*. (Johns Hopkins University Press).

Hobbes, Thomas. 1651. *Leviathan or the Matter, Forme, & Power of a Common-Wealth Ecclesiastical and Civil*. Andrew Crooke. Republished in 2002 as an eBook on Project Gutenberg. gutenberg.org/files/3207/3207-h/3207-h.htm.

Bibliography

Hollis, Richard. 2016. "History and the Graphic Designer." In *Graphic Design History and Practice*, edited by Antonio Benincasa, Giorgio Camuffo, Maddalena Dalla Mura, Christian Upmeier, and Carlo Vinti. Bozen-Bolzano University Press.

Howcraft, Elizabeth. 2021. "Sotheby's to sell 'first' NFT in online auction." *Reuters*, June 7. reuters.com/technology/sothebys-sell-first-nftonline-auction-2021-06-01.

I

Illich, Ivan. 1980. "Vernacular Values," *Philosophica* 26: 47-102.

J

Johnson, George. 1903. *The All Red Line; The Annals and Aims of the Pacific Cable Project*. James Hope & Sons.

K

Kantorowicz, Ernst H. 1955. "Mysteries of State: An Absolutist Concept and Its Late Mediaeval Origins." *The Harvard Theological Review* 48 (1): 65-91.

Karatani, Kojin. 2001. "The Principles of the New Associationist Movement (NAM)." *NetTime*, May 18. nettime.org/ Lists-Archives/ nettime-l-0105/ msg00099.html.

Keshavarz, Mahmoud. 2018. *The Design Politics of the Passport: Materiality, Immobility, and Dissent*. Bloomsbury.

Kim, Eunsong. 2016. "Poetry without Poets." In *Forms of Education: Couldn't Get a Sense of It*, edited by Aeron Bergman, Irena Borić, and Alejandra Salinas. Institute for New Connotative Action Press.

Koch, Paul.1933. "The Making of Printing Types." *The Dolphin: A Journal of the Making of Books* (1): 24-57.

Krauss, Rosalind.1979. "Grids." *October* 9: 50-64.

L

Langfur, Hal. 1999. "Myths of Pacification: Brazilian Frontier Settlement and the Subjugation of the Bororo Indians." *Journal of Social History* 32 (4): 879-905.

Laranjo, Francisco. "Critical Graphic Design." *Modes of Criticism*. Accessed December 3, 2024. modesofcriticism.org/critical-graphic-design/.

Latour, Bruno. 1986. "Visualization and Cognition: Drawing Things Together." *Knowledge and Society Studies in the Sociology of Culture Past and Present* 6: 1-40.

LeCavalier, Jesse. 2016. *The Rule of Logistics: Walmart and the Architecture of Fulfillment*. University of Minnesota Press.

Leonhardt, Megan. "Congress Is Increasing Childcare Funding by Nearly $585 Million—But It Won't Fix the 'Sweeping, Systemic Problems.'" *Fortune*, March 10. fortune. com/2022/03/10/congress-isincreasing-child-care-funding.

Lorenz, Chris. 1998. "Can Histories Be True? Narrativism, Positivism, and the 'Metaphorical Turn.'" *History and Theory* 37 (3): 309-29.

Lorusso, Silvio. 2023. *What Design Can't Do: Essays on Design and Disillusion*. Set Margins'.

M

Maiocchi, Massimo. 2019. "Writing in Early Mesopotamia: The Historical Interplay of Technology, Cognition, and Environment." In *Beyond the Meme: Development and Structure in Cultural Evolution*, edited by Alan C. Love and William C. Wimsatt. University of Minnesota Press.

Mansfield, Daniel. 2021. "How Ancient Babylonian Land Surveyors Developed a Unique Form of Trigonometry—1,000 Years Before the Greeks." *The Conversation*, August 4. theconversation.com/how-ancient-babylonian-landsurveyors-developed-a-unique-formof-trigonometry-1-000-years-beforethe-greeks-163428.

Marx, Karl. 1867. *Capital: A Critique of Political Economy*. Vol. 1, *The Process of Production of Capital*, edited by Frederick Engels. Translated by Samuel Moore and Edward Aveling. Republished on Marxists. org. marxists.org/archive/marx/ works/1867-c1/ch27.htm.

Mason, William Albert.1920. *A History of the Art of Writing*. Macmillan Company.

Mattern, Shannon. 2017. *Code and Clay, Data and Dirt: Five Thousand Years of Urban Media*. University of Minnesota Press.

McKendrick, Neil. 1970. "Josiah Wedgwood and Cost Accounting in the Industrial Revolution." *The Economic History Review* 23 (1): 45–67.

McLuhan, Marshall, and Quentin Fiore. 1967. *The Medium Is the Massage: An Inventory of Effects*. Bantan Books.

Meggs, Philip B., and Alston W. Purvis. 2012. *Meggs' History of Graphic Design*. 5th ed. John Wiley & Sons.

Metahaven. 2008. *White Night Before a Manifesto*. Onomatopee.

Mignolo, Walter D. 2017. "Coloniality is Far from Over, and So Must be Decoloniality." *Afterall: A Journal of Art and Inquiry* 43: 38–45.

———. 2009. "Epistemic Disobedience, Independent Thought, and De-colonial Freedom." *Theory, Culture & Society* 26 (7–8): 1–23.

Moore, Jason W. 2010. "'Amsterdam Is Standing on Norway' Part II: The Global North Atlantic in the Ecological Revolution of the Long Seventeenth Century." *Journal of Agrarian Change* 10 (2): 188–227.

———. 2014. "The End of Cheap Nature or: How I Learned to Stop Worrying about 'the' Environment and Love the Crisis of Capitalism." In *Structures of the World Political Economy and the Future Global Conflict and Cooperation*, edited by Christopher K. Chase- Dunn, and Christian Suter. Lit Verlag.

———. 2017. "The Capitalocene, Part I: On the Nature and Origins of Our Ecological Crisis." *The Journal of Peasant Studies* 44 (3): 594–630.

Morison, Stanley. 1980. *Selected Essays on the History of Letter-Forms in Manuscript and Print*, edited by David McKitterick. Cambridge University Press.

Morris, Edmund. 2019. "Thomas Edison and the Birth of the Stock Ticker." *Forbes*, October 25. forbes.com/sites/ forbesdigitalcovers/2019/10/25/thomas- edison-birth-of-the-stockticker-edmund- morris-book-excerpt.

Moten, Fred, and Stefano Harney. *The Under- commons: Fugitive Planning & Black Study*. New York: Minor Compositions, 2013.

Munro, Silas. 2018. "Introduction to the Plates." In *W.E.B. Du Bois's Data Portraits: Visualizing Black America*, 2018, edited by Whitney Battle-Baptiste and Britt Russert. The W.E.B. Du Bois Center at the University of Massachusetts; Princeton Architectural Press.

N

Nader, Laura. 1972. "Up the Anthropologist: Perspectives Gained from Studying Up." In *Reinventing Anthropology*, edited by Dell Hymes. Pantheon Books.

Nakamoto, Satoshi. 2008. "Bitcoin: A Peer-to- Peer Electronic Cash System." Bitcoin. org, bitcoin.org/bitcoin.pdf.

Newman, Eric P. 1967. *The Early Paper Money of America*. Whitman Publishing Company.

North, Peter. 2007. *Money and Liberation: The Micropolitics of Alternative Currency Movements*. University of Minnesota Press.

"N. Van Staphorst." n.d. *parlement.com*. Accessed November 2, 2021. Parlement. com/id/vg09llwr8aw4/n_van_staphorst.

O

Obach, Eugene F. A., and A. Dupré. 1897. *The Journal of the Society of Arts* 46 (2353): 97–116.

———. 1897.*The Journal of the Society of Arts* 46 (2354): 117–36.

Bibliography

Overmann, Karenleigh A. 2016. "The Role of Materiality in Numerical Cognition." *Quaternary International* 405 (A): 42–51.

P

Paput, Christian. 1998. *La Lettre: La Gravure du Poinçon typographique—The Punchcutting*. TVSO Éditions.

Parikka, Jussi. 2014. *The Anthrobscene*. University of Minnesota Press.

Park, Angle. 2013. "LaunchPad: Coin Production in the Roman World." The Art Institute of Chicago. YouTube video, April 11, 2 min., 35 sec. youtube.com/watch?v=b6T_ZutXzNQ.

Pater, Ruben. "What Design Can Do: The Refugee Crisis and Problematic Design." *Dezeen*. April 21, 2016. Accessed December 3, 2024. dezeen.com/2016/04/21/ruben-pater-opinion-what-design-can-do-refugee-crisis-problematic-design/.

Peña, Elizabeth S. 2006. "Wampum Diplomacy: The Historical and Archaeological Evidence for Wampum at Fort Niagara." *Northeast Historical Archaeology* 35 (20): 15–28.

Peters, Arthur K. 1996. *Seven Trails West*. Abbeville Press Publishers.

Poggi, Gianfranco. 1978. *The Development of the Modern State: A Sociological Introduction*. Stanford University Press.

Poirier, G. Phil. 2015. "Art, History, and Process of Guilloché Engraving." *Santa Fe Symposium Papers*. santafesymposium.org/2015-santafe-symposium-papers/2015-arthistory-and-processes-of-guillocheengraving.

Popova, Maria. 2017. "W.E.B. Du Bois's Little-Known, Arresting Modernist Data Visualizations of Black Life for the World's Fair of 1900." *The Marginalian* (blog). October 9. themarginalian.org/2017/10/09/w-e-b-du-boisdiagrams.

Powell Jr., Marvin A. 1972. "The Origin of the Sexagesimal System: The Interaction of Language and Writing." *Visible Language* 6: 5–18.

Poynor, Rick. 2015. *The Debate: The Legendary Contest of Two Giants of Graphic Design*. Monacelli Press.

R

Ramsden, Jenny. 2015. "Snapshots from the History of Mathematics: Robert Recorde." *Mathematics in School* 44 (5): 28–29.

Riedman, Jamie. 2022. "Ten Years Ago Satoshi Nakamoto Logged Off—The Final Message from Bitcoin's Inventor." *Bitcoin.com*, December 13. Accessed January 24, 2022. news.bitcoin.com/ten-years-ago-satoshinakamoto-logged-off-the-finalmessage-from-bitcoins-inventor.

Riley, James C. 1973. "Dutch Investment in France, 1781–1787." *The Journal of Economic History* 33 (4): 732–60.

Roberts, William. 1893. *Printers' Marks: A Chapter in the History of Typography*. George Bell & Sons. Republished in 2008 as an eBook on Project Gutenberg. gutenberg.org/files/25663/25663-h/25663-h.htm.

S

Sakamoto, Ryuichi (@ryuichisakamoto). 2021. "Launching the sale for single note NFTs of 595 music notes from the melody of 'Merry Christmas Mr. Lawrence' by Ryuichi Sakamoto. Auction for original handwritten music sheet available for NFT buyers," Twitter, December 20. twitter.com/ryuichisakamoto/status/1473065850831835142.

Satoshi., 2010. "Re: PC World Article on Bitcoin." *bitcointalk.org*, December 11. 11:39:16 PM. bitcointalk.org/index.php?topic=2216.msg29280#msg29280.

Sawyer, Laura Phillips. 2019. "U.S. Antitrust Law and Policy in Historical Perspective." *Harvard Business School Working Paper* (19–110).

Schmandt-Besserat, Denise. 1991. "Two Precursors of Writing: Plain and Complex Tokens." In *The Origins of Writing*, edited by Wayne M. Senner. University of Nebraska Press.

Shaw, Paul. 2020. "The Definitive Dwiggins No. 81A—W.A. Dwiggins and 'Graphic Design': A Brief Rejoinder to Steven Heller and Bruce Kennett." Paul Shaw Letter Design, May 23. paulshawletter design.com/2020/05/the-definitive-dwiggins-no-81a-w-adwiggins-and-graphic-design-a-briefrejoinder-to-steven-heller-and-brucekennett.

Simpson, Leanne Betasamosake. 2013. "Restoring Nationhood: Addressing Land Dispossession in the Canadian Reconciliation Discourse." Lecture presented by Vancity Office of Community Engagement, Simon Fraser University, Burnaby, Canada, November 13. Posted May 16, 2016. YouTube, 1:08:14. youtube.com/watch?v=SGUcWih74Ic.

Scott, James C. 1998. *Seeing Like a State: How Certain Schemes to Improve the Human Condition Have Failed*. Yale University Press.

———. 2009. *The Art of Not Being Governed: An Anarchist History of Upland Southeast Asia*. Yale University Press.

———. 2017. *Against the Grain: A Deep History of the Earliest States*. Yale University Press.

Singh Grewal, David. 2008. *Network Power: The Social Dynamics of Globalization*. Yale University Press.

Slanski, Kathryn E. 2013. "The Law of Hammurabi and Its Audience." *Yale Journal of Law & The Humanities* 24 (1): 91–110.

Société Réaliste. 2011. *Empire, State, Building*. Editions Amsterdam.

Sontag, Susan. 1999. "Posters: Advertisement, Art, Political Artifact, Commodity." In *Looking Closer 3: Classic Writings on Graphic Design*, edited by Michael Bierut, Jessica Helfand, Steven Heller, and Rick Poynor. Allworth Press.

Soth, Amelia. 2020. "Beating the Bounds." *Cabinet of Curiosities* (blog), JStor Daily, May 7. daily.jstor.org/beating-the-bounds.

Souchon, Cécile, and Marie-Élisabeth Antoine. 2003. "La formation des départements." *Histoire par l'image*, October. histoire-image.org/etudes/formation-departements.

Soule, Jake. 2020. "How The Urban Eclipsed the City: An Interview with Ross Exo Adams." *Failed Architecture*, May 18. failedarchitecture.com/how-the-urban-eclipsed-the-city-aninterview- with-ross-exo-adams.

Sotheby's. 2021. "Natively Digital: A Curated NFT Sale: Lot 2." Online auction, June 3–10. sothebys.com/en/buy/auction/2021/natively-digital-acurated-nft-sale-2/quantum.

Steinberg, S.H. 1955. *Five Hundred Years of Printing*. Penguin.

Standish, David. 2020. *The Art of Money: The History and Design of Paper Currency from Around the World*. Chronicle Books.

Struik, D.J. 1959. "Simon Stevin and the Decimal Fractions." *The Mathematics Teacher* 52 (6): 474–78.

T

Taylor, Diana. 2003. *The Archive and the Repertoire: Performing Cultural Memory in the Americas*. Duke University Press.

Taylor, Keeanga-Yamahtta. 2019. *Race for Profit: How Banks and the Real Estate Industry Undermined Black Homeownership (Justice, Power, and Politics)*. University of North Carolina Press.

Ten Grotenhuis, Elizabeth. 2006. "Stories of Silk and Paper." *World Literature Today* 80 (4): 10–12.

The Code of Hammurabi. Translated by L.W. King, 1907. Accessed August 19, 2021. avalon.law.yale.edu/ancient/hamframe.asp.

Thierry, François. 2010. "Fausses dates et vraies monnaies: Rites, information, propagande et histoire dans la numismatique chinoise." *Extrême-Orient Extrême-Occident* (32): 41–59.

Thomas, Kier. 2010. "Could the Wikileaks Scandal Lead to New Virtual Currency?" *PC World*, December 10. pcworld.com/article/499375/could_wikileaks_scandal_lead_to_ new_virtual_currency.html.

Bibliography

Thompson, Ralph. 2021. "Richmond Park
     and the Georgian Access Controversy."
     The National Archives (blog), June 23. blog.
     nationalarchives.gov.uk/richmond-park-
     and-the-georgianaccess- controversy.

Thompson, Wayne. 2018. "The Most Innovative
     Vehicle of Its Time." *Wells Fargo Stories*
     (blog), March 16. stories.wf.com/
     innovative-vehicle-time.

Tuck, Eve, and K. Wayne Yang. 2012.
     "Decolonization Is Not a Metaphor."
     *Decolonization: Indigeneity, Education and
     Society* 1 (1): 1–40.

Tully, John. 2009. "A Victorian Ecological
     Disaster: Imperialism, the Telegraph,
     and Gutta-Percha." *Journal of World
     History* 20 (4): 559–79.

Willis, Anne-Marie. 2006. "Ontological
     Designing." *Design Philosophy Papers* 4 (2):
     69–92.

Wilson Gilmore, Ruth, and Léopold Lambert.
     2018. "Making Abolition Geography
     in California's Central Valley."
     The Funambulist, December 20.
     thefunambulist.net/ magazine/21-space-
     activism/interview-makingabolition-
     geography-californiacentral-valley-ruth-
     wilson-gilmore.

Winant, Gabriel. "Professional-Managerial
     Chasm." *n+1*. October 12, 2019. Accessed
     December 3, 2024. nplusonemag.com/
     online-only/online-only/professional-
     managerial-chasm/.

U

Ulbrich, Chris. 2004. "Currency Detector
     Easy to Defeat." *Wired*, January 1.
     wired.com/2004/01/currency-detector-
     easy-todefeat/? currentPage=all.

W

Wark, McKenzie. 2019a. *A Hacker Manifesto*.
     Harvard University Press.

———. 2019b. *Capital Is Dead*. Verso.

Weber, Johannes. 2006. "Strassburg, 1605:
     The Origins of the Newspaper in Europe."
     German History 24 (3): 387–412.

Weymans, Wim (2004). Michel de certeau and
     the limits of historical representation.
     History and Theory 43 (2): 161–178.

White, Hayden. 1986. "Historical Pluralism."
     Critical Inquiry 12 (3): 480–93.

Wikipedia s.v. "eurion constellation." Last
     modified May 25, 2022. Accessed August
     20, 2021. en.wikipedia.org/wiki/EURion_
     constellation.

Wikipedia, s.v. "Secure Hash Algorithms."
     Last modified May 31, 2022. Accessed
     August 20, 2021. en.wikipedia.org/wiki/
     Secure_ Hash_Algorithms.

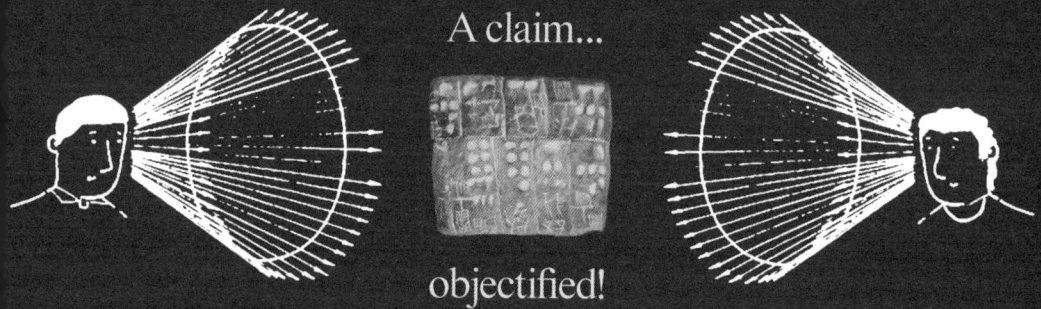

A claim...

objectified!

Colophon

Designing History: Documents and the Design
Imperative to Immutability

Written/designed by	Chris Lee
Edited by	Benjamin Tiven (Immutable),
	Rachel Valinsky (Immutable, Designing History)
Copy edited by	Rachel Valinsky

Typeset in Starling (Mike Parker),
and 凸版文久見出しゴシック Toppan Bunkyu
Midashi Gothic (字游工房 Jiyo-kobo)

The print edition of this book is published by Onomatopee
(Eindhoven, NL). It was printed at Petro ofsetas, Vilnius, LT.

The eBook version of this book's *Immutable: Designing History*
section was first published by Library Stack (librarystack.org).
It was generously supported by Arts Council England and NN
Contemporary Art (Northampton, UK) in 2022.

Print edition ISBN 978-90-834041-0-3

Every effort was made to obtain the permission of copyright
holders for the use of copyright material. Notification of any
additions or corrections that can be incorporated in future
editions of this book would be greatly appreciated.

This project was largely conceived and developed in territories
stewarded and claimed by the various Indigenous peoples whose
living sovereignty has been overcoded by centuries of violence
premised upon illegitimate claims made through documental
artifacts: Buffalo lies in the lands claimed by the Six Nations of
the Haudenosaunee Confederacy (Mohawk, Cayuga, Onandaga,
Oneida, Seneca, and Tuscarora); Tkaronto is located in the lands
claimed by the Huron-Wendat, the Seneca, and the Mississaugas
of the Credit; New York City is located in Lenapehoking, the
place from which the Delaware Tribe was heinously displaced
by the colonial settler-state.

Set Margins' Publications #37